CLASSIC MOMENTS OF
BOXING

Classic Moments of

BOXING

Jack Hails

MOORLAND PUBLISHING

Published by:
Moorland Publishing Co Ltd,
Moor Farm Road,
Ashbourne,
Derbyshire DE6 1HD
England

First edition 1983
Enlarged second edition 1989

British Library Cataloguing in
Publication Data

Hails, Jack
    Classic moments of boxing
    1. Boxing — History
    I. Title
    796.8′3′09   GV1121

ISBN 0 86190 317 X

The Author wishes to thank
John Grainger who compiled the
index for this book.

Printed in the UK by
Richard Clay Ltd,
Bungay, Suffolk

Contents

	Introduction	6
1	Jack Johnson v Tommy Burns, 1908	7
2	Jack Dempsey v Jess Willard, 1919	12
3	Jim Driscoll v Charles Ledoux, 1919	16
4	Ted (Kid) Lewis v Johnny Basham, 1920	21
5	Jimmy Wilde v Pete Herman, 1921	25
6	Jack Dempsey v Georges Carpentier, 1921	28
7	Georges Carpentier v Battling Siki, 1922	32
8	Joe Beckett v Frank Moran, 1922	36
9	Luis Angel Firpo v Jack Dempsey, 1923	39
10	Mickey Walker v Tommy Milligan, 1927	43
11	Gene Tunney v Jack Dempsey, 1927	46
12	Teddy Baldock v Alf (Kid) Pattenden, 1929	49
13	Jack Petersen v Jack Doyle, 1933	52
14	Max Baer v Primo Carnera, 1934	56
15	Harry Mizler v Gustave Humery, 1935	60
16	John Henry Lewis v Len Harvey, 1936	63
17	Johnny King v Jackie Brown, 1937	67
18	Joe Louis v James J. Braddock, 1937	71
19	Joe Louis v Tommy Farr, 1937	75
20	Benny Lynch v Peter Kane, 1937	80
21	Joe Louis v Max Schmeling, 1938	85
22	Eric Boon v Albert Danahar, 1939	89
23	Henry Armstrong v Ernie Roderick, 1939	94
24	Joe Lewis v Tony Galento, 1939	98
25	Freddie Mills v Len Harvey, 1942	102
26	Nel Tarleton v Al Phillips, 1945	106
27	Gus Lesnevich v Freddie Mills, 1946	110
28	Tony Zale v Rocky Graziano, 1946	115
29	Joe Louis v Jersey Joe Walcott, 1947	120
30	Jersey Joe Walcott v Rocky Marciano, 1952	125
31	Rocky Marciano v Ezzard Charles, 1954	129
32	Rocky Marciano v Archie Moore, 1955	133
33	Floyd Patterson v Ingemar Johansson, 1959	137
34	Floyd Patterson v Ingemar Johansson, 1961	141
35	Floyd Patterson v Sonny Liston, 1962	145
36	Sonny Liston v Cassius Clay, 1964	149
37	Muhammad Ali v Joe Frazier, 1975	153
38	Eusebio Pedroza v Barry McGuigan, 1985	160
39	Sugar Ray Leonard v Marvin Hagler, 1987	162
40	Mike Tyson v Leon Spinks, 1988	165
41	Sugar Ray Leonard v Danny Lalonde, 1988	166
42	Lloyd Honeyghan v Marlon Starling, 1989	168
43	Dennis Andries v Tony Willis, 1989	170
44	Mike Tyson v Frank Bruno, 1989	172
	Index	175

INTRODUCTION

What makes a classic moment in sport? Usually it is a performance of great skill, like a brilliantly-executed goal in a soccer match, a superbly-created innings by a batsman in cricket, or a finely-judged race on the athletics track. But boxing ... well boxing is different, isn't it? Of course, there has to be the great textbook performances where all the rules of the coaching manual are exquisitely performed. That is a classic moment. But boxing is not just about text-book displays. It is also about courage, determination, sheer guts if you like, and these can produce classic moments. Two men can be a little short on the technique of the sport, but if they produce a rare battle in which no quarter is asked or given, then the boxing crowd will feel they have had their money's worth.

So, the criteria used in selecting thirty-seven fights to include in a book entitled *Classic Moments of Boxing* had to be, not just the text-book fights, but also the fights which excited, the fights which had the fans sitting on the edges of their seats gripped with the sheer thrill of it all, and astonished by the sights which met their eyes. In short, they had to be fights which people *talked* about long after they were over, fights which are recalled today and discussed, even by people who were not lucky enough to be there in person.

Of course, when presenting a selection of such fights there is the ever-present problem of missing out the one fight which someone else felt should have been included, though it must be underlined that what follows does not purport to be the thirty-seven *best* fights of all time. It does not try to be a definitive list of the greatest. Perhaps Sugar Ray Robinson, pound for pound, probably the greatest of them all, should have figured; perhaps Randy Turpin on the night he beat Sugar Ray; perhaps another Sugar Ray — Leonard — and his fight with Roberto Duran in 1980. Any selection has to be personal; boxing, more than most sports, is well known for its arguments, outside the ring as well as within the hemp.

Note:
Professional boxing has been notorious for the tangle of world championships over the years when different governing bodies have recognised their own world title-holders. Wherever possible those contradictions have been explained in this book. Some boxing records, too, are sketchy and distinguished books on the sport have often disagreed on dates and places. Great pains have been taken to produce the correct details but some facts may never be firmly established.

JACK JOHNSON v TOMMY BURNS
World Heavyweight Championship
26 December 1908

In 1899, the year in which James J. Jeffries beat Bob Fitzsimmons for the heavyweight boxing championship of the world, a young coloured boxer was setting out on his own career in the sport. As Jeffries stunned the world of boxing by beating the Englishman Bob Fitzsimmons in the eleventh round of a savage fight at Coney Island, Jack Johnson was an unknown black fighter whose early life had been spent hitch-hiking around the United States in search of a living. But before he was finished John Arthur Johnson became the most hated man in America. In those days no one in white America liked a black man, they certainly did not like a successful black man, and they had absolutely no love for a successful black man who had affairs with white women. Jack Johnson was to become all of these things.

Gradually Johnson made progress through the ranks, scoring fine victories over some of the best coloured boxers of the day — men like Sam McVey, Joe Jeannette and Sam Langford — and all this time there had inevitably been other changes in the heavyweight boxing scene, with Jeffries giving way to a man called Noah Brusso, alias Tommy Burns, a squat Canadian. Jeffries announced his retirement in 1905 and nominated Marvin Hart and Jack Root to fight for his vacant crown. At Reno, Nevada, on 3 July 1905, the referee — Jeffries himself — stopped the fight in the twelfth round with Hart proclaimed the new champion. Now, however, dissention arose from people who claimed that there were other fighters worthy of the chance to battle for the heavyweight crown and angry at Jeffries's action. One of them was Tommy Burns — at 5ft 7in tall and smallest man ever to win the

modern heavyweight title — and he soon set about proving that he was the real champion. Burns set himself a frantic series of fights. On 23 February 1906 he beat Marvin Hart on points over twenty rounds in Los Angeles.

He then took on all-comers in all parts of the world, beating Jim Flynn and Philadelphia Jack O'Brien (twice) in Los Angeles, Bill Squires in Colma, California, Gunner Moir and Jack Palmer in London, Jem Roche in Dublin, Jewey Smith in Paris, Bill Squires again, also in Paris, Bill Squires once more in Sydney and Bill Lang in Melbourne. That fight was on 2 September 1908, so Tommy Burns had been world heavyweight champion for over two years, defending his title eleven times.

But if Tommy Burns was the reigning champion then there was a man coming up hard on his heels. Jack Johnson had come a long way since the days when he bummed around the United States. Now he was a boxer successful enough to own fast cars, smoke fat cigars, and — what angered white America most — attract the company of pretty white women. Bob Fitzsimmons and Jim Flynn had felt the weight of his punches to their cost; and so when Burns came to London, Jack Johnson followed him. Burns knocked out Gunner Moir, the British champion, at the National Sporting Club in December 1907, the Briton hitting the canvas in the tenth round, and Johnson was on his tail. When Burns quickly disposed of Jack Palmer at the old Wonderland, Johnson was pressing for a meeting with the world champion. When Burns rid himself of Roche in less than one round in Dublin, Johnson had the interest of the National Sporting Club. They were keen to match him with Burns for

Jack Johnson became the world's first coloured heavyweight champion. He also became the most unpopular because of his affairs with white women.

Johnson may have been more wealthy than he had ever been — but he still did not have the kind of money which would enable him to sail to the other side of the world with no guarantee of a fight at the end of it. The National Sporting Club came to the boxer's rescue, offering him the money to go to Australia on condition that if he met and defeated Burns, then he would come back to England and meet Sam Langford. Johnson needed no second bidding. Getting to Australia, however, was the easy bit. Setting up a world title fight with Tommy Burns was a different matter. For weeks the arguments raged and then, at last Burns agreed to meet Jack Johnson for the title. The date was set for 26 December 1908 at Rushcutter's Bay, Sydney. Johnson wanted — and got — McIntosh to referee the fight: 'For every point I'm given I'll have to earn two,' he said, 'because I'm a negro. There is only one white man I trust and that is Hugh McIntosh.'

Burns was guaranteed $30,000 (£7,500), which was the greatest sum ever offered to a fighter at that time. It was really the start of the big purses which eventually led to the million-dollar fights of the post World War I era. The pre-fight publicity rivalled anything which went afterwards. Johnson's mother was alleged to have remarked that her son was 'a rank coward' and that was used to fan the flames during the build up to the encounter. All manner of bizarre stories were published, public interest was sky-high, and whoever won the fight, there was now the certainty that McIntosh would be a winner either way. There was also the story that there was a great deal of ill-feeling between Burns and Johnson. Certainly, throughout the fight there was a constant barrage of words with Burns allegedly calling his opponent 'yellow'. There were 20,000 people packed into the stadium on that Boxing Day morning over seven decades ago. Many of the people were in Sydney for the races and they swelled the receipts to £26,000. Johnson was first into the ring and he received a very good reception. He stood five and a half inches taller than the Canadian and held a weight advantage of

the title and offered a purse of £2,500 with the winner taking £2,000. 'That will suit me fine', Johnson told them. But Burns wanted £6,000 — win, lose or draw. It was the first time that such terms had ever been suggested and, not surprisingly, they were refused.

However, if the National Sporting Club were not prepared to meet Burns's terms, then Mr Hugh D. McIntosh of Sydney was. He cabled the Canadian in London and Burns was on his way, pausing long enough in France to beat Jewey Smith and Bill Squires.

about two and a half stones. But Burns, while secretly respecting his opponent, was not overworried about these statistics. He had a longer reach and, besides, he had fought six-foot men before. Burns was the favourite and there were not many people in the throng who expected the Canadian to fall to the black man.

Yet the fight really started long before the bell went to signal the beginning of the first round. Sitting in his corner, Johnson noticed that Burns was wearing bandages around his elbows. At once the American was on his feet and protesting to the referee. McIntosh went over and examined the champion and decided that the bandages were not against the rules. But Johnson was not satisfied. The challenger insisted that the champion removed the offending bandages. There was a heated argument and for a while it appeared that there would be no fight after all. Then, amid loud cheers from an impatient crowd, Burns began to unwrap the bandages and at last the two men came together in the middle of the ring. The moment for which Jack Johnson, from Galveston, Texas, had waited for so long had arrived. After following Tommy Burns halfway around the world, Johnson now had his chance.

Johnson's intention was to dictate this fight from the start and as the two men came together from the bell, the negro smashed a left into Burns's ribs. Burns countered with a left to the American's stomach. When the boxers broke from a clinch Burns, whose first priority was usually to have his face and solar plexus well covered, dropped his guard for a split-second. It was exactly the moment for which the challenger had been waiting. In a flash Johnson sent a tremendous upward right swing towards Burns's exposed jaw. The champion might have seen it — he certainly had no opportunity to avoid it, it caught Burns full on the jaw and down he went for a count of eight. Johnson smiled hugely, a gold-toothed grin which inflamed the Canadian's corner. But Burns was soon up and apparently unshaken by the ferocity of the punch which had felled him. He immediately took the fight to his opponent

and they went at it hammer and tongs for the rest of that round. In the second round Burns was caught again and as he rose Johnson taunted him: 'Poor old Tahmmy!' Johnson had drawn blood and Burns was suddenly aware that he needed every ounce of his vast experience, his skill — and his raw courage — to survive this onslaught, so devastating had Johnson's attack become.

'Come right on in Tahmmy', taunted Johnson as the two men sparred in the centre of the ring. It was just as Johnson had hoped. His jibes began to creep under Burns's skin. The Canadian countered by calling Johnson 'yellow' and 'a coward'. No one needs to be told that the last thing a boxer must do is lose his temper. By the fourth round it was becoming clear that the world would soon have a new heavyweight champion — and its first black one at that. Burns seemed now almost incapable of landing one effective blow on Johnson, who continued to rain blows on the champion's head and body. Yet in the fifth round Burns came back into the fight. He went after Johnson and the referee had several times to part the two fighters as the exchanges became more bitter. Johnson and Burns continued to taunt each other. 'Come on Tahmmy, hit me, hit me,' called Johnson. Then Johnson actually allowed Burns to land a blow or two.

Of course, it was all part of Johnson's carefully laid plan to take Burns apart. Burns could hardly control his temper and yet there was Johnson, ice-cool and in total command of this fight, letting his opponent do just as much as he, Johnson, wanted. At the end of the eighth round, with Burns now trailing badly on points, the champion was a shocking sight. Blood poured from an injured eye and yet he refused to throw in the towel. When the bell went to start the ninth round Burns knew that his only hope of retaining the title was to score what would be a quite sensational knockout. But that was not to be and Johnson knew, at this point, that he had won the fight and could already feel the weight of the world heavyweight crown resting on his head. Yet the Galveston Giant as Johnson was known,

Tommy Burns looks in desperate trouble as Jack Johnson pounds him to defeat at Rushcutter's Bay, Sydney, on Boxing Day 1908.

seemed reluctant to end the fight, rather more content to play a cruel game of cat and mouse with Burns. Perhaps he wanted to relish this crowning hour of triumph, or perhaps he was annoyed that he had been forced to trek halfway across the world to find this crown. It was almost as if he wanted to punish Burns for all the inconvenience he had caused him. Johnson landed hard punch after hard punch and still he did not do quite enough to put Burns out of his misery. Burns, meanwhile, was still gamely fighting on, refusing to give in.

In the eleventh round Johnson made what was obviously a particularly hurtful remark to Burns. The Canadian came at Johnson like a devil. His fury might have stopped some boxers in their tracks — but against Johnson it merely added to Burns's already lost cause. His blind attack on the Texan turned the fight from a sporting spectacle to one of the most ugly, sickening sights that the boxing ring has ever witnessed, the sort of fight that is meat and drink to the anti-boxing lobby. The two men stood toe to toe, hammering blows at each other with Burns, in particular, looking like a wounded animal fighting for its life. In the twelfth round it

was only the incredible courage of the champion that kept him on his feet. Johnson was so much in control that he actually found the time to laugh and joke with the crowd. When Burns came out for the thirteenth he presented a ghastly sight. His face was badly swollen and he lurched around the ring, seemingly unaware of where he was going.

The bell went to end the thirteenth round and it seemed that the fight was surely over. But the fourteenth-round bell went and out came Burns again, to be sent crashing to the canvas again, this time for a count of eight. He was almost unconscious but somehow, as if by remote control, he gathered himself up only to be punched around the ring by Johnson once more. At this point even the most bloodthirsty members of the crowd were calling for the fight to be stopped and it was no surprise when the local police force intervened. It had been agreed before the fight that if the police did see fit to step in and stop the fight, then the referee would award the decision on points. McIntosh had no problem in deciding that Johnson's was the hand which he would lift to the Sydney sky. But the shame of it all was summed up by one

10

writer who penned later: 'This was one of the most disgusting spectacles of its kind ever witnessed in this country.'

Burns was finished. Johnson's world heavyweight championship career was just beginning. His win was deserved. He was quicker, cleverer and made full use of his extra height and weight. However, he now showed a different side to his character from the willing boxer who had impressed the official of London's National Sporting Club. When he was asked to honour his pledge of going back to England to meet Sam Langford, Johnson — the man who had been sent to Australia by that club — told them, 'My terms are £6,000.' By now he also had the reputation of a cruel man who had made his opponent suffer, but those who saw him fight maintain that Johnson was not an attacking boxer, indeed, it was almost as if he could not finish his opponents off. Johnson, said some of his contemporaries, was an idle boxer. He was certainly a hated one after this victory. A black man who was world champion at the expense of a whipped white man was certainly not a popular figure in early twentieth-century America. Johnson's affairs with white girls made his an even more detested figure and for some twenty-five years the hatred that people felt for Jack Johnson grew like a cancer in boxing. Not until Joe Louis came on the scene was a black man even allowed to fight for the title — though there were certainly several who were worthy of the chance.

Johnson held his title for almost seven years. His first defence was at Colma, California, ten months after he won it. That October day in 1909, Johnson met Stanley Ketchel, the 'Michigan Assassin' The middleweight champion conceded 35lb to Johnson, nevertheless, for one moment in the twelfth round it looked as though America had finally come up with the white hope for which they had been searching. Ketchel put Johnson on the canvas, but in the same round

it was Ketchel who was counted out. Johnson successfully defended his title five more times — in Reno, Nevada, against Jeffries, who was persuaded out of retirement; against Jim Flynn in Las Vegas; and in three defences in Paris, against Andre Spoul, Jim Johnson, and Frank Moran. The fight against Jeffries was an embarrassing affair with the former champion only a shell of his old self. It was indicative of all that was bad with boxing at that time.

Jack Johnson's reign came to an end on the Oriente Race Track in Havana, Cuba, on 5 April 1915. He met Jess Willard, the 'Pottowatomie Giant' and the 'Great White Hope' for which America had searched. Johnson was now thirty-seven years old, in poor physical shape, and in some financial distress after squandering his fortune enjoying the highlife in Europe. Willard knocked out Johnson in the twenty-sixth round — the longest fight of its kind under modern rules — but then Johnson later claimed that he had 'thrown' the fight, pointing to a photograph of his knockout and alleging that it showed him hiding his face from the sun with his gloves. Willard, the 6ft 6in boxer who did not take up the sport until he was twenty-eight, was one of the most limited of all world heavyweight champions. It was perhaps the scorching Cuban sun which finally beat Jack Johnson, his energy sapped. Did Johnson throw the fight? His later confession, sold to *Ring Magazine*, was perhaps done out of need for the cash. Whatever the truth Johnson later served a jail sentence.

Jack Johnson, the first black heavyweight champion of the world, was also one of the finest. His superb defence, punishing short jabs, and his artful feinting made him that. Sadly, after his defeat by Willard he was forced through financial problems to go on boxing for another thirteen years in the twilight. He loved fast women and fast cars. It was a car which killed him at Raleigh, North Carolina, on 10 June 1946.

JACK DEMPSEY v JESS WILLARD
World Heavyweight Championship
4 July 1919

On the day that the big Texas cowboy Jess Willard took the world heavyweight title from Jack Johnson in Cuba, another boxer, who fought his early bouts under the name of Kid Blackie, was losing a four-round contest to a man called Jack Downey in Salt Lake City. There was nothing to link Kid Blackie with Jess Willard on that April day in 1915. But four years later Willard came up against that unknown — now known as Jack Dempsey — and surrendered to him the world heavyweight crown. A new era was then born and Jack Dempsey known as Manassa Jack — he was born in the town of that name in Colorado on 24 June 1895 — or quite simply called The Champ, became the great idol of the sport, a man who was one of the greatest.

Christened William Harrison and the ninth child of Mormon farmers, Jack Dempsey took the first name by which he was always to be known from a nineteenth-century boxer with whom he shared a surname. In his teens Dempsey ran away from home and bummed around earning his living with a succession of jobs — miner, lumberjack, saloon 'bouncer' — and that last job taught him that he could also earn his corn with his fists. So Jack Dempsey took on all comers, fighting them for as little as a dollar or two. Soon Dempsey's prowess as a fighter came to the notice of a man called Jack Kearns, a young, up-and-coming manager of boxers on America's West Coast. Dempsey needed no second bidding when Kearns offered the promise 'stay with me and I will make you a champion.' That tie-up with Kearns, a flamboyant and ambitious fight manager, was the decision which changed Jack Dempsey's life. Up until then he had

been a small-time fighter on the 'tank town' circuit in Utah, Nevada, and Colorado, coupled with an unsuccessful brush with New York. After meeting Kearns in 1917, however, Dempsey's career took off and within twelve months he was being talked of as the outstanding contender for the world heavyweight championship still held by Jess Willard who had defended the title only once during the three years since he claimed it.

The fight which really earned Jack Dempsey a crack at the title was a bout — if we can call if that — against Fred Fulton, the Sepulpa Plasterer, at Harrison, New Jersey, on 27 July 1918. In that fight Dempsey sent Fulton crashing to the canvas, never to beat the count, within just eighteen seconds of the bell. That was enough to send Kearns out in search of that long awaited title fight with Willard. In December of the same year, another heavyweight, the big Carl Morris, was flattened within fourteen seconds of the first bell when he met Dempsey in New Orleans. With no less than forty-two knockouts under his belt, he met Willard; in fact in his five previous fights before the world title shot, Dempsey had finished each of his opponents in less than one round. Yet it has been said that the promoter Tex Rickard, a one-time cowboy, marshal and prospecter and one of the most colourful boxing promoters of all time, was reluctant to match Dempsey with Willard. Rickard's objection was apparently based on the fact that Dempsey was a good five inches smaller than Willard and conceding something like 53lb to the champion. Kearns kept plugging away and eventually Rickard called a press conference and allowed the two boxers to

12

Jack Dempsey, known as the Manassa Mauler, Manassa Jack or just simply as The Champ.

put forward their case for a title meeting. Of course, this was all part of the Rickard technique which ensured that the public would now be hungry for a Willard-Dempsey confrontation.

Having now assured himself of the financial success of the fight, Rickard now put his plans into motion and when the two men met at Toledo, Ohio, on 4 July 1919. Though only half the seats were occupied, the takings were still in the region of $380,000 (£95,000) with the cheapest seats being sold at $8 (£2). The day of the fight was one of the hottest that Toledo had ever known and as the sun rose higher into the Ohio sky, the temperature climbed with it to somewhere between 110°F and 115°F. Jack Dempsey and his manager were confident of success and they wagered $8,000 (£2,000) of their $28,000 (£7,000) on Dempsey winning in the first round. They also asked for — and got — odds of 10-1 which was surprising considering Dempsey's record as the Manassa Mauler. One writer even went so far as to describe Dempsey as 'a murderer in the ring who should be barred from the sport'.

Jack Dempsey, the challenger, was first into the ring on that blistering day. He paid little attention when the champion entered the arena, though Dempsey was reported later to have said, 'When he took off his dressing gown I have to admit that my heart jumped right into my throat and fluttered there'. Willard was certainly an awesome sight, standing a head taller than the challenger. His reach of eighty-three inches was in contrast to Dempsey's which was five inches shorter. Yet let us not forget that Dempsey, though smaller than Willard, was no midget. Indeed, this was to be a battle of the giants. Dempsey took a corner with his back to the sun, though both boxers were protected from the direct heat by large umbrellas which had been erected over their respective corners. On several occasions before the fight Dempsey had insisted that whatever happened his manager should not throw in the towel. As he left his corner for the first time, Dempsey turned to Kearns and told him, 'If I am to be beaten, then let me be counted out.'

The referee was Ollie Pecord and he called up the two giants for their final instructions. At nine minutes past four o'clock the gong went for the first round and the crowd sat forward on their seats anticipating an epic struggle. Dempsey came out and immediately surprised Willard by abandoning his usual rushing tactics. It was Willard who laid the first blow, a light left to Dempsey's head, and the champion followed this with a right and then another left to the head. Willard now felt confident and he towered over Dempsey, crowding the challenger. But this was exactly what Jack Dempsey wanted. After all, he was the master of the short blow. Dempsey let fly with a short, but powerful right to the heart. As it landed Willard's mouth dropped open and he gasped in pain and surprise. It was the moment for which Dempsey had been waiting. The challenger brought round a left hook to Willard's head. The blow landed high on the Texan's cheek but was still enough to send him to the canvas. Willard stayed down only long enough for the count to reach two and then he was back on his feet and into the fray once more, but he walked right into more trouble. This time Dempsey landed a left to Willard's eye and again the champion went down. The crowd roared and Willard this time rose at nine, complaining that he could not hear the count for the noise of the spectators.

In fact Willard had little time in which to register his complaint. Within seconds he was back on the canvas again, this time on the receiving end of a tremendous right to the chin. Down he went for another count of nine — and this time he had great difficulty in beating ten. Willard climbed unsteadily to his feet just in time and staggered on to the ropes. Then Dempsey let fly and again Willard went down — the fourth time in the opening round that he had stretched his length on the canvas. It seemed that Dempsey and his manager, with $8,000 (£2,000) riding at odds of 10-1 on a first-round finish, were about to become very rich men. Willard took his third count of nine and then got up to wade back for more punishment. In the final minute of that first round Jess Willard, the heavyweight champion of the world, was put down no less than seven times. On the seventh occasion Willard slumped down in a neutral corner, eyes glazed, blood streaming down both nostrils, as the referee counted '. . . seven, eight, nine, out.' Pecord raised Dempsey's hand as the winner and Dempsey raised both hands in triumph as the new heavyweight champion of the world. But he was not — not yet anway. In the pandemonium which had followed Willard's seventh visit to the canvas, no one had heard the bell go. The timekeeper confirmed that the gong had saved Willard with count at seven. But now the ring was full of people and Dempsey, after seeing that he could not get to Willard to console the man he thought was now the vanquished champion, got out of the ring to receive the backslapping of fight fans who crammed the narrow aisles leading to the ring. Then manager Jack Kearns was in the ring and screaming for Dempsey to return: 'For God's sake, Jack, get back in the ring,' he bellowed, 'the fight isn't over yet!'

Dempsey rushed back and fought his way into the ring once more. Pecord explained to a befuddled Willard that he was still the champion and the fight continued into the second round. We now have to put ourselves in Dempsey's position. In a few seconds he had known elation and complete anticlimax. One minute he thought he was the new world champion and $80,000 (£20,000) rin company with his manager; the next he saw the real world champion — albeit bloodstained and shell-shocked — coming at him, and his chance of that $80,000 had gone forever. It must have been quite an emotional shock to Dempsey who now found himself with the job still incomplete. His concentration must have been disturbed as Willard confronted him.

Fortunately for Dempsey, Willard had taken such a battering that he was in terrible shape and had only just made the second round. Yet he did not go down in this round. Perhaps Dempsey needed time to compose himself and get back his wind and concentration. Undoubtedly, Willard showed amazing courage. He had lost two front teeth, his nose and mouth were bleeding freely, his right eye was almost closed, and his forehead was swollen and bruised. Somehow he managed to stay on his feet as Dempsey proved he was unable to finish the job, but the challenger did manage to get some telling righthanders on to Willard's right eye and by the time the bell went to end the torture of the champion, the eye had closed completely. The third round was much the same story. Willard came out of it looking a pitiful wretch, like the victim of some horrible accident. Dempsey hammered him on the face and body, landing blow after blow, wrecking any hopes that Willard might have nurtured for a knockout. Poor Willard was quite unable to land one blow of any consequence. He could only stumble and be hit. Dempsey drew blood again with a right to the mouth. Willard made a feeble attempt at saving some pride but his punches found fresh air — and then Dempsey hammered him again — 'like a giant riveting machine' one reporter wrote — and the blood streamed down his swollen face in

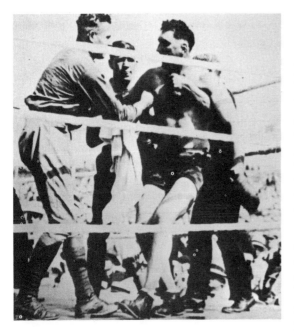

The fight is over for Jess Willard but the ex-champion still needs assistance to leave his corner for the dressing room after his hammering at the hands of Dempsey at Toledo in July 1919.

little rivulets, finding their course between the folds of puffy skin. When the bell went to end the third round Willard stumbled back to his corner and crashed down on to his stool. The crowd were now in no mood to witness any more bloodshed. They bayed at the referee to stop the fight: 'Murder, stop it, for God's sake!' cried one man close to the ringside, and there were many others whose voices could not be heard. Meanwhile, Willard's seconds were working desperately on their man's face.

This time there was nothing to be done. The referee was called to the champion's corner and there was a brief moment of debate before Dempsey knew that he was the new king. The old monarch could not go on; Willard had received such a battering that it was impossible for him to continue. Dempsey's hand was held high and the world had a new heavyweight champion. Willard had not held Dempsey in particularly high esteem and was not in the best possible shape — mentally or physically — for this fight. He

had done little serious training and had paid for his indiscretion by having to abdicate while sitting on a stool. Not until the fight had been over for a full ten minutes was Willard able to move from that stool. In that time Jack Dempsey, now to become one of the greatest names in boxing history, had gone over and offered his sympathy. Willard mumbled some reply. He probably was unaware that it was the new champion talking to him. Willard was given restoratives and examined by a doctor before he was allowed back to his dressing room.

Jack Dempsey's title win had been achieved with one of the most remorseless exhibitions of boxing ever seen. Seldom, if ever, has a world champion taken such a beating as he lost his crown. Not surprisingly in view of the ferocity of Dempsey's punches there was controversy after the fight. 37-year-old Willard had held the title for four years and three months when he lost to 24-year-old Dempsey under the boiling sun in Toledo. Now came stories that Dempsey had something other than bandages in his gloves. The favourite story was that the new champion had sprinkled his bandages with plaster of Paris and then soaked them in water so that they set hard like concrete. It was a highly unlikely story and yet even Willard was convinced that there was something in it, though men who had seen the bandages wrapped round Dempsey's hands firmly refute such a possibility. Harry Carpenter, the BBC television boxing commentator, wrote in his book *Boxing - A Pictorial History* (William Collins, 1975): 'From personal experience I know that Willard, a bitter old man, went to his death in 1968, not far short of ninety, still convinced that Dempsey had *something* in those gloves, other than his hands.' What was for certain was that the Jack Dempsey era saw the start of the sport as a multi-million dollar business. The devastated Willard, slumped on his stool, was left in another age. Jack Dempsey led the charge to wealth. He was the first and others would now follow in his golden wake.

JIM DRISCOLL v CHARLES LEDOUX
_____ European Bantamweight Championship _____
20 October 1919

'Jim Driscoll is the master. He is the greatest man I have ever met or ever shall meet. He played with me for fourteen and a half rounds and I could do absolutely nothing.' So said the great French boxer, Charles Ledoux, of one of Wales's classiest fighters. Jim Driscoll, who returned to the ring after his career had been over for six years and might well have scored one last magnificent victory had it not been for the fact that the duration of his final appearance had been changed at the last minute. As it was Driscoll lost. But he went out after giving one of the most classic displays of the art of boxing that the ring has ever seen.

Jim Driscoll was born in Cardiff in 1881, a man who never knew anything other than hardship and suffering in his early years. Jim's mother was a widow who lived in the most reduced circumstances. As soon as he was able, young Jim, small and good-looking with dark, curly hair, left school and found a job in the printing works of a local newspaper. When the other workers in the composing room decided to form a boxing club, Jim Driscoll was the first to put down his name and as a popular lad he soon found himself elected club captain. Money for boxing gloves was in very short supply in the Cardiff of the late nineteenth century and the boxers of this particular club had to innovate. They used waste paper, picked up from the floor of the printing room, scrounged some string from the packing department, and made their gloves from that. It did not, however, prevent them from acquiring considerable boxing skills, and club captain Jim Driscoll was the star of the company. Naturally, it was not long before Driscoll's prowess came to the attention of the more wealthy and organised clubs in Cardiff and two local enthusiasts took him under their wings. Before long Jim was boxing in the local clubs and polished up his skills by touring with a boxing booth for several years.

Jim Driscoll's reputation had now spread far beyond the borders of the Principality and in 1906 he went to London and shocked the members of the National Sporting Club by beating Joe Bowker, then considered the best boxer of the day at both bantamweight and featherweight. Now Jim Driscoll's name was being spoken of not just in British boxing circles, but internationally. He was known in the United States and before long he was across the Atlantic to do battle in America. Soon he was a big attraction in American cities where the little Welshman's classy style was a revelation. Driscoll's great weapon was a flashing blade of a left hand which he used to drive his opponents into the ground with remorseless hammering. Then, when all was lost with the other man, Driscoll would employ his right hand to deliver the final crushing blow. Though not the sort of boxer who went after his man with the intention of finishing the bout in the shortest possible time, Jim Driscoll had his fair share of victories which finished well inside the distance and this, coupled with his ability to produce such a textbook style made the Americans send forward their best featherweights in a bid to bring this little Welshman down. All of them failed and eventually Driscoll was matched with Abe Attell, the man who was recognised as the featherweight champion of the world. Attell, a Jew from San Francisco, had first laid claim to the world title in 1901 when The

Charles Ledoux, the French hero of the ring.

Little Hebrew, as Attell was known, beat the former champion George Dixon on points over fifteen rounds in St Louis. The two had met a week earlier in that October when they boxed a draw. So Attell had the vacant title to himself and proceeded to defend it against allcomers.

On 13 October 1904, eight months after stopping Harry Forbes in five rounds, Attell met Tommy Sullivan in St Louis and was knocked out in the fifth round. But after complaining that Sullivan was over the weight, Attell kept his world featherweight crown and continued to defend it successfully until 1912 when he lost to Johnny Kilbane on points over twenty rounds at Vernon, California. One of his most difficult fights before Kilbane took the title from him was against Jim Driscoll on 19 February 1909 when the Welshman's success against every other featherweight that America could produce earned him a shot at the world title. It was a fight which turned out to be one of the most thrilling in boxing history.

The crowd at the National Athletic Club of New York witnessed one of the greatest performances ever achieved by a British boxer on foreign soil. For fully ten rounds Abe Attell was given a lesson in the art of boxing by the little Welshman. Driscoll finally underscored his reputation for being a *clever* boxer. He would surely have beaten the world champion had it not been for the fact that the fight was staged on a 'no decision' basis. That is to say that to claim the fight, Driscoll had either to knock out his opponent, or stop him. Some States forbade fight officials to give decisions and it was the fact that Driscoll was fighting in one such State which cost the Welshman victory. It did earn him the nickname for which he became well-known. One American writer — no less a person than the legendary United States marshal Bat Masterson, the scourge of Dodge City, who had taken up the pen — described Driscoll as Peerless Jim, a name which stuck.

Back home in Britain, hailed as the world champion by the sporting press who paid no heed to the rules of American States, Peerless Jim was matched against Seaman Arthur Hayes in a fight for the British championship. Hayes was disposed of in six rounds and Driscoll was the new British featherweight champion. Driscoll claimed the first Lonsdale Belt awarded for the featherweight division. He subsequently beat Spike Robson on two occasions to become the first British boxer to win a Lonsdale Belt outright. Driscoll's second contest with Robson was the Welshman's only fight of 1911. In 1912 he again made only one appearance — but it was enough to win him the European title when he knocked out the Frenchman, Jean Posey, in the twelfth round. Driscoll's infrequent appearances were not of his own choosing. It was simply that there were no featherweights available who could be put in the ring

17

Peerless Jim Driscoll's classic straight left has Ledoux's knees bending.

against Peerless Jim and stand much chance of winning. Indeed, it would have been rank stupidity to have matched him with some of the young boxers who clamoured for the chance. In 1913 he again had only one contest: against Owen Moran who had just returned from an American tour. The fight should have been in Birmingham for what was billed as the world title, but someone lodged a complaint — professional fighting was unpopular in many quarters — and the men were charged with attempting to cause a breach of the peace. The fight was moved to the National Sporting Club and after twenty rounds a draw was declared. Peerless Jim Driscoll then announced his retirement.

Eighteen months after Driscoll's decision, Britain plunged into war with Germany and Driscoll was immediately drafted as an Army physical training instructor. Driscoll set himself a massive workload teaching soldiers to box, first in France and then at Aldershot, and boxing many hundreds of rounds himself each year. At the end of World War I, Driscoll got together and trained the British Army boxing team which won the Allied Tournament at the Royal

Albert Hall. After the war most people in boxing were amazed to learn that Driscoll was going to resume his career. It had been widely thought that he would turn his energies to training boxers, but in 1919 Driscoll met and beat another veteran the Box o' Tricks himself, Pedlar Palmer. But another fight, against a young Welshman named Francis Rossi, found Driscoll unable to finish his younger and much less experienced opponent and in twenty rounds the fight was declared a draw. Driscoll now realised that after six years out of the competitive ring, a comeback was not possible. Later that year, however, officials of the National Sporting Club approached him to fight one last time in the Covent Garden arena. Driscoll readily agreed and when his opponent was named as the French pastrycook, Charles Ledoux, eleven years his junior and one of the best boxers in France at that time, even that did not cause so much as a raised eyebrow from Peerless Jim.

Ledoux was well-known as a brave and tough boxer. The French bantamweight champion, he had beaten many fine British opponents including Digger Stanley, Joe Bowker, Bill Beynon, Walter Ross, Jim Higgins, Tommy Noble, Curley Walker and Tommy Harrison, his defeat of Stanley in 1912, Ledoux knocking him out in the seventh round, being for the world title in Dieppe. Ledoux lost his title to Eddie Campi in America a year later, but he was still a formidable opponent when he was chosen to face Driscoll. He was also the European champion — a title he held with a short break until 1923 — and it seemed a foolhardy venture for Driscoll. The fight was first scheduled for fifteen rounds but later changed to twenty and we shall see how crucial was that alteration. The fight was also made at 8st 12lb and again one has to question the wisdom in making Driscoll's 'swan song' at weight and over the full championship distance. There must have been several worthy men who could have provided his final opposition. As it is, this fight with Ledoux is still listed as a European title affair.

*Ledoux's head is bowed but it was Peerless Jim
who finally succumbed in this, his last fight.*

Yet for fourteen rounds of this contest it appeared as though Jim Driscoll had lost none of his old speed, dash and cunning. His immaculate style was more than a match for Charles Ledoux, the European champion, and from the first round the Frenchman knew that he had a real battle on his hands. Although Ledoux made the opening moves he failed to lay a glove on Driscoll. A left to the face and a flashing uppercut both failed to find their target and Peerless Jim feinted and weaved with ease. Even at this stage there was the sight of Jim Driscoll upright in the truly classic pose, while Ledoux bowed down and bent his back almost in submission. For those fourteen rounds it was all Jim Driscoll. The images of the fight remained in the minds of those who were privileged enough to witness it for years afterwards. There was Driscoll, drawing off the Frenchman before jabbing in one of those famous lefts; and Ledoux frantically attempting to get through Driscoll's classic guard. There was Driscoll making the younger man come off his stool at the start of each round and forcing him to walk across the ring to meet him; then there was Driscoll working the pattern of the fight so beautifully that, at the end of each round, he had almost the position where he only had to bend his knees to find his stool, whereas Ledoux had to walk back across the ring to his.

Driscoll obviously was not going to expend one more ounce of his own energy than was absolutely necessary. He knew that if he allowed the pace to become frantic his chances of staying the twenty rounds were not high. So he set out to wear down Ledoux by constantly changing the pattern of the fight. His instincts, his vast experience, told on the French champion. Anticipating a flurry of blows, Driscoll would sway back and then counter with a right or left as Ledoux came rushing past; or he would crack him on the chin with an uppercut of crisp, stunning power. Driscoll would sway his head the merest inch — but it would be enough to diffuse any attack that Ledoux might mount. All the time there was Driscoll's nagging, penetrating left hand, stabbing out to swell his opponent's face. Ledoux's lips were swollen, his left eye half-closed. When he failed to land a blow he would almost raise his hands in questioning astonishment: 'Just what do I do now?'

They came out for the fourteenth round and again it was Ledoux who did the rushing while Peerless Jim was content to let him. Driscoll was now even managing to deflect Ledoux's punches by gentle little nudges to the Frenchman's shoulders which meant that intended blows were misdirected without Driscoll having to bother swaying out of the way. Seldom can a boxer's limitations have been shown up in the way that Jim Driscoll exposed Charles Ledoux's technique that day.

But halfway through that fourteenth round came the punch that changed the course of this fight. Ledoux, who despite the punishment he had received, and all the energy he had had to use to get precisely nowhere, still packed a powerful punch. Ledoux might have been out of this fight if it had been the original fifteen-rounder. But Driscoll knew that he still had another seven rounds to go. He knew that the younger man would stand the pace better; he perhaps felt that it was now time to finish the job. He began to score points quickly and Ledoux, almost in sheer desperation, swung an almighty punch to Driscoll's body. It was the sort of punch that the Welshman had been comtemptuously avoiding all afternoon, but this time Ledoux was in luck. Peerless Jim was a fraction slow and the punch, a cracking right, thumped into his midriff. For a moment Driscoll's face went ashen, his legs buckled, and his strength drained away with the need to cope with pain. He recovered to launch a quick attack and then the bell went. When the fifteenth round started it was obvious that Driscoll had shot his bolt. He had no strength left — it had all been sapped by that thunderbolt of a punch — and

it was a mystery how he survived. Ledoux came at him like a devil, slamming rights and lefts into Driscoll's body. The Welshman avoided some, took many others in full, and was quite unable to lay a punch in return. His ability for attack was gone. In the previous fourteen rounds there had been great cheering; in the fifteenth there was only a stunned silence. It was now all Ledoux and the spectators prayed for the bell. When it came to spare Driscoll further agony there was a great sigh of relief.

Right at the start of the round Driscoll had been caught a tremendous right hand to the head and that, together with the punch which caught him in the previous round, meant that he could not cope with the barrage of punches which Ledoux had then laid upon him. When the bell went for the sixteenth round Driscoll got to his feet and tottered to the centre of the ring. He wanted to go on, but his corner did not. For a moment there was a strange, unreal moment as Driscoll prepared to fight on, unaware that his corner had surrendered for him, and with Ledoux in full possession of the facts and now not willing to come out of his corner, Driscoll looked somewhat bemused. Then he was led away by his seconds, much to the relief of the spectators and of Charles Ledoux who obviously did not want to continue the slaughter of this gallant old master.

Charles Ledoux boxed on for several more years and became quite a personality, becoming mayor of a French spa town and ending his days a rich man after putting his earnings from professional boxing into land, unlike so many boxers who frittered away the money they won with their fists. Ledoux never forgot the boxing lesson that he received that day from Peerless Jim Driscoll. He knew that, but for a chance punch, he might well have lost that fight. Driscoll, of course, did not box again. He was dogged by ill-health and died in January 1925, remembered for his classy style, his wonderful defence, his magnificent left hand, but, most of all, for his last fight when he came back to give a magnificent boxing lessson.

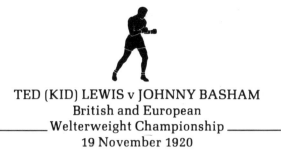

TED (KID) LEWIS v JOHNNY BASHAM
British and European
Welterweight Championship
19 November 1920

There can have been few return fights so eagerly awaited by the boxing public as that between Ted (Kid) Lewis and Johnny Basham for the welterweight championships of Great Britain and of Europe and scheduled for the Royal Albert Hall on 19 November 1920. Five months earlier, at Olympia, London, Lewis, the local boy, had taken the titles by stopping Basham in the ninth round of a bloody contest. Basham lost his British title that night — the European title was vacant after Switzerland's Albert Badoud had relinquished it because of weight problems — and he was in a tearing hurry to regain the British and to take the European championship, especially since he felt somewhat outdone after the Olympia affair. Basham, a Welshman from Newport who learned his boxing as a private in the Royal Welch Fusiliers, had been unwise enough to go into that first fight with Lewis minus a gumshield. In the third round of the fight Lewis had caught Basham a terrific blow and a tooth had been driven into the roof of the defending British champion's mouth. Blood had continued to pour from a severe wound for the rest of the fight and though it had developed into a thrilling affair, it was perhaps as well that Basham failed to convince the referee that he could continue, hard though he tried to impress the official. In November of the same year, Basham was ready for another crack. He felt sure that he could outfox and outbox Lewis, the former world champion. Now he had the chance to prove it.

Not unnaturally, Johnny Basham's style was most orthodox, as you would expect from a man who learned his noble art in the service of King and Country. He had a lovely straight left and, though not many of his victories were as a result of the knockout punch, the boy from Newport could deliver a blow of the required quality when the occasion demanded. Within three years of starting out in the professional ranks, Basham had risen to the top of his division and took the British title for the first time by knocking out Johnny Summers in the ninth round at the National Sporting Club just before Christmas 1914. Summers needed the victory to win the Lonsdale Belt outright: he had won the required three title fights, but one of them was at Liverpool and the dispensation of the Belts was at the pleasure of the National Sporting Club where he had won two title fights. Thus he was obviously keen to get the coveted award outright and can be considered a most difficult opponent. Basham then went on to become the first welterweight to win the Lonsdale Belt outright, a feat he accomplished on 1 May 1916 against Eddie Beattie, and took the defence of the title a stage further on 13 November 1919 when he won on points over twenty rounds against Matt Wells in London.

Lewis was born in Aldgate and was four years younger than Basham. He was raised in the tough world of Whitechapel — Jack the Ripper country — and first fought for pennies at the Judean Club in the heart of London's East End. His frail appearance belied his furious style and in 1912, Lewis, then a featherweight, got his big chance with a fight at the National Sporting Club. His opponent that day was a young man from Camberwell called Duke Lynch. In the first round Lynch landed a crushing blow on young Lewis's jaw and he was counted out. At the age of eighteen it was a devastating

Johnny Basham, the boy from Newport who learned his boxing in the Royal Welch Fusiliers.

blow for a young fighter to suffer, but Lewis was born to box and he was soon back in the ring, shrugging off the defeat as all part of his training for bigger and better things.

Lewis fought back and in the following year was considered good enough to dispute the British featherweight title with Alec Lambert at the National Sporting Club. On 6 October 1913 Lewis surprised everyone except himself when he forced the referee to stop the fight in the seventeenth round. Lewis was not in the featherweight division for long, however, for he had trouble in maintaining the weight. After returning his Belt to the NSC he moved up a division and went to Australia where he scored a famous win over the well-known Hughie Mehegan. Then Lewis was off again, this time to America, where he developed his speed and punching power to the point where he was the logical contender for the world welter-weight title. In 1915 Lewis took the title and until he was knocked out by Jack Britton in 1919, he monopolised it, save for one spell when Britton took it from him in the interim. Back home in England, Lewis proved too good for his challengers and this earned him his first crack at Johnny Basham and the resultant titles at the Olympic arena when Basham was left rueing the fact that he wore no gumshield.

The return fight had all the ingredients of the sell-out it became, with the fast and furious style of Ted (Kid) Lewis winning him many followers, while the more classic style of Basham gave the purists the view that he would win, and had been unlucky to lose in the first place. The two men also had differing styles of approach to the fight. Where Lewis remained impassive, Basham kidded and joked his way through, even during the weigh-in. Seldom can there have been two more dissimilar fighting men vying for a title. Poker-faced Lewis refused to be moved by Johnny Basham's clowning. In the ring that November evening Lewis boxed in the same cold, merciless manner, wearing down his opponent with a show of remorseless punching in the later rounds.

It was the man from Aldgate who opened the attack, swinging a right to Basham's head. The Welshman anticipated it and

Ted (Kid) Lewis, born in Aldgate as Solomon Mendeloff, and grew up in the tough East End.

swayed to the side to let the blow faintly brush his face. Basham then jabbed out his left which the champion took but by which he did not appear to be bothered. Instead, Lewis countered with a left and a right to Basham's head which did check the former champion for a second or two. Lewis went after Basham but the Welshman countered too, laying three left jabs with machine gun-like rapidity into Lewis's face. They found themselves on the ropes and Lewis, refusing to be bottled up, smashed away with lefts and rights, some missing, but others finding the target. When Basham managed to get away to the middle of the ring he was able to come back again and land two punches — both left jabs — on Lewis's face. Although they were not as strong as the champion's they still raised a swelling above the Kid's left eye. For the next four rounds it was all Johnny Basham. Whenever possible Lewis tried to get to close-quarters where he could be assured of keeping Basham mainly on the defensive. Lewis and Basham each had totally different plans of campaign. For Lewis it was to be an in-fight; Basham, on the other hand, wanted everything carried out at long distance.

In the early stages of the fight Basham achieved this, but as the bout wore on he allowed Lewis to have his own way. Basham was letting the fight slip away from him at this stage. If he could keep the fight at arm's length, and keep his left going, then he was assured of the title once more, but he would keep getting in close and occasionally trying to join in the fray by swinging a right at Lewis's head, which left his own entirely unprotected. The sixth round saw a fluke which might have had far-reaching conse- quences. Lewis tried a haymaker of a right to Basham's jaw but aimed too high. At the same time Basham ducked and the punch hit him full on the top of the head. He lurched backwards while Lewis inspected a burst glove. He showed it the referee, but Basham told him loudly, 'Come on, that doesn't matter!' as if to imply that, gloves or bare knuckles, he was ready for the champion.

By the halfway stage Basham had won every round by the smallest of margins and except for the occasional bout of foolhardi- ness had suffered no real damage. When the bell went for the eleventh round the cham- pion came out with renewed determination. He was behind and he knew it. Though not at the stage where he should have been worried, Lewis knew that he had to speed up the pace. He set about Basham from first to last bell of each round after that, but still Johnny Basham took it all in his stride, weathering the storm which Lewis was unleashing on him. He was still scoring points himself and fully aware that, if he could keep this up, the title would be his once more. But in the thirteenth round Lewis landed a cracking blow which split Basham's right ear and caused it to bleed freely. The blow stunned the challenger and he was still reeling from it when the bell went to signal the end of the round. In the fourteenth round Lewis cracked the ear again and made the injury still worse. Basham was now more concerned with protecting the ear, and Lewis then went to work on the rest of the former champion's exposed body. By the end of that round Basham was a different fighter from the confident one of the earlier rounds.

For the first time he had lost a round and from then on he lost each one. In the fifteenth round he suffered the first knockdown of the fight, going down as much through sheer exhaustion as anything else. The next three rounds saw Lewis again go after Basham's ear and again Basham allowed himself to be hit elsewhere. The end was surely not far off and it came in the nineteenth round. Basham's early lead meant that if he could stay on his feet then he would still win; but staying on his feet was the problem. Basham tried a haymaking right, missed, and was dumped on the floor with a left to the body, followed by a right to the jaw. He got up at nine, but could only stagger across the ring, whereupon Lewis went after him. The cham- pion opened up Basham's feeble defence and delivered a left, then a right, to the chin. Down went Basham again, like the prov- erbial sack of potatoes.

Amazingly, Basham managed to get up

Ted (Kid) Lewis lets go a right-hander as
Basham prepares to take evasive action.

again and as Lewis came in to deliver what would surely be the final blow, the referee stepped in and raised the champion's hand. In fact, in the general uproar, the challenger had been counted out and no one had noticed. So Lewis won by a knockout and retained the titles of Britain and Europe after one of the greatest battles of the ring. Ted (Kid) Lewis was one of Britain's greatest boxers of his era. He met Basham twice more. In 1921, after Basham had won the British and European middleweight titles from Gus Platts, Lewis stopped him in the twelfth round and ended his career. Sadly, Basham was foolishly persuaded out of retirement in 1929 when he met Lewis in a charity fight at the Hoxton Baths. It got as far as the third round before Lewis won again. But it will be for his great contribution to boxing that Basham will be best remembered, not least the night he fought that classic with Ted (Kid) Lewis.

JIMMY WILDE v PETE HERMAN
Catchweight contest at the
Royal Albert Hall
13 January 1921

They called him 'The Ghost with a Hammer in his hand'. Jimmy Wilde was one of the greatest flyweights of all time. The veteran of literally hundreds of fights — no one is quite certain just how many if one includes those in the boxing booths of his native South Wales — Wilde, or 'The Little Atom' to give him his other nickname, took on all comers and in a career which lasted from 1911 to 1923 scored seventy-five knockouts and was defeated only four times. Wilde is probably remembered as well for one of these defeats as for any of his famous victories; a defeat at the Royal Albert Hall in the winter of 1921 which reduced many hardened boxing fans to tears.

In 1916 Jimmy Wilde became the first official world flyweight champion in the new class invented by the British exclusively for boxing's smallest men. Though still several pounds lighter than the poundage limit of the time (108lb) and, indeed, of the eventual limit which was settled at 112lb (8 stones), Wilde was by the far the outstanding fighter in the class. On 18 December 1916, at London's Holborn Stadium, he scored an eleventh-round knockout over the Italian-born American, Young Zulu Kid (alias Joe de Melfi) to take the world crown. A year earlier, Wilde had suffered one of his rare defeats when Scotsman Tancy Lee stopped him in the seventeenth round of his British title fight at the National Sporting Club. It should be recorded, however, that Wilde had been suffering from influenza, while Lee was more than a stone heavier than the champion. Wilde soon regained his title, for after Lee had lost to Joe Symonds, Wilde stopped Symonds at the National Sporting Club on 14 February 1916, and

when he stopped Tancy Lee at the same venue four months later, The Little Atom took the Lonsdale Belt outright. Later that year, Wilde took the first world title and held it for the next seven years. For the rest of World War I, The Little Atom boxed exhibitions and non-world title fights in Britain and when the Armistice was signed in 1918 he went to America where he created a great impression.

Wilde's success in the United States stirred up a tremendous amount of interest in the flyweight class and he boxed such fighters as Little Jack Sharkey, Babe Asher, Micky Russell, Young Zulu Kid, Battling Murray and others. Wilde's American campaign was a busy one, though it did mean that he had to give up his European and British titles, and when he returned home he was given something of a hero's welcome. Though small and with an almost under nourished look about him, Wilde packed an incredibly powerful punch and lived up to that name of 'The Ghost with the Hammer in his hand', given to him by the great bantamweight, Pedlar Palmer. The small, skinny, pale-faced man from South Wales packed a punch like a mule's kick and this, coupled with his impeccable timing, made him an opponent to be avoided if at all possible.

All this meant that Jimmy Wilde was hot property at the box office and in January 1919 he was matched against the American Pete Herman. Although his career in the ring went back seven years, this was to be the first time that Herman had boxed abroad. Herman began boxing in his sixteenth year, a native of New Orleans who took the world bantamweight title when he beat Kid Williams on points over twenty rounds in

Jimmy Wilde, the world's first official flyweight champion.

Peter Herman, from New Orleans, who was hot property at the box office.

his native city in 1917. Herman held the bantamweight title until December 1920 when he was outpointed by Joe Lynch in New York. Three weeks after losing that crown, Herman was in London for a fight with Jimmy Wilde set at 118lb. The Wilde-Herman fight was one of the main features of this tournament which also included a fight between Bombardier Wells and Battling Levinsky, and with the Prince of Wales, later the Duke of Windsor, in attendance, the evening promised to be a memorable one. Yet it very soon looked as though it would degenerate into a farce. First it was announced that Levinsky had pulled out; then there was a bitter argument over the lighting arrangements which, it was alleged, obscured the view of many of the paying customers; and finally there was the news that the Wilde-Herman fight might not, after all, take place. All this after one of the preliminary contests had been so hopelessly mismatched that it had the crowd in fits of laughter.

The arrival of the Prince of Wales resulted in loud cheering and calls for the royal visitor to make a speech, which he duly did from the centre of the ring. Then came three rousing choruses of 'For He's a Jolly Good Fellow', and more cheers. All this time there was the most fierce argument going on in the dressing rooms. The contest between Wilde and Herman was now based on the weights for the fight. The contracts had allowed for Herman to be more than a stone heavier than

Wilde. Wilde wanted to ensure that Herman weighed in immediately before the fight. At that afternoon's weigh-in the American had barely made the agreed weight. Now, after a meal, Wilde felt sure that his opponent was well over the stipulated maximum. The rows went on and the crowd grew restless. Wilde, and the men guiding him, were adamant, but eventually, after being told that the Prince of Wales himself would like Wilde to fight, the little Welshman declared, 'Well, if the Prince wants me to fight, then I'll fight.' Lord Lonsdale breathed a sigh of relief, and the two boxers began to make their final preparation for the fight. Wilde, not unnaturally, received the greatest cheer as he climbed into the ring and it has been said that the Prince of Wales leaned forward and said, 'Thank you Wilde — and the very best of luck.'

From the very first round Jimmy Wilde realised that he was up against one of the most formidable opponents of his life. The huge crowd was with the Mighty Atom to a man, but this did not deceive Wilde, nor the experts who were watching. The betting veered sharply from 2-5 on Wilde to even money and in the second round it appeared as if even they were generous odds as Herman almost had Wilde beaten there and then. However, the Welshman fought back like a tiger and carried the fight to the American. Wilde knew that his opponent possessed a skill and fighting ability to match his own; and, more to the point, the weight disadvantage which he had always suffered was now critical. Yet, as so often when fighting men of much greater weight, Jimmy Wilde carried the fight to his opponent. For a while he started to take points and at one stage was actually in front.

For fully six rounds Jimmy Wilde held his own against the heavier Pete Herman. But in the seventh, the American's extra poundage began to tell. He increased the pressure and put more power into his punches with Wilde now fighting with his back to the wall. The eighth round went much the same way and it was only Jimmy Wilde's indomitable spirit which kept him in the fight during the ninth. He soaked up all the punishment which the bigger, heavier American meted out and just when it seemed that the bantamweight would outbox the flyweight to the point where he would succumb, Wilde fought back courageously and in the twelfth round actually got on top of his opponent for a brief spell. Unfortunately that incredible show of attacking bravery sapped the last ounces of stamina from Wilde's wilting body. The thirteenth and fourteenth rounds came and went with Wilde hanging on desperately: in the fifteenth it was little short of amazing that at the end of it, Wilde was still on his feet. It was the same again in the sixteenth, at the end of which The Little Atom's corner administered smelling salts to their charge.

Jimmy Wilde (right) covers up in the face of a Herman attack. The Mighty Atom had the crowd in tears after his courageous display.

The bell went and Jimmy Wilde left his corner for the seventeenth and last time in this fight.

Wilde was in bad shape as he tottered to the centre of the ring to meet Herman once more and a swinging right hand sent him crashing through the ropes and half out of the ring. The count started and it was up to eight before the gritty little Welshman managed to disentangle himself and meet Herman again. When he did he found the American waiting for him with another haymaker which felled Wilde again. Up again, this time just before the count of ten ...and down again when Herman lashed him with another right. Once more the gallant Welshman struggled to his feet — and now many of the spectators were weeping openly at such a display of raw courage. Wilde was ready for yet more punishment but the referee, Jack Smith, reckoned that he had suffered enough and led him away to his corner. Game to the last, Jimmy Wilde protested that he wanted to carry on, but his seconds would have none of it. People were still in tears; some had even left the arena seconds before, unable to stomach the sight any longer. That display of guts and fire has never been surpassed in the ring to this day.

Herman won back his bantamweight world title six months after beating Jimmy Wilde, though he held it for only a further two months. Wilde remained world flyweight champion until June 1923 when he was knocked out in the seventh round in New York by Pancho Villa. Wilde was then thirty-one-years old and perhaps it was the folly of meeting the bigger, stronger Herman which finally cost the Welshman the world title. Pete Herman never had any doubts about Wilde's quality. He was always ready to tell people, 'Jimmy Wilde was the greatest fighter I ever saw in my life — make no mistake about it.'

JACK DEMPSEY v GEORGES CARPENTIER
World Heavyweight Championship
2 July 1921

After taking the world heavyweight championship from Jess Willard in July 1919, Jack Dempsey defended it twice the following year, stopping Billy Miske in three rounds at Benton Harbour, Michigan, and then accounting for Bill Brennan in twelve at Madison Square Garden towards the end of that year. But it was not until the Manassa Mauler was pitted against the idol of France, Georges Carpentier, that the Golden Era of world heavyweight boxing really came into being. When Killer Jack met Gorgeous George (or the Orchid Kid as he was also known) on a site known as Boyle's Thirty Acres, Jersey City, on 2 July 1921, boxing saw its first million-dollar gate, even though some 36,000 of the 117,000 seats remained unoccupied. It was the start of an era which has catapulted boxing towards the multi-million dollar world heavyweight title fights of today which are beamed live by communications satellites across the globe.

Dempsey's opponent on that July day over six decades ago was the best-known boxer that France ever produced. Born in 1894, Georges Carpentier was the world light heavyweight champion when he came to Jersey City for a shot at what was now the richest prize in boxing. Carpentier took the light-heavyweight crown by knocking out Battling Levinsky in the fourth round of their title fight in New York in October 1920. Carpentier was also heavyweight and light-heavyweight champion of Europe. He took the heavyweight title from Bombardier Billy Wells at Ghent in 1913, and the light-heavyweight crown by beating another British contender, Bandsman Rice, at Paris, also in 1913. Carpentier also held the European middleweight title from 1912 to 1920 when he gave it up to concentrate on the two heaviest classes. He also held the European welterweight title in 1911, again giving up that for the heavier weights, and, of course, he was the French champion at every weight from welter to heavy. He was, then, the outstanding contender for Dempsey's world crown at that time.

It was a natural match and though Carpentier was really only a light-heavyweight, his accurate long-range punching, particularly his right hand, and his graceful, dancing style which ghosted him around the ring, gave the American public every confidence that here was a man who would test their champion to his utmost. Promoter Tex Rickard was not so sure. He had seen Carpentier sparring at his training camp in Long Island, New York, and he could not help but feel uncomfortable when partners got in close to crowd the Frenchman. Rickard could not help wondering if the glamorous Frenchman would be vulnerable to the savage attack of the world champion. However, that was not his immediate worry. His prime concern was to fill the seats in the huge stadium he had constructed on Boyle's Thirty Acres. Carpentier had been promised $200,000, Dempsey $300,000, and the cost of erecting a stadium big enough to house the anticipated crown was $50,000. So before a punch was thrown in anger, Rickard was looking for takings of well over half a million dollars just to break even. If the American sporting press got to see Carpentier, they would surely spot that he was not likely seriously to test the champion. If they wrote as much, then Rickard was likely to be hundreds of thousands of dollars out of pocket. Rickard, however, was a promoter of the most extraordinary quality, thinking far ahead of his next move. He made Carpentier into a mystery boxer. By refusing to let the press in to the Frenchman's workouts, which decision he blamed on Carpentier's manager, he brought about a situation whereby the Dempsey-Carpentier fight was being called 'The Battle of the Century', and that was exactly what Tex Rickard wanted.

Indeed, quite apart from his place at the top of European boxing, Georges Carpentier had many other qualities which endeared him to promoter Rickard. He was tall and handsome; and a war hero. Gorgeous George had interrupted his boxing career to fly for France and then resumed his sensational run of successes in the ring. He would have almost as much of a female following as he had from America's fight fans. But Rickard's bid to get Carpentier over the Atlantic had not been easy. The Frenchman had first signed up with the British promoter C.B. Cochrane and when Rickard responded by obtaining Dempsey's signature, there followed a series of rival bids for the fight until Rickard offered Cochrane a partnership. It was agreed but Cochrane then became seriously ill and, unknown to him, his wife withdrew the bid on his behalf, leaving Rickard a clear field. That was how George Carpentier came to be in America in the summer of 1921.

Rickard's stadium in Jersey City was started on 26 April and finished only days before the fight. He sold huge blocks of tickets to speculators and two weeks before the fight was due to be staged Rickard knew that he would make a profit. It was to be the first million-dollar gate in boxing history. Thousands poured into Jersey City on the day of the fight, many of them only to find that they had bought counterfeit tickets and were unable to gain admission, though many seats were still unoccupied in the huge wooden bowl. As the stadium filled up Dempsey and his manager looked at the 'octagon of teeming humanity' as one newspaper reporter described it, and rued the fact that they had opted for a guaranteed purse instead of a share of the gate money. Rickard

told them. 'You've talked yourself out of a fortune. There's over a million and a half dollars down there.' But Jack Dempsey just shrugged his shoulders and replied, 'When I've licked this Frenchman you'll be talking to me like a million dollars.'

Carpentier's reception when he climbed into the ring surprised even the French boxer and his manager, Francois Descamps. The challenger was greeted by loud cheering and it took him a minute or two to drink it all in. Then Gorgeous George responded by throwing kisses to the crowd and waving to them. Dempsey, in sharp contrast, just sat and glowered, a week's growth of beard making him look even more ferocious than ever. The referee called the boxers together. Carpentier came across dancing and smiling; Dempsey offered him a sullen nod of the head and they went back to their corners, instructions duly noted.

When the bell went to start the contest, Carpentier astounded the fans by launching himself into a ferocious attack, obviously of the opinion that he could do it, though it had been generally thought that he would rely on his speed and boxing ability to get him through. Certainly, no one anticipated that the Frenchman would carry the fight to the champion. Two lightning lefts jabbed into the champion's face, then two equally flashing rights, and the Manassa Mauler winced and shook his head in surprise and not a little pain. Dempsey was checked momentarily, but he was soon back in his stride and caught the Frenchman with a vicious blow to the stomach. The left which buried itself deep in the Frenchman left him breathless and a look of pain came over his handsome countenance. Carpentier was soon back on the attack, however, and this was a mistake. He left himself no time to recover, being too eager to return to the offensive, and Dempsey took advantage. If the Frenchman had kept the fight at long distance where he could outdance his heavier opponent, then he might have stood a chance, but he was no match for Jack Dempsey when it came to infighting and soon the American was pounding away mercilessly. Carpentier took all these body blows and then stepped back, danced away a little, and then let fly with the famous right hand which was his one hope of becoming the world champion. It caught Dempsey full on the jaw and the big man was halted in his oncoming stride. The champ visibly buckled at the knees.

The crowds were on their feet and roared on by them Carpentier struck again, another cracking right which smashed against Dempsey's jaw. The mystery boxer from across the Atlantic had set the stadium alight. Again Dempsey buckled, and then he found his pride driving him on. Dempsey came forward once more and rained a succession of blows on Carpentier, some to the body, some to the head, all of them taking their toll on the Frenchman. One left in particular caused Carpentier problems. It smashed into his nose and drew blood, sending him reeling back across the ring. Carpentier was not thinking straight now. He should have been taking evasive action, dancing out of reach for a few vital seconds. Instead he came back at Dempsey and the champion fought away a series of rights and lefts and refused to let Carpentier get through. Carpentier went on to the ropes — indeed, halfway through them — and when the bell went to end the first round the two men were standing exchanging blows toe-to-toe.

Dempsey came out for the second round intent on finishing the Frenchman. Carpentier rode the attack and then let fly with a couple of hard right handers to Dempsey's head which rocked the champion. Dempsey halted in his tracks and Carpentier rained a succession of blows on the American. Dempsey's only reaction was to come back punching harder. It was hell-raising stuff, as Dempsey split Carpentier's cheek with a crunching right, and in the very next second Carpentier almost finished the fight. A left to the body brought down Dempsey's guard and then that lightning right shot out to crack Dempsey on the chin. It was the most crucial punch of the many great punches thrown in this title fight. It stunned Dempsey and all but laid him his full length on the

The referee's finger is raised over Georges Carpentier who has just been felled by Dempsey. Dempsey walks away unconcerned. Gorgeous Georges failed to beat the count.

canvas, and it broke Carpentier's right thumb in two places and sprained his wrist. Perhaps worst of all, the refusal of Dempsey to succumb to a punch which contained every ounce of Carpentier's strength sapped the Frenchman's resolve. He got into a clinch and was subject to a battering from close range. Then he wriggled free and delivered a series of lefts to the champion's face. The bell went to end round two and Dempsey was glad to hear it. But Carpentier had given almost his all and the champ was still on his feet. What could he do now?

The third round found a more wary Dempsey advancing more slowly than his earlier charges. Carpentier, too, retreated, anxious not to get into close quarters. He jabbed out the left, using his injured right hand far more sparingly. But Dempsey's short punches had reduced Carpentier's face to a mass of blood, his nose and mouth now spilling blood freely. Dempsey switched his attack to the Frenchman's body and this was now having its effect. Punches rained about the challenger's rib cage, yet still he fought back, cracking Dempsey with a left and then grimacing in pain as he landed a right. Again Dempsey delivered a barrage of body blows, again the courageous Carpentier tried a right, his only hope of salvation, injured hand or not. When the bell went to end the third, it was the handsome Frenchman who was most pleased to hear it.

Carpentier came out fresh-looking for what was to be his last round, so well had his seconds worked on that bleeding face. But Dempsey now knew that victory was his for the taking. The champion launched another heavy attack on Carpentier's body. A right just under the heart, followed by another to the jaw sent Carpentier crashing to the canvas. Surely, said the fans, this was the end? Not quite. Dempsey was surprised to see Carpentier stagger up at nine. But not too surprised to brush aside contemptuously a feeble left from the challenger before delivering another one of his own to the body, then a stunning right to the chin. Carpentier thudded to the floor. This time he did not beat the count. Dempsey helped the referee to carry the gallant Frenchman to his corner and it was some time before he was able to leave the ring. The 'Battle of the Century' was over. The French challenger had come and gone. Jack Dempsey still wore the world heavyweight crown.

GEORGES CARPENTIER v BATTLING SIKI
World Light-Heavyweight Championship
24 September 1922

Paris in the late September of 1922 was a happy place for anyone with money. World War I was now slipping out of immediate memory, and the atmosphere of 'Gay Paree' assisted people to forget that bloody conflict, the whole of Parisian society settling down to a life of wine and song. On one particular day in that month there was one special event at which the women in their finery, and the men, in good suits with a good cigar and good wine, wanted to attend. That was to be among the 60,000 people who packed into the Velodrome Buffalo in the French capital where Gorgeous Georges Carpentier, the toast of French cafe society, was fighting Battling Siki, the Singular Senegalese, for the light-heavyweight championship of the world. No one expected the powerfully built black man who two years earlier had been almost unknown, to beat Carpentier. But there was something rather romantic about a world title fight between the handsome Frenchman and a boy from the jungle who had learned his boxing in a French territorial army regiment. The huge crowd was in for all the romance they could expect. They were also to witness one of the greatest boxing upsets of the twentieth century — and certainly the most bizarre end to any world title fight.

Since Carpentier had lost his bid for the world heavyweight crown against Jack Dempsey in 1921, he had fought only once for a title, defending his world light-heavyweight title against Ted (Kid) Lewis in London. The European heavyweight title was also on the line that night at Olympia, but any hopes Lewis harboured evaporated in the first round when he was knocked out in controversial circumstances. Lewis went for a quick knockout and attacked furiously. The referee warned the Briton not to hold, Lewis turned to appeal, and Carpentier, who weighed two stones more, hit him with a right from which Lewis never recovered. There was uproar, a bottle was thrown into the ring, but Carpentier was still the world champion.

If that was considered a sensation, however, it had little to compare with the end of Carpentier's next world title defence. Battling Siki was noted for his speedy footwork, and a series of impressive victories culminated in the defeat of the French heavyweight champion, Marcel Nilles. That earned him the chance to fight Carpentier for the world light-heavyweight title, as well as the European heavyweight and light-heavyweight crowns. To the question of whether the French idol would have been better employed meeting a boxer of more distinguished pedigree there was a simple answer. Carpentier had beaten all the challengers that Britain could offer him — and beaten them in quite stunning fashion. Siki, the wild man of the ring, might have been a joke to some, but the fact remained that he was the only logical contender who had not yet pitted himself against handsome Georges. Battling Siki boxed with his heart, not with his head. His technique was limited and he probably won as many fights by frightening his opponents with his wild rushes as with scientific boxing. He had a fierce temper, an over-fondness for drink, and when he became world champion he took to walking the streets leading a lion cub on a leash. A measure of his bizarre lifestyle can be drawn from the manner in which he met his death three years after meeting Carpentier. He was murdered, shot dead in Hell's Kitchen, New York, where a policeman found him in the early hours of one morning, lying in the gutter with a bullet in his back.

But that grisly end was a million miles away when Battling Siki climbed into the ring at the Velodrome Buffalo on 24 September 1922. The 'orphan of the jungle' as one pressman labelled Siki, looked nervously across at the smiling Carpentier when the champion joined him in the ring. Perhaps he was thinking of the champion's famous right hand. It is said that Siki, like the rest of the people that day, did not rate his own chances too highly. Maybe he was daunted by the presence of film cameras which were there to record Gorgeous Georges perform yet another clinical execution on yet another hapless contender, for, make no mistake, Carpentier saw this contest only as an annoyance. Siki had usurped his way into the same ring as the world champion. Georges would soon put him in his place.

The first round found Carpentier content to play a cat and mouse game with the challenger. Carpentier danced around, landed a light blow here and there, and generally appeared to be treating the fight as though it was an exhibition bout of no consequence. Siki looked a worried man. He had a habit of covering up his face with a glove and when Carpentier laid a not-too-fierce punch on that glove, the Senegalese dropped down on one knee, though he was up in a flash and boxing on. The crowd hooted and jeered at the African who had gone down so easily and for the rest of the round Carpentier teased him, obviously thinking that he wanted some more film footage before finishing off the upstart. In the second round Siki went down again, also from a blow of little real power, and this time he stayed down for a count of six. Many who had paid their money were already feeling cheated by this display from the challenger and again the arena echoed to the boos and catcalls. But then an astonishing thing happened. As if spurred on by the taunts of the spectators. Siki launched a ferocious

The bizarre character, Battling Siki, after his sensational defeat of Carpentier.

attack on the champion. Carpentier, too, was surprised, none more so than when a left and a right caught him full on the chin. Carpentier's knees buckled and down he went. He was up at two but after missing with a carefully aimed right, he was the subject of another fearful battering from the African. Carpentier was most certainly glad to hear the bell for the end of round two.

When the bell went for the third round Carpentier came out knowing that he could no longer afford to play around. He was in real danger of losing his world title to this 'jumped-up African' who, he was still convinced, did not deserve to be in the same ring as himself. Enough of this tomfoolery, Carpentier would settle the issue now, beyond doubt. He had let Siki off the hook for too long. But Battling Siki had other ideas. 33

Carpentier began by hammering the African to the canvas with a hook to the jaw that should have ended the fight. But Siki did not even bother to take a count and he was back on his feet in a flash and ready for more. He rushed at Carpentier who side-stepped and slipped. Siki went to help him up and was rewarded with a smashing left to the face. The crowd were not pleased with their Gorgeous Georges. Siki now seemed relieved that the fearsome punches which Carpentier was said to deliver had not really bothered him. He had nothing to fear and when the bell went to end the round it was Carpentier who was saved from further punishment.

With the bell still echoing. Siki dropped his hands, and Carpentier hit him full in the face with a right before turning for his corner. The crowd booed again and now Siki, who shook his woolly head in disbelief at such an action, knew that he had the spectators on his side. It was a critical moment for the African and when he came out for the fourth round it was with renewed confidence. Siki also had his ire well and truly raised and he slammed into Carpentier. Tremendous blows drew blood from the Frenchman's face, his nose, mouth and right eye all streaming red. Carpentier tried to get into the clinch, but Siki contemptuously thrust him away and then continued to launch his merciless attack on the champion. Round five was a massacre. How Carpentier managed to stay on his feet for three rounds no one will ever know. His manager, Francois Descamps, peered under the bottom rope in horror as his man was knocked all around the ring. Carpentier was now functioning on automatic pilot. His attempts to fight back were feeble; and his attempts at defence were no better. The bell went and the whole crowd knew that Georges Carpentier was about to drop from the world of sporting heroes and into the land of mortal men.

Round six and Carpentier, his handsome features now almost unrecognisable, came forward and tried a right which lacked any of his old power. Descamps was near to tears and yet he knew that he dare not rescue his

The opening round of the fight and already the Frenchman looks apprehensive.

man. Carpentier had to win, he had to retain his championship for his future depended on it. But the champion could not see, so swollen were his eyes. Siki showed him no mercy, taking what Carpentier had to offer and then raining blow after blow from every angle at the champion. Siki had him on the ropes and then a fierce uppercut lifted Carpentier, doubled him up. Siki went after him, there was an untidy tussle, and Carpentier appeared to fall over Siki's outstretched leg and went over on his back. Pandemonium broke out. Siki's corner was jubilant. The African was not so sure and stood there in bewilderment. People came into the ring and Carpentier was carried back to his corner. The crowd called for the result to be announced and when it was there was further sensation. Siki had been disqualified for tripping Carpentier! Seldom, if ever, has a fight ended in such chaos.

People spat at Carpentier, the man they had come to cheer, and he made his way to the dressing room amid a hail of boos and abusive shouts. Siki looked about as dispirited as a man can be when he has just hammered an opponent into the ground, only to be told that he has been disqualified for an accident. There was no natural justice in the decision and certainly there was no jubilation from Carpentier's corner. Officials met and an hour after the fight had ended the reason for Carpentier's lack of interest became apparent. It appeared that, seconds before he fell over Siki's inadvertently outstretched foot, Carpentier had been rescued by his corner when the towel was thrown in to save the champion from further punishment. The world had a new light-heavyweight champion.

The aftermath of that day was almost as sensational as the day itself. Battling Siki became virtually uncontrollable. The Home Office in London refused to allow him to fight Joe Beckett, and when he came to defend his title in the ring in Dublin, on St Patrick's Day the following year, he had already been technically stripped of it by the French boxing authorities for professional misconduct. In the Dublin hall that night, with soldiers with fixed bayonents on the streets at the height of rebel troubles, and with no one knowing for certain whether the hall had been mined, Battling Siki lost his title to Irishman Mike McTigue after twenty energy-sapping rounds. The fight went on with the sound of gunfire in the streets and when it was over it spelled the end of the Singular Senegalese as a boxer. He was reviled in Paris and went to America where, after a few minor bouts, he found himself in trouble with police and eventually met a murderer's bullet. For Carpentier there were slightly happier days ahead, though he never recaptured his position as darling of the French. He made a comeback with a one-round win over Joe Beckett and then went back to America in search of a return with Jack Dempsey. He was too ambitious. Defeats at the hands of Gene Tunney and Tom McGibbons saw him return to France where he announced his retirement.

JOE BECKETT v FRANK MORAN
_____ Heavyweight contest at Royal Albert Hall _____
12 October 1922

There were not enough seats for those who wanted to watch British heavyweight Joe Beckett have a second shot at the American dentist from Pittsburgh on a chill October evening in 1922. True, there was not a hall worth hiring in the entire United States for on that side of the Atlantic there was little interest in a fight between two men who had shown themselves both to be below world class. In London, though, it was different. Joe Beckett was still a great favourite, the fight fans remembered only too well his two-rounds knockout at the hands of the dentist in London at the end of 1920. They were keen to see if their Joe could this time escape the sleep-inducing power of the dentist's right hand, the punch he called his 'Mary Ann.' They were not to be disappointed. If the fight lacked exceptional skill, then it more than made up for it with excitement, dash and bravery, and a result which was in doubt from first to last.

The dentist who was lined up to meet Joe Beckett was a man called Frank Moran, a rugged, hard-punching fighter who learned his boxing skills in the navy and who after qualifying as a dentist in order to please his mother who thought her son ought to have a professional career, took up the gloves in professional earnest and elected to knock teeth out rather than extract them painlessly in the surgery chair. Moran was due to fight the big Jim Coffey at Madison Square Garden one day and refused to take to the ring without first seeing his purse money. It was understandable. Twice in recent times Moran had fought for money which he then never saw. The promoter threatened him with a breach of contract but Frank Moran was not impressed: 'No dough — no fight!' he

told them. It was as simple as that. One of Coffey's seconds was present: 'Just get in the ring, Moran,' he sneered, 'and let Jim Coffey put you where you belong — on the floor.' Moran's retort was instant; 'Go and tell that big ham that I'll kiss him with my Mary Ann,' said Moran, kissing his right glove, 'Tell him that he won't know what hit him when my little sweetheart gets to work.'

That was how 'Mary Ann' was born. The money was duly paid over, Frank Moran went into the ring that night, duly 'kissed' Coffey with his 'little sweetheart' and saw him off with a third-round knockout which impressed the punters. Moran's pedigree was never world-class however. He fought Jack Johnson, in Paris, and Jess Willard, in New York, and although edging them both close, failed on each occasion to lift the world title. All this was before the United States became embroiled in World War I. Now that conflict had been over for four years and Moran was nearly thirty-six when he met 28-year-old Joe Beckett for the second time.

Beckett was born in a village near Southampton and had earned his early living, as did so many fighters of his generation, at the boxing booths attached to fairs. He joined the army on the outbreak of war and, again like so many fighters of the age, became a boxing instructor. In 1918, while still in the service of King and Country, Beckett fought Sergeant Dick Smith for the British light-heavyweight title at the National Sporting Club, losing on points over twenty rounds as Smith won his third Lonsdale Belt. The same year, Beckett was outpointed over three rounds by Bombardier Billy Wells in the final of the King's Trophy Heavyweight

Joe Beckett, the Hampshire-born heavyweight champion.

Competition. When he took up boxing in earnest in 1919 and made a determined assault on the British heavyweight title, Joe Beckett found himself not wanting. He knocked out Wells, the British title-holder, in five rounds, only to find that, though the public were ready to accept him, the National Sporting Club, outside whose immediate jurisdiction the Wells-Beckett fight had been staged, were not. They installed Frank Goddard as champion and Beckett was obliged to beat him in two rounds to confirm his claim. A win over the American, Eddie McGoorty, then set Beckett up for a crack at Georges Carpentier's European heavyweight title but a seventy-four-second defeat by Carpentier in London in December 1919 brought that challenge to a swift end. Beckett, though, was encouraged to try again and knockouts over Dick Smith, Billy Wells and Tommy Burns — the latter having been retired for a decade — led to the first fight with Moran. Defeat of the Pittsburgh dentist would have meant another shot at Carpentier, and possibly at Dempsey's world crown, but Beckett failed to get out of the way of 'Mary Ann' and in the second round he was knocked out.

With Beckett obviously not ready to test the world champion, Noel (Boy) McCormick was looked upon as a possible successor and a fight for Beckett's British title was arranged in London for 12 September 1921. Joe, however, was not willing to give up his title and after twelve rounds Boy McCormick was stopped. Beckett then took the British Empire title by beating the Australian, George Cook, and the time now seemed right to stage a return match with Frank Moran. The crowd wedged themselves into the Royal Albert Hall on 12 October 1922 and when referee Moss Deyong called the two men together, the spectators rubbed their hands in growing anticipation of the battle they felt sure was to follow. Never mind that Beckett and Moran had fallen short of world class, this had all the makings of a real thriller. Moran stood three inches taller and weighed in at twenty-two pounds more than the Hampshire man. But that was to make no difference.

Joe Beckett went straight into the attack and seemed oblivious to the dangers of 'Mary Ann', the crushing right hand which had delivered the *coup de grace* on so many boxers, Beckett himself included. When the round ended it was the American who had taken most of the punches, mostly to his midriff. The second round continued with Beckett's star in the ascendant. He punished Moran's face and body and soon the American's features were a sorry mess. His cheek was swollen, a long, raking gash had appeared over his left eye, and blood mingled with the sweat running into his mouth. He was not yet done for, however. He stood exchanging blow for blow with Beckett and the atmosphere in the Royal Albert Hall was electric. Then came a sensational incident in a sensational fight. Moran swung a left hook under which Beckett ducked. The British champion countered with a right to Moran's body and the American doubled up in pain and fell. There was no cause for the British camp to be elated, for the blow looked foul. Moran got up at seven but collapsed immediately. The count was not resumed and there was an awful silence as the crowd waited. Would the Briton be disqualified and this tremendously exciting fight ended? Then

Joe Beckett's left is blocked by Frank Moran.

the bell went. The crisis was over and Beckett, who, it has to be said, did not deliberately foul his opponent, lived to fight again.

Moran was not desperately hurt and he came out for the third round as if he meant to end the fight within the next ten seconds. Beckett had taken but a pace from his corner when a mighty blow from 'Mary Ann' crashed into his ribs, followed by a right to the head. It sent Joe Beckett down on one knee. Moran withdrew and Beckett was up in a flash to carry the fight back to the American. The two men met in the centre of the ring and there followed an exchange of blows the like of which had seldom been seen in a British ring. With no regard for their own defence, both men hammered away, toe to toe. It continued until the bell, with Beckett again having the better of the exchange. His reach was seven inches shorter than Moran's, while the American was handicapped at close quarters.

Moran's right eye was closing rapidly and he came out for the fourth round again intent on swift destruction. A left to the body, a right to the jaw, and Moran had Beckett on the retreat. The British champion came back and Moran was waiting for him, first with a left which halted Beckett in his stride, then

with a long right — 'Mary Ann' — to catch Joe Beckett full on the jaw. The British champion was lifted off his feet, on to the ropes, and down on to the resin. His body was on the canvas, his head resting on a rope, and it was the way in which he fell that saved Joe Beckett that night. At the count of five the blood flowed back into his head which was tipped backwards over the rope. Three seconds later, and after much urging from his corner, Beckett was back on his feet. It seemed like a miracle to the champion's aides. Moran foolishly allowed Beckett to get into a clinch and here the Briton rested until the referee dragged them apart. There was another furious exchange of blows and Beckett was down again. His own ferocious attack had been halted by 'Mary Ann'. Yet he was up in an instant, raining blows on Moran's face. When the bell sounded it was the American who was on the retreat. The fifth round was all Joe Beckett. Frank Moran did not have the strength in his arms to defend or attack. He launched his famous right on a couple of occasions, but each time it found nothing but fresh air.

The picture was repeated at the start of the sixth round. Moran was losing the exchange of punches by six to one. His face was a mask of blood and 'Mary Ann' was sent into action many times, but landed on target only once, a blow which Beckett took without blinking. Moran refused to be knocked down, so Beckett drove him to the ropes and proceeded to rain blows down on the hapless American's body. Blow after blow hit the target which the tired, beaten Moran presented. Referee Deyong could do only one thing and mercifully he knew it. He stepped in between them and held up Joe Beckett's hand in victory with Frank Moran lying a bloody, aching body across the ropes. At the same time the towel was flung from the American's cornermen. Joe Beckett, who was to retire as undefeated British champion a few months later, went to his corner and grabbed a bottle of champagne. It was hurriedly uncorked and Beckett then took it first to Frank Moran's corner. It was a gesture which summed up this great fight.

LUIS ANGEL FIRPO v JACK DEMPSEY
_____ World Heavyweight Championship _____
14 September 1923

Though it lasted less than two rounds there is no doubt that the world heavyweight title fight between Jack Dempsey and the 6ft 3in tall Argentinian Luis Angel Firpo — the man they called the 'Wild Bull of the Pampas' — was one of the most exciting in boxing history. In three minutes and fifty-seven seconds of boxing there was more action than is normally seen in the fifteen rounds of a full title fight. With a record number of knock-downs, action all the way, and some of the most sensational events ever seen in the ring, Dempsey's toughest fight defies the imagination. It is easy to let the superlatives run amok. In this fight there was so much excitement that the written word cannot do it full justice.

Since defending his title successfully against Georges Carpentier in July 1921, Jack Dempsey had defended only once in the following two years when he met Tom Gibbons at Shelby, Montana, in July 1923. The fight turned out to be a fiasco for everyone save Dempsey and his manager, Jack Kearns. Even Dempsey had to look back and admit that it was the worst fight of his life. Gibbons, of Montana, took the champion the full distance and cut Dempsey's eye into the bargain. In this fight the real losers were the people of this Montana city. Kearns somehow persuaded the authorities to guarantee his boxer no less than $300,000. When only 7,202 spectators paid to watch, which was the lowest attendance of Dempsey's championship career, the money did not even cover the champion's purse. Four local banks went broke, poor Gibbons got nothing for his part in providing opposition for Dempsey, and it was one of the most embarrassing flops in the history of the

world heavyweight championship. Two months later, though, Dempsey was taking part in the greatest fight of his career.

It is a surprise to learn that Jess Willard was still on the scene in 1923. The former champion, was experiencing financial difficulties, and tried to make a comeback at the age of forty-one. Rickard matched him with the big Argentinian, Firpo, with the promise that the winner could have a shot at Dempsey's crown. Firpo came to the United States as just another big, shambling fighter with no reputation and hardly worthy of climbing into the same ring as the world champion. A series of build-up fights soon left the public in no doubt that Firpo was, after all, a worthy contender. In the space of five months Firpo won no less than eight knock-outs, two points decisions, and took nine victories in a row including wins against Bill Brennan, Willard, Jack McAuliffe, Charlie Weinert and Joe Burke. His defeat of Willard in eight rounds finally convinced the doubters and Firpo was soon looking forward to his biggest fight.

After struggling so badly against Tom Gibbons only two months earlier, Dempsey ought to have known that the coming scrap with the Argentinian was going to be a tough one, though even he could not have known that it would be so sensational. Ninety thousand people packed the New York Polo Grounds that evening, and not all of them came to see the home man win. Dempsey was not as popular a champion as we might imagine sixty years later. He had been accused of dodging a title fight with Harry Wills, a black boxer who had pressed hard for a chance. This was not entirely true, but the public is fickle and they cared not. They

39

Jack Dempsey goes through the ropes after a made charge by the 'Wild Bull of the Pampas'.

paid over $1,188,000 to see Dempsey defend his title against Firpo, and made sure that the Argentinian felt at home when he entered the ring on what was to be one of the most eventful evenings that boxing has ever seen. Firpo came to the centre of the ring and accepted the cheers, his long, ankle-length dressing gown exaggerating his tall body still further. Dempsey waved and was then lost from view as he returned to his seat. With a few last-minute instructions from referee, Johnny Gallagher, the two men returned to their corners once more to await the bell. When it sounded it signalled the start of an amazing fight.

Jack Dempsey was well-known for his furious opening attack and this fight was to be no different. He swept forward, meeting Firpo, almost before the challenger had risen from his stool, and set about him with a terrific left swing aimed at the Argentinian's jaw. The blow was woefully short of its target and the champion was sent off-balance. Firpo, however, did nothing to capitalise on that and Dempsey was able to recover and land a left to Firpo's midsection. The big South American staggered

backwards and in a flash Dempsey was after him. Left and rights found their target on Firpo's body, and then the challenger landed his first punch of the night. A right smashed into Dempsey's face, but it checked him for only a moment. Then he was back with two punches, left and right, to Firpo's face, one cracking right to the chin, and then another. Firpo responded and the two men went into a clinch. The referee called break, and a man at the ringside glanced at his watch and noted that all this had happened in the first quarter of a minute of the fight.

They came out of the clinch amid a thunderous roar from the spectators and Firpo lowered his arms and looked towards the referee. Dempsey saw his chance. He smashed out a left which caught the Argentinian full on the jaw. He dropped to the canvas like a stone and the count was taken up. Now the Wild Bull of the Pampas showed his inexperience for he jumped straight up instead of taking his time. Even if his seconds did claim that he was hit on the break, it was a foolish thing to do in allowing Dempsey that free hit. Before Firpo had time to gather himself, Dempsey dropped him

40

again. Once more he scrambled straight back to his feet and this time clubbed Dempsey with a right which had the champion reeling. Back came Dempsey and both men had forgotten about defence. They stood exchanging blows with a ferocity which had the crowd roaring their approval and gasping in amazement. Both men were hitting hard, but it was Jack Dempsey who was finding his target more precisely with scientific boxing as opposed to Firpo's wild rushes. Dempsey dropped the South American on to the canvas once more. This time there was no springing straight up and many felt that Firpo had failed to beat the count. When he did get to his feet, a flashing left hook put him on his back for the fourth time.

It was a blow which would have laid out most heavyweights. Although he was again slow in rising, Firpo did beat the count again, and this time he caught the champion a stunning right to the ribs which had Dempsey staggering back on his heels. Dempsey demonstrated his experience here, unlike Firpo, he took a breather before resuming the attack. When he did, another wicked right to the South American's jaw dumped him on the canvas for the fifth time in this first round. Unbelievably, Firpo was up at six and wading into Dempsey. Right after right slammed into Dempsey's body while the champion counter-attacked just as strongly. A left to the body and a right to the jaw sent Firpo down for a sixth time and this time the Wild Bull only just beat the count. The champion went in for what would surely be the final blows of this sensational fight. But again he was met by a terrific onslaught from Firpo, yet again, Dempsey fought back too. The two boxers stood and smashed punches into each other until Dempsey made one really count and for the seventh time in this first round the challenger kissed the resin. For the seventh time he got to his feet and came at Dempsey. A smashing right brought the champion to the canvas for the first time in many years, though he was up in a flash. Now stung into indignation, Jack Dempsey piled into the South American with renewed strength.

It was Firpo, however, who looked the stronger. He drove Dempsey on to the ropes until the champion lowered his head and doubled up, his right shoulder now poking through the rope above where the pressmen sat. Firpo saw his chance. He launched a mighty right which smashed full on Dempsey's jaw, lifting the world champion clean through the ropes and into the laps of the world's press. The timekeeper began to count off the seconds ... one ... two ... three; and the stadium erupted. The crowd were on their feet — could the world champion get back into the ring? Or were they about to see the Wild Bull of the Pampas crowned as the new king? There was a fury of activity down below where reporters were shoving the champion off themselves and back into the ring! Dempsey just made it with the help of pushing hands. He was covered in blood, staggering and dazed, but he was back in the

Luis Angel Firpo, the 'Wild Bull of the Pampas' who caused a sensation against Dempsey in 1923.

ring. It was all against the rules, of course, but it was allowed. Now Firpo had the chance to finish his job.

He had the world champion out in front of him. shattered and pained, waiting, asking indeed, to be finished off. But the events of the previous few seconds had also surprised Firpo and he wasted valuable time before getting back into the champion. Instead of hammering Dempsey as soon as he was back on his feet, Firpo waited and it was the champion who finally landed the next blow. When Firpo did wake up to the possibilities and launch a frenzied attack, Dempsey was ready to weather it. The round ended with both men slugging it out once more. When the bell sounded it ended the most sensational first round in boxing history. Never before had a man been knocked down seven times in the first three minutes. Firpo had survived all that to still be there with a fighting chance.

Dempsey was being lectured by his corner on the dangers of letting the unsophisticated Firpo get in with his haymaking right hand. With that weapon, the South American could afford to acknowledge his own technical shortcomings. Jack Dempsey had now enjoyed some moments to reflect and when he came out for the second he was more wary, weaving and swaying out of the way of the Argentinian's main weapon. Then Dempsey began to lay his own blows on the challenger, punishing blows which smacked hard into the body and began to drain the strength away. Firpo tried to get into a clinch but Dempsey was soon out of it and swinging a devastating right hook to the challenger's jaw. Down went the South American once more, but once more he was up in the twinkling of an eye. Firpo knew that his last hope rested with the swinging right hand, so he swung in the general direction of Jack Dempsey's jaw. But before it was halfway to its target, Dempsey had countered with a crunching left hook, followed by the most classic right to the point of the chin that you could ever wish to see. That was the punch which ended this incredible fight. Firpo went down again and this time Dempsey knew that he would not beat the count. Before the timekeeper had reached five, Demspey was back in his own corner accepting the congratulations of his helpers.

It had been a tremendous fight with both men intent only on one thing: knocking the other out. Yet it might have been so different a result if Luis Angel Firpo had been guided by a manager of the class of Kearns. The controversial incident when Dempsey was literally pushed back in the ring really meant that Firpo should have been awarded a technical knockout. If the roles had been reversed once could hardly have imagined Kearns allowing the matter to be forgotten without some form of instant protest. It was also felt that, given the circumstances, Firpo deserved a return with Jack Dempsey, but he never had the chance and soon after he was on his way back to the Argentine where, after a few more fights, he disappeared from the scene. Dempsey was to be champion for another three years, although he had only one title defence ahead of him. Thus, Jack Dempsey never won another title fight after that sensation in the New York Polo Grounds.

MICKEY WALKER v TOMMY MILLIGAN
World Middleweight Championship
30th June 1927

After Cornishman Bob Fitzsimmons retired as world middleweight champion at the end of the nineteenth century, Britain did not have another world champion at that weight until Randolph Turpin, the coloured boxer from Leamington Spa, sensationally defeated Sugar Ray Robinson at Earl's Court in July 1951. Yet from the time Fitzsimmons, who won the title in 1891 by knocking Jack Dempsey, 'The Nonpareil', retired from the middleweight division to concentrate on the heavyweight championship, which he won in 1897, the only British-born boxer ever to hold that crown, Britain made several noble attempts to win back the middleweight title. There was Jim Sullivan's courageous effort against Billy Papke in 1911 before being knocked out in nine rounds; there was Ted Moore who went the distance with Harry Greb in New York before losing on points in 1924; and there was Len Harvey who was outpointed by Marcel Thil in London in 1932. But it was in 1927 that Britain felt it had a middleweight champion who really could unseat the world champion.

He was Tommy Milligan, Edinburgh-born, who took the British title in 1926 by stopping George West in London. The Scot had already enjoyed success in the welterweight class and he first sprang to prominence in that class. In November 1924, aged twenty, he had outpointed the famous Ted (Kid) Lewis to win the British title and followed up this with the European middleweight title by defeating the Italian, Bruno Frattini. Then followed the British middleweight title at the expense of West, which he successfully defended on two occasions, against Ted Moore when the referee stopped both fights in the fourteenth round.

Strangely, his first title win against West had achieved exactly the same result.

Milligan had already been to America to try for a shot at Mickey Walker's world welterweight title. The Boston-based fighter was having trouble in making the weight and therefore the Americans did not want to pit their man against Milligan, who they thought might be capable of taking the title out of the United States. Milligan hung around in the hope that a world title fight would be arranged, but two defeats in three fights against other leading American welterweights meant that the Americans had their excuse and the Scot went home without testing himself at the highest level. Milligan came back to Britain and announced that he was moving into the middleweight division. Roland Todd was the official British champion but he had gone to America and the authorities turned to Milligan, who had won the European middleweight title from Frattini, and matched him with Guardsman George West. West was beaten inside fourteen rounds, the well-known Plymouth middleweight Ted Moore twice went the same way, and Tommy Milligan was the undisputed top middleweight in Britain. Charles B. Cochrane knew it and soon Mickey Walker was on his way from the United States for a world title fight for which Milligan had dreamed, albeit at a different weight.

Mickey Walker was known in America as the Toy Bulldog on account of his frenzied attack. When Milligan was in the United States, Walker had problems in keeping within the welterweight limit. On 20 May 1926 he lost the world title to fellow American Pete Latzo, being outpointed over ten

43

rounds; by the end of that year he had won the world middleweight title from Tiger Flowers, outpointing him over ten rounds in Chicago. So when Cochrane came in for him to fight in London for that title, Walker this time had no reservations about meeting Milligan. To tell the truth, Walker felt that Milligan was less of a danger than many of the useful American middleweights clamouring for a shot. Then there was the fact that Milligan was really a welterweight fighting in the higher division. The icing on the cake was that Cochrane, to ensure that he got his fight, had offered the American champion a sum well in excess of £20,000, though manager Kearns no doubt bargained much of that for the champion. Milligan, in contrast, picked up only about £3,000, though it was his position as British champion on which Cochrane had based much of his pre-fight ballyhoo. For the record, Cochrane had to charge £11 for ringside seats, and when the bills were added up at the end of the promotion he had lost around £15,000.

The fight was originally due to be staged on Blackpool's South Shore, in a specially constructed stadium to cost £15,000. The date was set for the last day of June, when Blackpool would be full of holidaymakers, and the stadium would then be used for other big sporting events. But there were problems in getting the scheme off the ground, and when both boxers held Cochrane to the date, the promoter had to switch the fight to London's Olympia. So, on 30 June 1927, Milligan and Walker stepped into the London ring under the watchful eye of referee Eugene Corri. Many felt that the Scot could take the title, but they were unaware that Walker had lately acquired the ability to deliver the most tremendous body punches while at the same time being able to soak up an enormous amount of punishment himself.

The first round found Milligan hammering straight into the attack. It was a grave mistake, for, while he was no stranger to bouts of twenty rounds or so, Walker had not often boxed as long. It was in Milligan's best interests, then, to take the fight as near to its scheduled end as possible, and yet there he

Mickey Walker stands over Tommy Milligan as the brave Scotsman goes down for a count.

was trying to finish it within the first round. Walker allowed himself to be struck, soaking up the Scotsman's punches without apparent ill-effect. Then the American got on to the offensive and smashed lefts and rights into Milligan's body. The two men stood and exchanged blow after blow with Milligan refusing to take a rest. His usual tactics had been thrown to the wind. It was the same at the start of the second round. The Fighting Scot went in hammering and when he received a gut-wrenching blow to the stomach it only served to spur him on to greater effort. Through the third, fourth and fifth rounds it was the same. Milligan would smash away with dozens of punches — but when the champion laid one to rest it did far more damage than four of Milligan's put together. And when the sixth round came it was obvious that where Milligan's efforts had tired him, Walker's tactics of conserving his energy to the occasional telling punch had now left him with much still to offer. Walker was now getting home to the body and jaw with some terrific blows. Then the Fighting Scot stumbled and in a flash Walker was into him, The Toy Bulldog unleashed all his strength on Milligan and when the bell ended the round the Scot looked the more thankful.

Round seven followed the same route and in the eighth round Milligan actually came out with his guard down and Walker dropped him for a count of eight with a smashing left to the side of the head. Thirty seconds later Milligan was on the canvas again, once more to rise at eight. Now the crowd saw a remarkable display of courage from the Scot. He refused to go down again and actually launched a counter-attack. He tried so hard to lay the one punch which would have rescued this fight for him. But Walker took advantage of the Fighting Scot's need to abandon defence and he got home some bruising punches to Milligan's body. The ninth round was just as bad for the Scotsman, worse in fact. Walker measured a left and dumped Milligan on to the floor once more. He was up again at eight, but now absorbing the most awful punishment. Momentarily, Milligan lost his bearings and referee Corri stepped in between the two boxers. For a moment it looked as though the fight had been stopped, but it was simply to let Milligan resume some semblance of a boxing stance. The crowd wanted it stopped there and then, but when Milligan astonishingly began a counter-attack, it looked to justify the referee's decision to allow matters to continue.

But again Milligan's violent rush was met with one telling punch as a right uppercut put him down for the count of six. It was the bell to end that round which saved Milligan from being smashed through the ropes. But the end was nigh and in round ten when Walker scored a cruel left and right to the stomach, then another one-two to the head. Milligan went down face first, got up at nine, and was then hammered down again with a left to the body and a right to the jaw. This time he did not get up and the count of ten and the towel from Milligan's corner arrived more or less at the same time. It was a brave attempt to win the world title — but it cost Tommy Milligan his career. Nine months later he lost his British title to Alex Ireland, being disqualified in the ninth round of their fight in Edinburgh. And five months after that, in August 1928, he was knocked out in the first round by Frank Moody. That defeat finished The Fighting Scot's boxing career. At the age of twenty-four he retired, still in possession of a pair of blood-stained gloves — a grim reminder of the day he fought so bravely to bring home a world title.

GENE TUNNEY v JACK DEMPSEY
_____ World Heavyweight Championship _____
22 September 1927

Put the explosive mixture of two Irish-Americans in the ring for the world heavyweight title and you have the sure-fire ingredients for a fight that will be argued about for years to come. That was exactly what happened when Gene Tunney met Jack Dempsey for the title on 22 September 1927. Tunney already had the crown; he had won it from the Manassa Mauler just a year earlier. This return fight had everything, including one of the most controversial incidents ever to light up even this most colourful of sporting events. It became known as the Night of the Long Count, when Gene Tunney was rescued by a somewhat benevolent referee just when Dempsey thought he had regained the prize he was sure was rightfully his.

The first fight between these two characters took place in Philadelphia's Sesquicentennial Stadium on the evening of 23 September 1926. It was yet another million-dollar affair and drew 120,757 spectators, who in fact paid nearer two million dollars to see this fight. Tunney was a 28-year-old ex-US marine at the time of that first fight and had learned his boxing in the tough school of that service. From his background of the New York sidewalks, he defeated twenty opponents to win the American Expeditionary Force light-heavyweight title in 1919. In 1922 he took the American light-heavyweight title from Battling Levinsky and in the same year suffered the only defeat of his professional career when Harry Greb beat him for that title. But a year later, Tunney was national champion again when he regained the title from Greb in fifteen rounds. After defending the title against Greb once more, Tunney then decided to go after Jack Dempsey's world heavyweight title. A series of successes led him towards that goal and in 1926 he had his chance.

Promoter Tex Rickard had wanted to stage the fight at New York's Yankee Stadium, but there were political problems. A black called Harry Wills had been pressing hard for a shot at Dempsey's title but Dempsey refused to fight him and, not for the first time, a title fight between Dempsey and the now nationally-known boxer fell through. The Boxing Board appealed to Rickard to stage the fight but he refused, hinting that Governor Al Smith did not want a mixed-race title fight in the city. This was refuted by the New York State Athletic Commission chairman, and when Dempsey was matched against Gene Tunney instead, the Commission refused to sanction the fight at Yankee Stadium. Instead it went to Philadelphia and on 23 September 1926, Jack Dempsey stepped into the ring to lose his title, though he was about to pick up over $700,000 in prize money.

As the two men came to the ring, torrential rain hammered down over the open-air arena. The canvas was slippery, the boxers and the huge crowd were soaked through, and Dempsey floundered through the fight like an unconsequential challenger rather than the champion he was. Killer Jack, apart from one moment in the fourth round when he almost knocked Tunney down, seemed to have lost most of his punching power. After that left hook had almost downed Tunney in the fourth, Dempsey found himself cut in the fifth. When the bell ended the tenth and final round, Jack Dempsey had a badly swollen left eye, a bruised face, and a pair of rubbery legs. Gene Tunney, with a display of clean

Gene Tunney lost only one fight out of a career of seventy-seven bouts.

hitting and precise, scientific boxing, had won the world heavyweight title. Dempsey fans began to look around for excuses. Perhaps the weather conditions had dulled their Jack from embarking on a display of power boxing similar to those which had destroyed Willard, Carpentier and Firpo; perhaps he was suffering from the strained relationship which had developed between himself and his manager. The fact was that Gene Tunney was one of the cleverest boxers ever to contest the world heavyweight crown. Despite having fallen out with Kearns and with retirement on his mind, Jack Dempsey was persuaded into the ring for a return with Tunney. First he was matched with Jack Sharkey, who had beaten Harry Wills at the Yankee Stadium on 21 July 1927. In the early stages of the fight Sharkey's long range tactics took him in front. But when he decided to mix it at close quarters Dempsey was the master. Over 75,000 fans saw Sharkey stunned by a

suspiciously low looking punch in the seventh. Sharkey turned to appeal to the referee, Dempsey hooked him to the jaw, and Sharkey was counted out.

With Sharkey disposed of, Dempsey's path was now clear for a re-match with Gene Tunney. The return was set for the great Soldier's Field football stadium in Chicago where nearly 105,000 people paid an all-time record sum of $2,658,660, with the champion taking $990,445. Tunney wanted a million-dollar cheque, so he wrote Rickard one for the balance and then received his seven-figure fee. Tunney had struck oil with this fight (Rickard and Dempsey did not do so badly out of it either) and this time the betting men laid even on the outcome. As Dempsey came into the open there was prolonged cheering, for he was still a popular figure, and Tunney's appearance was greeted with similar enthusiasm. That was soon to dampen down, however, because before referee Dave Barry had time to call the two boxers together, the heavens opened and down came the rain once more. It is important to remember that this fight was being staged under the neutral corner rule. In the event of a knockdown the man still standing was to go to a neutral corner while the count was taken. Early in the first round Tunney got in a telling blow to Dempsey's head and for the rest of the round completely outboxed the former champion. For the next five rounds it was a similar story; Tunney doing all the boxing and Dempsey looking slow and unable to compete. Tunney looked to be in little danger of losing his title when he came out for the seventh round — a round which was about to go down as one of the most controversial in boxing.

Tunney opened with a left and right to the head, while Dempsey replied with several lefts and rights to the champion's body. The progress of all this took the boxers to the ropes and when Tunney came at Dempsey once more the crowd were stunned to see a left hook from the former champion put Tunney down. It was the first time in his career that the champion had been down and Dempsey could not contain his excitement. 47

Tunney goes down and, as Dempsey does not move away immediately, enjoys the benefit of the infamous 'long count'.

He stood over Tunney, gloating at him much the same way as he had done when Firpo kept going down four years previously. But Dempsey had forgotten all about the neutral corner rule. One man who hadn't, however, was referee Dave Barry. He refused to start the count until Dempsey had moved into a neutral corner, though even when he did, Barry decided that it was too near Tunney and waved Dempsey to the farthest one before starting the count. All this time precious seconds were ticking away and only when Barry was absolutely satisfied that Dempsey was out of the immediate way, did he begin the count from one.

At least five seconds had elapsed, probably more, and when Tunney eventually raised himself to his feet at nine it meant that the champion had been down for something like fourteen seconds. Whether Dempsey's over-excitement in forgetting the rule would have made any difference to the result of this fight is one of the great imponderables of sport. Could Tunney have made it if Dempsey had retired immediately and the count started at once? Tunney maintained that he

could and that 'nine' was his signal to get up. He had simply been waiting for that. Perhaps Dempsey would then have been able to deliver the final blow, however, for there appeared to be no doubt that the champion was stunned. Those extra five seconds made all the difference to his ability to recover. Whatever the answer, Dempsey had missed his chance. Tunney rested for the remainder of the seventh round and then fought back hard in the eight and ninth, cutting Dempsey on both eyes, dumping him on the canvas briefly in the eighth, and being heralded as the clear victor when the bell ended the contest after ten rounds. Dempsey retired and did not fight again. Gene Tunney had one more fight, defending his title against the New Zealander Tom Heeney on 26 July 1928 when the referee stopped the fight in New York in the eleventh round. Then he too retired. Both Dempsey and Tunney were rich men. Dempsey alone had netted two and a half million dollars from world title fights. But could he ever forgive himself for allowing Tunney breathing space on that Night of the Long Count?

TEDDY BALDOCK v ALF (KID) PATTENDEN
_____ British Bantamweight Championship _____
16 May 1929

Boxing titles — world, European and national — have sometimes been disputed by several boxers at once. The bantamweight division was a classic example in the late 1920s when Britain had two fine boxers both claiming, each with some justification, that they were the rightful British championship holder. To compound matters both were products of the tough East End of London. There was only one course of action to be taken and they took it. The ensuing fight, which settled the immediate ownership of the crown, was one of the most thrilling and memorable ever to be staged in a British ring. Down in the East End they still talk about the night that Teddy Baldock, from Poplar, and Alf (Kid) Pattenden, from Bethnal Green, settled once and for all who was top dog. It was the East End's very own title fight.

Teddy Baldock was a schoolboy sensation. At the age of thirteen he fought in the great local boxing venue of Premierland and his flashing left hand accounted for opponent after opponent as little Teddy left the East End's fight fans stunned by his incredible speed, agility and power-packed punching. For six years he was the talk of the area and at the end of that time he had reached the top of his class in the flyweight division, though he was never able to get to grips with the British champion of the day, Elky Clark. In 1926 Teddy went across the Atlantic and proceeded to cause the same kind of sensation in America that he had in his native London. He fought twelve fights, won eleven, drew one and missed out on a shot at the world flyweight title only because the retirement of the reigning champion, Fidel La Barba, had left the ownership of it in some disarray. On 21 January 1927, La

Barba beat Elky Clark on points over twelve rounds in New York; by the time Izzy Schwartz outpointed Newsboy Brown in December of that year to settle the world flyweight issue, Teddy Baldock was back home and enjoying great success in the bantamweight division.

Around that time there was also some conflict about the true identity of the world bantamweight champion and in February 1927 Bud Taylor outpointed Eddie Shea in Chicago to claim the title abdicated by Charles Rosenburg after he had failed to make the weight for a defence against Bushy Graham. Taylor's claim was recognised by the NBA, but there was another claimant in America's Archie Bell. Bell was brought over to meet Baldock in a fight which carried a 'world title' label and when the East Ender outpointed the American, he was held to be world champion in some quarters. Baldock's narrow points victory over Bell was celebrated more in the East End than in boxing at large and in the same year Baldock was beaten by the South African, Willie Smith, who outpointed him. In the meantime, Taylor had vacated the NBA title and another claimant to the world bantamweight throne, Bushy Graham, beat Izzy Schwartz. Not until Panama Al Brown held the title for six years, from 1929 to 1935, was the issue really clear.

The British bantamweight title was also in contention between several boxers. Johnny Brown, who with three victories had won the Lonsdale Belt outright, had not fought for three years for want of a worthy challenger and the National Sporting Club declared the British title vacant and staged a fight between Kid Nicholson of Leeds — the

Teddy Baldock tries to get off the ropes by jabbing a left into Pattenden's face.

A rather ludicrous situation had now developed. Baldock had defeated the British champion who had in truth allowed his title to lapse through want of decent opposition; Pattenden had emerged victorious from a British title fight set up by the National Sporting Club. It became even more complicated when Pattenden then defended his 'title' against Johnny Brown's younger brother and stopped him in twelve rounds at the National Sporting Club. So Pattenden had the Lonsdale Belt, traditionally the property of the rightful champion; Baldock had defeated the 'real' champion; and both men thus claimed that they were the champion. A fight between them was the logical answer and on 16 May 1929, the NSC staged a triple-championship night at Olympia. Len Harvey challenged Alex Ireland for the British middleweight title; and Harry Corbett, the holder, met Johnny Cuthbert in another fight in their intense battle for the featherweight crown. Three attractive fights, but the one the crowd really wanted to see was the final decider of the bantamweight puzzle.

The two men could hardly have been further apart when it came to boxing style. Pattenden's usual way of stopping his opponent from scoring points was to attack him furiously from the opening bell. Defence was something he knew very little about and what he lacked in the scientific arts of his chosen sport, he more than made up for with a tremendous frenzy of attacking boxing. Baldock was the real boxer of the two, possessing more textbook skill and more scientific application. On this May evening in 1929, both men, however, went hammer and tongs from the first bell. It was Tommy Baldock who got on top in the early rounds with Pattenden continually laying himself wide open to the crunching power of Baldock's famous right hand which carried a punch capable of laying out many a heavier fighter. But though Pattenden received more and more punishment as the fight wore on — his mouth and lips were cut and his face a mass of swollen, bruised skin — the Bethnal Green boy absolutely refused to go down.

only other fighter to have scored a victory over Baldock when the East End man was on the wrong end of a foul decision — and Alf (Kid) Pattenden. Pattenden was the other East Ender, and when he knocked out Nicholson in twelve rounds at the National Sporting Club in June 1928, it made him the British champion so far as the NSC was concerned. But Johnny Brown still considered that he was the rightful champion and though Baldock and Pattenden were the best of pals outside the ring, there was enough rivalry in the East End to set up a battle between these two, especially since Teddy Baldock had until fairly recently held a version of the world title. The initial development was a rival British title fight between Brown, whose title had not been defended for three years, and Baldock. On 29 August 1928, at Clapton Greyhound Track, Baldock was the complete master. Brown was a pale shadow of his former self and he lost the title when he was stopped in only the second round. How much better it would have been if this fine bantamweight had remained in retirement undefeated.

The pace actually intensified as the contest went into its final third. Baldock was hammering away punch after punch at Kid Pattenden and Pattenden was refusing to go down.

Baldock was well in front by the tenth round, of that there was no doubt. But the question now on everyone's lips was, if Pattenden did not crack in the face of this incredible pressure, was it just possible that Baldock, after finding that all his efforts could not knock Pattenden down, would crack himself. Baldock had never boxed better in his life. He was sharp, scoring the most punishing blows on Pattenden's body, and yet still the Bethnal Green man was there and fighting back. Pattenden had only to land his own right hand once in the right place and that might turn the fight on its head. As Baldock began to tire from the enormous amount of work he was doing, that became a real possibility. Yet when Pattenden did land some body punches of real quality, Baldock showed that he could take it. Round and round the ring they went and when the fifteenth and final round came it was the same story. Baldock laid a great one-two on Pattenden's jaw, but instead of going flat down on his face, the Bethnal Green boy fought back and lashed into Baldock with a hail of punches. Baldock was forced on to the ropes, slipped and fell out of the ring, and then the two were at it again.

Again Baldock went through the ropes and when he scrambled back this time it was obvious that he was badly shaken. He fell into a clinch and Pattenden fought to free himself and get after his man again. When the last bell went the two were still toe-to-toe exchanging blows.

There was no doubt that Teddy Baldock had won. After the first ten rounds he only had to stay on his feet to do that. But what a tremendous fight it had been. From first to last bell both men had attacked each other. Baldock received a deafening cheer as his arm was raised. Pattenden possibly received an even bigger ovation. It had been a credit to boxing. Throughout all the frenzied action there was never any hint of needle from either man. On the two occasions when Baldock went through the ropes, Pattenden stood back and let him stand fully erect before going after him again. Baldock relinquished the title in due course, and eye trouble bought the retirement of Pattenden in 1931, soon after his great rival had given up. Eighteen months after their title fight they had met again in the Blackfriars Ring, but those expecting a repeat performance of that sensational night at Olympia were disappointed. Baldock won easily unlike the night that the Kid pushed him every inch of the way to the unofficial championship of London's East End.

JACK PETERSEN v JACK DOYLE
_____ British Heavyweight Championship _____
12 July 1933

Jack Doyle can hardly be rated as a classic boxer; nor was his British heavyweight title fight with Jack Petersen in July 1933 a classic fight in the textbook sense. But for sheer thrills, spills and colour, there can surely have been few fights in a British ring to equal it. Doyle, the former Irish Guardsman with a sledgehammer punch and a sensational record of one and two-round knockouts behind him, came within a whisker of taking the British title and all that went with it. When the fight was over Doyle and Petersen left the fight fans breathless and stunned. They could hardly believe their eyes and Jack Doyle, in particular, went down as one of the most colourful British boxers of all time, though his star flashed but briefly across the sky.

Doyle had first reached the attention of boxing's more informed public in 1932 when he boxed his first professional fight at the Crystal Palace where another of the highly-rated Sydney Hulls tournaments was taking place on 4 April that year. Doyle was billed to fight a Yorkshire miner named Chris Goulding and in the first few seconds of the fight it looked as if the raw Irish lad had bitten off far more than he could chew. The Irishman's crude defence was punctured with alarming regularity and blow after blow got home to his chin. But Doyle was unaffected by them, and he was soon returning the blows. Two hard lefts to Goulding's body made the pitman lower his guard. Doyle sized him up, let go a right to the jaw, and the fight was over in the first round with Goulding counted out before he had time to break sweat. Jack Doyle had arrived and fully vindicated the opinion of Len Harvey, the man who was to become British heavy-

weight champion before the end of that year. It was at Harvey's training camp at the Star and Garter Hotel, Windsor, that Doyle had first appeared on the scene. After two weeks of watching Harvey spar and shadow box, the big soldier wangled himself a few rounds in the ring with Harvey. Though he was obviously raw, the Irishman impressed Len enough for him to recommend Doyle to his manager. That is how, on that April evening in 1933, Doyle came to be dumping Chris Goulding on the Crystal Palace canvas.

One month after that speedy knockout, Doyle was in action again, this time against Arthur Evans, who was also a Rugby League player. Evans was still considering the best way to tackle the Irishman when he received the blow on his chin which ended another Doyle bout in round one. In the following twelve months Doyle scored another eight knockouts, all of them within the first two rounds. One of the most sensational was a two-rounds win over Jack Pettifer at the Crystal Palace. Pettifer was considered one of Britain's best young heavyweight hopes of the era, but a deadly right hand from Jack Doyle put him face down in the resin within six minutes of the first bell. Doyle's record after his first ten fights was five knockouts in the first round, five in the second. There are few boxers who have made such a sensational entry into the world of professional boxing. People now clamoured for him to be matched with the British title-holder, Jack Petersen of Wales, who had been on the same bill the night Doyle disposed of Arthur Evans, the Rugby League 'hard man' who could not stand up to one right-hander from Ireland's current favourite.

Irish heavyweight Jack Doyle was a natty dresser.

round knockout over Heine Muller followed and then came the offer to defend his title against Jack Doyle.

It was hardly a proper match, for while many of Petersen's opponents had been short of true championship class, he had still far too much experience for Doyle, even if Doyle had disposed of Pettifer in two rounds where Petersen had taken twelve. Apart from Pettifer, all of Doyle's fights had been against men of infinitely lower class than Petersen. Yet this was the fight which the public wanted and promoter Jeff Dickson's main concern, after all, was to fill stadiums. He certainly had no problems in selling tickets for this fight and to ensure that it went ahead he even had both fighters lodge £2,500 'appearance' money against their possible non-appearance, though the chances of either missing such a fight were slim indeed. Dickson's next problem was to find a venue, for there was no hall big enough to hold the thousands of fans clamouring for tickets. Dickson took the fight to the White City Stadium for the night of 12 July 1933 where more than 17,000 people were able to see the action out-of-doors.

The fight began with both men going straight to the centre of the ring and exchanging a barrage of punches. Doyle had been particularly keen to get on with the fight and had appeared to take absolutely no notice of referee C.H. Douglas's pre-fight lecture. Doyle stood three inches taller than the champion and weighed two stones more. He was two years younger and had a reach which was three inches longer. On the other hand, he had little experience. He swung several wild punches at the champion, one of which, a tremendous right, caught Petersen on the side of the neck. But the Welshman was finding scoring easy and he continually penetrated Doyle's woefully inadequate defence. Doyle countered by scrambling after his man and twice the referee had to rescue Petersen from the most undignified clinches, though Doyle seemed oblivious to the lecture which followed. All he wanted to do was to get back into the scrap. His next punch was a stinging left which caused the

Whereas Doyle had no pedigree at all, Petersen's rise to the top had been much more orthodox. Petersen was the ABA light-heavyweight champion of 1931 and a series of wins against impressive opposition when he turned professional led him to the Welsh light-heavyweight title against Dick Power. He disposed of Power in the first round, went on to knock out Charlie Smith, and was then put in the ring with Harry Crossley for the British title. They met on 23 May 1932 and after fifteen rounds Petersen was declared the winner. The new British light-heavyweight champion was then matched with Reggie Meen for the heaviest British title. On 12 July the same year he accounted for Meen in two rounds to become the only man to win the British light-heavyweight and heavyweight titles in consecutive fights. Six months later he defended the heavy-weight crown against Jack Pettifer and knocked him out in the twelfth round. A one-

champion to wince in pain, though it looked a highly dubious punch. Mr Douglas asked Doyle to keep his punches up, but even as he did Doyle came back with another debateable left. Petersen did not complain but crashed a right to Doyle's jaw. Doyle appeared not to notice and swung another low punch. This time, though Petersen again did not protest, referee Douglas intervened. Or at least he tried. Doyle was still not listening and again he waded in with both hands.

Petersen let go a magnificent left, then a right, but Doyle again took no notice and rushed his man once more. The champion hit the ropes and Doyle measured a swinging right at Petersen's jaw. He was quite a few inches out and instead managed to land it on Petersen's temple. It was misdirected, but it was still enough to send the Welshman staggering backwards. Petersen hit the ropes and his hands dropped to his sides. It was an open invitation to Jack Doyle to finish the fight. All the Irishman had to do, to pick up the British heavyweight title, was to land one good right on Petersen's exposed jaw. Incredibly, the Irishman smashed Petersen on the body with a left instead. It hurt the champion, of that there was no doubt, but it did not finish him. In fact, it did not even land where Doyle had intended. Instead it smacked into Petersen's right thigh. The referee stepped in to warn Doyle, but even as he did the Irishman slammed another left into the champion's thigh and was lining up a third when the bell called a halt to such ludicrous proceedings. Petersen limped to his corner and Doyle sprang to his, though not before Mr Douglas had again warned him. Indeed, the referee took the

54

Jack Doyle (left) shapes up to Jack Petersen.

trouble to visit Doyle's corner before the start of the second round to admonish him once more and ensure that he understood the gravity of these wild rushes which, while not malicious, were still contrary to the laws.

A warning that he would be disqualified if he hit low once more did not have any effect on Jack Doyle's tactics. He rushed out for the second round and as Petersen landed him a one-two, the Irishman laid two very suspicious blows to the region of Petersen's belt. Mr Douglas immediately stepped in, but Doyle was like a mad bull now. He pushed the referee aside and proceeded to hammer Petersen against the ropes. The champion fought back with a barrage of punches and worked Doyle back to the centre of the ring again. There the two men stood hammering away at each other. Blows were struck on exposed jaws and yet neither Irishman nor Welshman would succumb. Then Mr Douglas, who had been chasing around the ring since those two low blows from Doyle, managed to get between them at last. He pushed Doyle away and both men went to their corners. The verdict was that Petersen was the winner. Jack Doyle had been disqualified for punching low. Pandemonium broke out. Boos and whistles echoed round the stadium as the boxers and officials made their ways to the dressing rooms. No one wanted this contest to end.

But they had certainly had their money's worth, even in so short a space of time. Jack Petersen was so badly shaken by the onslaught from Doyle that he had to take a long cruise to summon back his strength. On his return to the ring he lost his title to Len Harvey, who outpointed him in London in November of that year, and then won it back in June the following year and held it until Ben Foord stopped him in the third round at Leicester in August 1936. Doyle's further career was in sharp contrast to that of Petersen. He was suspended by the British Boxing Board of Control and his purse of £3,000 impounded, though he was paid £5 per week, with another £5 per week going to his mother, for six months, the balance being forfeited. He went to America where Buddy Baer stopped him in the first round of a contest in which the Irishman claimed that he had been fouled. Back in England he scored a respectable points victory over King Levinsky and was then knocked out by Eddie Phillips in a two-round farce. In July 1939, all but six years to the day since he lost so sensationally to Jack Petersen, Doyle met Phillips for a second time. Again he was knocked out in quick time, and the venue was, ironically, at the White City Stadium where a moment of raw inexperience had once cost him the heavyweight championship of Britain.

MAX BAER v PRIMO CARNERA
World Heavyweight Championship
14 June 1934

The world heavyweight championship fight between the Italian giant Primo Carnera and the American playboy and jester Max Baer, fought out on New York's Long Island in the summer of 1934, has been called the Comedy Battle. Certainly, if one is looking purely at the greatest *skilful* battles between boxers in the professional ring, then this fight would not be even considered on a shortlist. But what is the qualification for a *classic* moment of boxing? Naturally, one looks mostly at the fights which have shown the greatest exhibitions of skilful scientific boxing. But then there are the fights which, although they lacked the highest skill, gave great pleasure because of the enormous courage shown by one or the other fighter. Then there are fights where the tables were turned in the most dramatic manner. All these will be remembered, not for the great exhibiton of technical boxing, but for the sheer thrill in the ring. They deserve to be called classics of their kind, for boxing can give intense enjoyment without offering the greatest exhibition of ring craft each time. But Carnera-Baer, where do they fit in?

The fact is that Primo Carnera and Max Baer were two of the most colourful characters ever to fight for the richest prize in sport. Carnera was a mountain of a man, laughed at and ridiculed since he could remember, and probably underrated as a boxer, though even then one would never place him in the top class. Baer, in contrast, was probably overrated, a man who, if he had taken boxing seriously enough, could have been a great champion, but who instead liked to fool around too much, and who is ultimately remembered more for that than for his boxing skills. The fight between these two in

which Baer wrested the world heavyweight title is still one of the best remembered, oft-quoted of all time. It lacked much in the way of skill, but more than made up for that with incident. At one time it looked likely that Primo Carnera, who was down and all but out, might yet pull off a sensation and retain his crown.

Primo Carnera was a product of the commercialisation of sport. Fifty years, even twenty years previously, he would not have got anywhere near a world title fight. But boxing in the 1930s had become show-business. Promoters investing millions of dollars had the greatest say in who fought who and when. Challengers were manufactured to suit a need, to fill a gap, and Primo Carnera, standing almost six and a half feet tall, was 'great box office'. He was born in the village of Sequals, near Venice, on 25 October 1906, the first-born child of Sante and Giovana Carnera who called him Primo in recognition of that fact. At the age of eight he was a big boy and the family apprenticed him to a local cabinet maker. By the time he was in his twenty-first year, Primo stood nearly 6ft 6in tall and weighed something over 266lb. It was then he decided to leave home and make for France to seek his fortune. The little money he took with him soon evaporated on his travels through southern France and his great height caught the attention of the proprietor of a travelling circus. Primo was offered a job wrestling all-comers and performing strongman tricks. With no money he was in no position to refuse and it was that decision which ultimately resulted in him taking the road which led to the heavyweight championship of the world.

Max Baer and Primo Caernera end up on the canvas together in their bizarre title fight.

Primo was spotted by Paul Journee, a former French heavyweight boxer, who saw Carnera as the way to make a fortune. He offered the big Italian the chance to see Paris, thinking that with a pair of boxing gloves wrapped around those giant hams of hands, Primo would be a great attraction in the boxing rings of the French capital. Carnera eagerly agreed and once there Journee introduced him to Leon See, his former manager. See was impressed with Journee's find. Primo, who was surprisingly quick on his feet despite his height, was soon knocking over all-comers in Western Europe and in London. Now his handlers thought it was time to take him to the United States and it took just seventy seconds to make Carnera into a sensation on that side of the Atlantic. That was how long it took him to knock over Big Boy Peterson at Madison Square Garden. After that people queued to see him train, followed him around the streets of New York, and all this encouraged See to embark on a tour of the States in 1930.

Wherever the Ambling Alp, as he had become known, fought, there were never enough tickets available. His contests never lasted long because Primo usually knocked out his opponent within the first round or two. This did not matter to See. The main thing was that Carnera was gaining a reputation as a knockout sensation, a giant of a man who no one would be able to stop. That, of course, meant dollars, and See took his

man to the big cities where successes were repeated in similar style. One of his few defeats had been at the hands of Jack Sharkey, who outpointed the Ambling Alp over fifteen rounds. Now Sharkey was heavyweight champion of the world; and when See pushed the Italian's claims for a shot at the title, Sharkey had no objection, for he felt that he had the measure of the big man. Certainly, for the early rounds Sharkey outboxed his man. But in round six Carnera let go a crippling body blow, followed by a cracking left to the jaw. As Sharkey's chin passed him on the way to the canvas, Primo let go another stunning left. The champion did not beat the count and the world now had a new and most unlikely champion.

That fight was on 29 June 1933 and Carnera lost no time in putting his title on the line. Less than four months later he fought Paolino Uzcudun in Italy and outpointed him over fifteen rounds. He then returned to America and did the same to Tommy Loughran in Miami. So Primo Carnera was not a champion afraid of defending his crown, though it must be said that it was promoters' interests more than anything which put him back in the ring so quickly. Nevertheless, it meant that there was more interest in Carnera than ever and Hollywood made him an offer, which he straightaway accepted, to star in a film called *Everywoman's Man*. The hero of the film was Maxmillian Adelbert Baer, a man who was

One of the eleven times when Baer had the Ambling Alp on the canvas.

nearly three years younger than the Ambling Alp, but who was himself challenging for the title. The script called for Baer to fight Carnera and knock him out. The Italian objected and the ending was changed to a draw.

Max Baer was a born comedian, raised on his father's ranch in Nebraska, and a natural athlete with a good physique and handsome features. He took up boxing for the same reason that he found himself in that Hollywood movie — he liked to be in the limelight. By the beginning of 1934 he had proved himself a good enough fighter to deserve a crack at Carnera's world title, particularly since he had scored a ten-rounds knockout over Max Schmeling. The New York State Athletic Commission wanted to rid themselves of Primo Carnera as champion as quickly as possible and they were happy to grant Baer a shot at the crown. The fight was set for 14 June 1934 at the Long Island Bowl, an enormous outdoor arena owned by the Madison Square Garden Corporation. Baer started his clowning long before the fighters got into the ring. He let it be known that he was not training properly and fooled around so much that the Commission did, at one stage, threaten to call off the fight until they were convinced that Baer was in the best possible shape. Indeed he was, and at the weigh-in he was at his clowning again. It

made no difference to what people thought of his chances. The bookmakers made him the clear favourite, the first time that a challenger had entered the ring as favourite since Dempsey beat Willard.

Fifty-five thousand fight fans were present when the bell went to sound the start of the world's most unlikely heavyweight title fight. It was Carnera who attacked first, rushing at Max Baer and landing some exceptionally heavy body punches which soon raised the challenger's blood. Baer got so steamed up that within ninety seconds of the start of this fight he had Primo Carnera down on the canvas. A searing right hand did the damage and the crowd howled their approval at the American's action. Carnera was up in a flash but he suffered a tremendous battering for his pains. The Italian countered by getting into a clinch but near the end of the round Baer had him down again. This time Baer fell over him and the two sprawled in an undignified heap on the canvas before rising. Carnera looked to have done some damage to his knee and spent the rest of the round hobbling in some pain. The second round again found Baer in control, slamming rights and lefts into Carnera's body. There was no science in all this; just good old-fashioned fisticuffs of the most elementary variety.

In the third round Primo went down again

Once more Caernera hits the deck as the Clown Prince of Boxing looks on.

and this time Baer danced over him and even hit him before he had risen to his feet. But no one cared and in the context of this fight it seemed that almost anything was acceptable. The fourth round saw Baer spring out to carry on his demolition work on the champion who was still limping from his injured ankle. This time, however, it was Carnera who looked the more positive boxer. A series of short-arm blows won him the round, much to the surprise of the crowd. In the fifth round Carnera again ended on top, save for one horrendous moment when a straight right from Baer landed smack on the challenger's nose and broke it. Blood sprayed everywhere, Carnera let out a little howl of anguish, and Max Baer burst out laughing! Baer was still grinning broadly when he landed another right on the same bloodied spot. Now Carnera displayed immense courage. He fought back and, for the first time in the fight, had Baer retreating back towards his own corner. Back came Baer and

when the bell went it was obvious that this fight was far from over.

Primo outboxed his opponent again in round six and he seemed to have found new strength and resolve while Baer was tiring from his earlier frantic efforts. The seventh, eighth and ninth rounds were more subdued than the frenzied start to this fight. Carnera now had the challenger's dangerous right under control and now the champion was collecting valuable points. It certainly quietened down the spectators and wiped the smiles off those who called Carnera 'Satchel Feet'. The Ambling Alp came out for the tenth round looking far more confident than at any other time in the fight. Baer tried a couple of low hits and Carnera shook him rigid with two tremendous body punches. This only served to anger Baer and he got through with a right which smashed home on Carnera's jaw and dumped him back down on to the resin. He was up at four but looked unsteady and the round ended with Max Baer slamming the champion round the ring once more. This fight might lack finesse, a man told his neighbour, but it sure as hell made up for it with excitement. It was a brave man who would now put his money on the result.

Carnera accelerated out of his corner for the eleventh round, evidently intent on attacking his man and battering him into submission. It was a grave mistake. Baer met him with a fusillade of punches and put him down. Up he got to struggle on and walked straight into another terrific right. Down went Primo Carnera once again and it seemed that this time he would never beat the count. Yet he was up at only three. That was his second and last big mistake of that round. He had absolutely no idea where he was and when Baer shaped to smash him down again, referee Arthur Donovan nipped between them, ushered Carnera back to his corner, and proclaimed Max Baer heavyweight champion of the world at the end of probably the most extraordinary fight ever to decide the fate of that title.

HARRY MIZLER v GUSTAVE HUMERY
Lightweight contest at the Royal Albert Hall
2 October 1935

That late, great boxing promoter Jeff Dickson served up some tremendous contests during his career. But for sheer sensation there was never one to equal the tussle between the former British lightweight champion, Harry Mizler, and that great Frenchman, Gustave Humery, who went on to win the European lightweight title. These two met at the Royal Albert Hall in October 1935 in a fight which had incident after incident and culminated in the man who had been knocked around the ring for most of the fight letting fly with a desperate last-ditch punch which found its target, caused serious damage, and won him the fight. That final round had everything and as it drew to its climax there was not an occupied seat in this great arena, as everyone was on his feet.

Harry Mizler was a brilliant amateur boxer. He won the ABA bantamweight, featherweight and lightweight titles in 1930, 1932 and 1933 respectively and was also British Empire amateur champion and represented Great Britain in the 1932 Los Angeles Olympic Games. The following year, after taking his third ABA title, Mizler turned professional and scored thirteen consecutive wins. It was a record which earned him a shot at Johnny Cuthbert's British lightweight title and on 18 January 1934, after only six months as a professional, he outpointed the champion in London to take the crown. Seven months later Mizler, a good-looking Jewish boy who was becoming hot property at the box office, defended his title against Billy Quinlan. It was another great night for Mizler and he outpointed the challenger at Swansea, a success which took him back to London and another title defence against Jack (Kid) Berg. On 29 October 1934,

Mizler met his match and it was no surprise when the referee stopped the contest at the end of ten rounds to save poor Harry from further punishment. A five-months lay-off was ordered, so badly was Harry Mizler mauled that night. But his return to the ring saw him win six consecutive fights before Dickson gave him the test of fighting Gustave Humery.

The Frenchman was twenty-seven years old, five years older than Mizler, and his professional career went back eleven years. Humery was noted for his whirlwind style of boxing and a powerful punch in both hands which had seen most of his opponents stopped inside the distance by the man they called Tiger. Twice in three fights he had beaten Jack (Kid) Berg, a fact which gave him an immediate moral boost over the Briton. That apart, this was an inspired piece of matchmaking, even by Jeff Dickson's own high standards. Mizler was keen to prove that he was far from finished and desperate to earn a crack at regaining his British title, even to go on for a world title shot. Humery, on the other hand, had already been promised a fight with the world champion, Tony Canzoneri, if he beat Mizler. Clearly, for both boxers there was much at stake. The prize was high, but defeat would mean that the loser's career would be severely checked. In addition there was tremendous interest in the differing styles of the boxers. Mizler was the more classical, the stylist, though with a notoriously weak mid-section which he had been busy toning up for this fight; Humery was the aggressive 'Tiger', a vigorous boxer who harried his opponents into submission.

It was with the ferocity of a tiger that

Humery came out of his corner at the start of this fight before 7,000 fight fans at the West Kensington arena in the autumn of 1935. But before he could land a blow, Mizler's famous straight left stopped him in his tracks and set him back on his heels. Another straight left momentarily checked the Frenchman when he came at Mizler again, but it was to be one of the rare occasions in the fight that Mizler was able to keep Humery at bay with that punch. Humery was soon back again and this time he forced Mizler on to the ropes with a barrage of body punches. When Mizler covered up his midriff, Humery quickly changed tack and it was the former British champion's head which was then the helpless target of this fusillade of lefts and rights. Mizler managed to free himself and scored with two lefts and a searing right to the Frenchman's jaw. Just as quickly Humery was back on the offensive and again Mizler found himself back on the ropes and taking the most terrible body punishment.

Mizler opened the second round with two fine point-scoring lefts, but again it was a short-lived success. Humery soon had him on the ropes once more and felled him with a savage blow to the kidney region. Mizler beat the count but from that moment until the bell ended the round, he soaked up more rough treatment. The crowd were on their feet, but even they could not have imagined the sensations to come in the very next round. Mizler just had time to land a right on Humery's chin at the start of round three before the Frenchman charged him once more. Against the ropes, Mizler tried to fight his way clear, but when he dropped his guard for a split second, Humery delivered a cracking right to the Briton's jaw. Down went Harry Mizler in a heap, this time for a count of nine. No sooner had he regained his feet than Humery hit him again, another right, this time to the body. Once more he went down, only to rise at eight, and he was now so dazed that Humery could pick his spot. He felled Mizler yet again and everyone felt certain that poor Harry would not rise again. But he did, only to receive a wicked left under the heart as he straightened up. Then a most amazing incident happened. Mizler fell across the bottom rope. He was

Humery is lectured by the referee while Mizler takes a breather on the ropes.

not out on the canvas; and yet he was certainly not in any condition to continue. Humery stood looking puzzled, unsure as to his rights. Referee Moss Deyong seemed similarly perplexed and Mizler hung there for over ten seconds without any count starting up, and without Humery applying another blow. It was a kind of 'no man's land'. Eventually the referee signalled for Humery to advance and finish the fight, but as he did so the bell went and Mizler was saved.

Mizler came out for the fourth round looking surprisingly fresh, but as soon as Humery landed the first blow, the Briton began to wilt. For the rest of that round Humery hammered Mizler, though the Briton also landed the occasional good right. Nevertheless it was staggering that Mizler was still on his feet when the end of the round came and there were many who thought that his corner must now throw in the towel, so much punishment had the plucky Jewish boy taken. Round five saw Mizler land a couple more good lefts, but he was fighting almost by instinct and it was no surprise when Humery put him down again. Mizler beat the count with a second to spare. Again he managed to get through the round.

In the sixth round Humery once more delivered a series of devastating blows to Mizler's body and towards the end of the three minutes he smashed a left hook into Mizler's stomach, followed by a hard right under the heart. Mizler went down and it was only the bell which saved him. He was helped back to his corner and there were now serious thoughts as to whether it was wise to allow him to continue. Deyong went to his corner during the interval and asked him if he really wanted to carry on. Mizler nodded and the referee reluctantly allowed the fight to continue. The seventh round saw another amazing incident. After shocking Humery with a series of rights and lefts to the body, Mizler was rocked by a right uppercut to the chin. It was the start of a barrage which forced him back on to the ropes where he was beaten into a kind of squatting position. Again both Humery and the referee were puzzled. Mizler was sitting on the middle rope, gloves over his face. The timekeeper could not begin the count, for Harry was again not technically down. Humery gave him another quizzical look. The referee, getting no response from Mizler when he ordered him to box on, beckoned Humery forward to finish the job. But as the Frenchman weighed up just where to hit Mizler, the bell saved the Briton from certain defeat.

The eighth round started with Humery boring into Mizler, anxious to have the thing over and done with. Mitzler let him have a hard left to the chin. The two men stood toe-to-toe hammering away and Mizler got in a right to the chin. There was no doubt that Humery had won this fight hands down . . . unless Harry Mizler could find one punch to end it all himself. The Briton wound up a right and sent it crashing through Humery's defence in one last, desperate effort. It was a punch which carried every last drop of energy in Harry Mizler's body. The right crashed home on the point of the Frenchman's jaw and rocked him back. Blood poured from his mouth and nose and he seemed incapable of defending himself. Mizler jumped in after him with a succession of punches. There was another right to the jaw, then a left which spun the Frenchman round towards his corner. At the same time the towel came in and the fight was over. Harry Mizler had, with that one last-ditch punch, broken Gustave Humery's jaw. The scenes in the ring were indescribable. Both men were cheered rapturously, though poor Humery was in tears at the thought of seven and a half rounds of total domination being lost in a blinding flash. At the end of that seventh round, with Mizler a beaten man, the Englishman's corner had advised: 'Just see if you can hit him with a right. Give it everything you've got!' Mizler took the advice and scored one of boxing's most sensational last-minute victories.

JOHN HENRY LEWIS v LEN HARVEY
_____ World Light-Heavyweight Championship_____
9 November 1936

It was an inspired piece of business that brought Len Harvey, British champion at middle, light-heavyweight and heavy-weight, to Wembley Stadium in 1936. Though still most active in the ring, the former champion had been hired, not for his boxing talents, but for his great experience of the sport in general. Arthur J. Elvin, managing director of Wembley Stadium, hired Harvey as a matchmaker for his boxing organisation. Elvin had staged varied attractions at the stadium, including ice hockey, indoor athletics, table tennis and professional tennis, and, of course, it was by now the permanent home of the FA Cup Final. But Elvin was convinced that Wembley could also be one of the major boxing venues in Britain. He was equally convinced that Len Harvey's expertise as a match-maker could help him achieve that dream. What he had not anticipated was that it would be Harvey himself who would be the challenger for a world title. As Harvey told him when he suggested the idea, 'It will be the fight they'll all want to see'.

Len Harvey was twenty-nine and had been boxing since he was twelve. His career, which had quite some way to go yet, boasted several impressive performances. He had dominated the British middleweight title from 1929 to 1932 before losing to Jock McAvoy on points; he had won and then relinquished the lightweight title; and had already held the heavyweight crown by beating Jack Petersen in an epic contest before Petersen regained it with an equally fine performance. John Henry Lewis, was a 22-year-old Negro. A native of Los Angeles, Lewis took the world light-heavyweight (or cruiserweight as it is also known) title by outpointing the holder, Bob Olin, at St Louis in 1935, and though twenty-seven of his fifty-seven bouts had ended in him knocking out his opponent, he was more of a boxer in the classic style than just a good old-fashioned slugger. In March 1936 he had outpointed Jock McAvoy after a rousing fifteen rounds, so he was no stranger to British boxers, and of course, London's fight fans had heard all about him.

Len Harvey was correct, then, when he said that this would be the fight that every-one in the capital would want to see. Yet Harvey was not even British champion at this weight, so how could he justify a title shot? The British title-holder was Eddie Phillips but, as Harvey was quick to point out, he had already beaten Phillips twice. Besides, if Phillips fancied his chances as world championship material, then Len Harvey would be pleased to give him the chance . . . if Harvey beat Lewis. The sugar coating on the pill was that Phillips was given a fight on the same Wembley bill as the world title fight and that left everyone happy.

Lewis said that he was more than pleased to come to London to defend his title, though it cost the promoter £4,000 in a flat fee, free of income tax, plus £200 for training expenses and four first-class return tickets from New York to London. Elvin was so keen to stage the fight that he agreed at once. Then, however came a snag. Lewis wanted his fee lodged in an American bank before the fight as it was felt that the absence of the no-foul rule in Britain might prove a little too risky. The matter was resolved when it was agreed that the money should be lodged in America, but not released until the fight had started.

63

Len Harvey, the Cornishman they called the 'modern Bob Fitzsimmons'.

John Henry Lewis's famous 'mean look'.

With everyone now apparently satisfied. Lewis and his party arrived at Southampton to be met by Harvey who was, of course, matchmaker as well as challenger. Lewis was installed at Harvey's own training headquarters at the Barn Club, and the challenger then went away to the Dumbell Hotel, Maidenhead, to prepare for his shot at the world title. The fight was now drawing attention from all over the world, for it was an intriguing match. The contenders weighed almost identical amounts and although Harvey was slightly taller, it was Lewis who had the shade longer reach. A scare when Lewis damaged an eye in training was quickly dispelled and on the evening of 9 November 1935 over 9,000 spectators, who had paid just under £13,000, wedged themselves into the Wembley arena to justify Harvey's claims about the compelling nature of the fight. There was an American promoter at the ringside, ready to take Harvey back to the United States if he was victorious that night. A barrage of press cameras, the presence of many celebrities from entertainment, sport, politics and London society all added to the glamour of the occasion.

The referee was Jack Smith, a veteran of such nights, and he called the men together amid all the hullaballoo going on outside the ring. Len Harvey looked surprisingly calm and relaxed, his face cracked by a broad smile. Lewis, on the other hand, appeared nervous and fidgity and a plaster covered the eye injury which had healed sufficiently for the fight to take place, but which perhaps still worried the champion. Harvey was normally a cautious boxer in the opening stages of a fight, but when the bell sounded on this evening, he bounded straight out of his corner and began to attack Lewis vigorously from the off. He began with a hard straight left to Lewis's face and followed up that with a right to the ribs. Lewis was forced back on to the ropes and had to get into the clinch to rescue himself. Harvey was in no mood for that sort of thing. He threw Lewis off and whipped in a right to the chin. There was very little that the American could do about it and he was forced to retreat for the rest of the round. When it ended, Harvey was clearly the winner.

Though Lewis had clearly settled into his stride during the second round it was still Harvey's. Lewis was warned for holding and when the two men broke there was Harvey, slamming in a right which crunched into Lewis's mouth. Lewis was forced to hold on whenever he could and the crowd now began to sense that Len Harvey was in with a fine chance of ending this night as champion of the world. In the third round though, Harvey, ironically, was to land a right which changed all that. He came out intent on continuing to force the champion back again, but when the Cornishman crashed a right high on Lewis's temple it was immediately obvious to everyone, especially Lewis, that the challenger's right had 'gone'. It was now apparent that Harvey was in some considerable pain and though he tried hard not to show it, Lewis knew that the fight had now turned dramatically in his favour. He came off the retreat and started to go forward, letting fly with lefts which hurt Harvey. It took all the challenger's experience not to let himself be damaged. Now Harvey was pleased to clinch whenever he could but Lewis showed that he was master of that kind of situation, hitting and holding with ease and letting Harvey know that he was in the ring with the world champion.

Lewis took the fourth round, for Len Harvey was now forced to defend for most of it, occasionally jabbing out a left but doing little to cause any real discomfort. The fifth round raised some British hopes when Harvey caught the champion with a hard left which sent the plaster over Lewis's eye dropping to the canvas. But this only served to make John Henry Lewis angry and he tore into Harvey with both hands working overtime. Harvey, to his great credit, held firm and there followed a period of in-fighting which greatly annoyed the crowd who were unaware that both men were inflicting great punishment on the other with a series of short but wicked punches to the body. The

referee eventually called a halt to that and pulled them apart, though Harvey received a rebuke for sending in a bristling right on the break which missed the champion's chin by a whisker. Then by putting in a volley of lefts, Harvey forced Lewis back again, though when the bell came it was obvious to the challenger's cornermen that the effort in clenching that right had caused Harvey more damage. The next seven rounds saw Harvey almost totally on the defensive with Lewis boxing exceptionally well and wiping out the early lead which the Cornishman had established. As the bell sounded to end the twelfth round everyone felt that Harvey had given all he had to give. But they were wrong.

Harvey seemed to have found new strength from somewhere. He drove forward and after crashing a left on to Lewis's chin, followed up that with a powerful right which also slammed into the champion's jaw. It all took the champion by surprise and Harvey now ignored the pain in his right hand and continued the barrage. Lewis decided to counter this with his own brand of furious hitting and although Harvey went back to his corner marginally ahead in that round, he did so at a cost. His body was bruised and blood streamed down his face from a cut over his left eye. The fight entered its final six minutes and Lewis now looked tired, while Harvey appeared to be brighter than at any time since the opening three rounds. Len Harvey's most fervent intent now was to drop Lewis on to the canvas and he went after him. Harvey hammered punch after punch into Lewis's body which gasped under the weight of them. The champion's injured eye was now also in a sorry state and back he went as Harvey drove forward. If only Harvey had not damaged that right hand so early in the fight then the end might have come at this point, but the pain which shot through his body every time he landed that punch severely restricted its power.

For the three minutes of that penultimate round there could have been no one in the

The lights bring out Len Harvey's features in stark relief as he wards off Lewis.

Wembley arena who stayed in their seat. Instead they stood and urged these two boxers on, or at least they urged Len Harvey on, for naturally the vast majority wanted a home victory. There was one more round to go and they could see the light-heavyweight championship of the world within Len Harvey's grasp. They looked at John Henry Lewis sitting on his stool as the American's seconds worked feverishly to restore some strength into his aching body, and they saw Len Harvey, also tired, but now just three minutes away from the world title. But he had to win this last round by a good margin, or else either knock down or stop Lewis.

At the bell Harvey set off to do just that. Hardly pausing to touch gloves he steamed into Lewis. Harvey ignored his own damaged eye and his aching right hand and lay punch after punch on Lewis. The champion was bombarded with every punch that Harvey possessed. But John Henry Lewis was a world-class fighter. He bore the signs of punishment but he would not go down.

Instead, though not matching Harvey's furious attack, Lewis found time to counter-punch his way through the last round. When the bell ended the fight John Henry Lewis was tired and battered, but he was still standing firmly on his feet and it was obvious that Len Harvey had not done quite enough. Without hesitation Jack Smith turned to Lewis and raised his hand. There could be no one in the arena who could argue with that decision. Len Harvey had been a game fighter but he had not done enough to become world champion. Nevertheless, the Cornishman had given one of the best displays of any British boxer between the wars. There could be no one who regretted paying money to see this fight. If Harvey had not injured his hand then things might have been different. He still had much of his career remaining and went on to more British titles. Yet he was right about that night at Wembley. This had been the fight that they all wanted to see and they were not disappointed.

JOHNNY KING v JACKIE BROWN
_____ Bantamweight Championship of Britain _____
31 May 1937

Most boxing managers would be happy to have one star performer at a particular weight in their stable, but occasionally there is a fight manager who finds himself in the enviable position of having two men of equal weight and ability. The position becomes less than enviable though, when the manager must choose one or the other when the time comes for the boxers to fight their own personal battle to see who will go on to greater things. Such a manager was Harry Fleming of Manchester who had in his stable, in the 1930s, the two boxers Jackie Brown and Johnny King. Brown was the former world flyweight champion, King the current British bantamweight title holder, and with Brown now having difficulty in making the weight in the flyweight division he moved up to bantamweight. It was then that Harry Fleming's dilemma began. The first climax came in 1935 when Jackie Brown forced himself into a position where Fleming could no longer put off the day when his two boys stepped into the ring to oppose each other.

Jackie Brown first won the British flyweight title in 1929 when he knocked out Bert Kirby in the third round of their championship fight at West Bromwich. He lost the title to Kirby the following year, when Kirby had his revenge with a three-rounds KO in London, but then won it back over fifteen rounds at Manchester in 1931, and then defended it successfully twice before Benny Lynch relieved him of it in 1935. That night also saw Lynch take the world crown which Brown had won in October 1932 when he stopped Young Perez in thirteen rounds at Manchester. With defeat by Lynch, Brown decided to become a bantamweight fighter

and it was not long before he was casting envious glances at his stable companion. Johnny King had recently regained his British title from Dick Corbett (these two kept that championship as their own special preserve between 1931 and 1934) and now that Corbett had relinquished the title King was out on his own. He was looking towards the featherweight title, but had no objections to meeting Brown, so long as his bantam crown was not at stake.

A meeting was arranged on 22 November 1935, but over only twelve rounds which meant that if Brown did defeat King, then the latter's title would not be at risk. Fleming could now decide either to side with one of the boxers, or wash his hands of the whole affair. He chose the latter and spent the evening of the fight in Blackpool, though he was on the telephone every few moments to check on the progress of the battle between his two protegés. The first two rounds of the Belle Vue bout were quiet enough as the two men sized each other up. Then Brown sped into top gear and scored some good lefts to the body while the champion attempted to land his famous right. Brown, however, was always that little bit faster and even when the right which had won King so many fights landed, it was always with Brown moving away so the full force of the blow was never felt. By the end of the fifth round Brown was well ahead on points and the champion's cornermen looked more than a little apprehensive. The sixth round changed all that. King opened it with a left to Brown's head while Brown was still looking for the right, and as the former world champion hit the ropes, another wicked punch, this time the right, smashed into his jaw. His eyes went glassy, his hands dropped to his sides, and only his peculiar flat-footed, legs-wide-apart stance kept him upright as King hammered away with lefts and rights. Only when the referee jumped between them and stopped the contest did Brown collapse. Honour was satisfied and everyone knew that Brown had been given his chance and had been found wanting.

Everyone except Brown, that is. He was still desperate to unseat King and set off again, this time from the bottom rung of the ladder. He scored six successive wins, lost to Johnny Cusick and then beat the same fighter in a return, and finally successfully challenged Len Hampston for the Northern Area bantamweight title. That led him into a series of eliminating contests to find King's challenger. The other leading contenders were Jim McInally, the Scottish champion, and the Welsh title-holder, Len Beynon. It was decreed that Brown should meet McInally, the winner should meet Beynon, and the winner of that final eliminator should challenge King for the British title. Jackie Brown opened up a big lead against the Scotsman before knocking him out in the last round. A hard-won points victory over the Welshman then earned Brown his long-awaited title shot.

The fight for the British bantamweight championship was set for the last day of May 1937 at, of course, Belle Vue, Manchester, where the number of people clamouring for tickets was so great that the promoters decided to move the fight from the King's Hall and stage it outside. The picture had now changed dramatically since their first meeting of eighteen months earlier. Then, King had scored an emphatic victory over Brown; now Brown actually started the fight as the bookmakers' favourite. Since their first meeting, Johnny King had fought for the featherweight title, but Nel Tarleton had beaten him on points at Liverpool. Since then he had been outpointed five times in thirteen contests and his career looked to be sliding back, but Brown's looked like taking off. After all, in fifteen fights since his last meeting with King he had been beaten only

once — a points defeat which he later reversed — and had beaten both of the other leading British bantamweights to earn himself the place as natural challenger. There was one other intriguing difference about this second fight. Jackie Brown had left the managership of Harry Fleming and was now in the stable of Tom Hurst, so King now had the advantage of Fleming in his corner, a luxury which both he and Brown had been denied a year and a half earlier.

Though the fight had been scheduled for the end of May, Manchester's weather was by no means hospitable and a spiteful wind gusted around the arena. At the weigh-in Brown had been ten ounces over the 8st 6lb limit, though he removed it without difficulty and when he visited the scales for a second time he was three ounces inside the limit, just one ounce heavier than the champion. The challenger bounced into the ring amid tumultuous applause and danced around acknowledging the crowd. There was a similar welcome for the champion, but his demeanour was much different, almost sullen. He gave only a stiff little bow, almost like a polite Japanese, and returned quickly to his corner, while Brown was enjoying the atmosphere so much that he could hardly contain himself. Certainly this was the fight that all Manchester wanted to see. After nearly two years of rivalry between these two, it had all come together on this special night. The referee called the men to the middle of the ring and gave them their final instructions. They returned once more to their respective corners, and Manchester waited to see who would be the victor.

Jackie Brown was renowned for his eagerness to take the fight to his opponent and so it was a major surprise that, when the bell went for the first round, he elected instead to approach King in a rather circumspect manner and it was the champion who was forced to do the attacking. King responded in style, jabbing out straight lefts which kept Brown well out of harm's way. Near the end of the round, King caught his opponent with a hard straight left to the body, followed it up with a right, and when the bell ended the

*Round thirteen and Jackie Brown is out for the
full count after being KO'd by Johnny King.*

first three minutes, Jackie Brown was glad to
retreat to his corner. Those two blows had
certainly shaken the challenger. Brown
changed his tactics in the second round and
came out quickly to launch a series of lefts
and rights on the champion's body. Some of
them must have hurt King but he did not
show it; instead he measured Brown with
that left, and occasionally let go a powerful
right. With the champion remaining cool in
the face of Brown's more positive approach,
it still seemed that the favourite who started
the fight would need all his skill to end it as
champion. There was the continual threat of
that wicked King right, and so far Brown had
shown precious little ability to combat it.
Both men were cautioned for holding at the
beginning of the third round, which King
again took with a stylish spell of long-range
boxing, and in the fourth Brown once more
took the fight to the champion. Rights and
lefts were exchanged but it was King who
was the heavier puncher and at the end of the
round Brown looked battered and tired, his
body bearing the marks of considerable
punishment.

Brown came back bravely in the fifth and
scored points with a two-handed attack
which found its way both to the champion's
body and to his face. Yet still King remained
calm and the champion was still collecting
points at the start of the sixth, even when
Brown was scoring too. This was Brown's
best round so far. He shook King with a
sharp left hook to the point of the chin and
when it came to close quarters, Brown was

on top, while King, for the first time,
struggled to get to grips at long range. The
first half of the seventh round belonged to
Jackie Brown who scored with several one-
twos of real class. But by the end of the
round, King, who still refused to be ruffled,
crashed home a right which met Brown's jaw
and sent the challenger staggering on to the
ropes. It was all Brown could do to cover up
and stay on his feet to wait for the bell to
rescue him.

There was no doubt that King was in the
lead and Brown started the eighth round by
darting forward and landing a right to King's
jaw, only to find that the champion's immediate response was to smash him back on
to the ropes with a right of his own and then
proceed to rain down a shower of body
punches that took away much of Brown's
strength. Even then Brown had enough
energy and courage to fight back furiously
with a spell of two-handed hitting, but King
took it all and was still meting out punishment when the round ended.

The ninth round was particularly damaging to the challenger's hopes. King opened it
by rocking Brown with a left to the jaw and
followed up that with a succession of rights
to the head. For almost the whole round it
was King on the offensive while Brown
soaked up all the punishment until people
were beginning to ask if he was incredibly
strong, or if King was indeed unable to find
the punch to knock his man down. The next
two rounds saw Brown again taking almost
all the knocks. A wicked right on the chin   69

found him hanging on until the referee eventually parted him from King; and the end was surely now in sight, thought the spectators, when King sent another right crashing against the challenger's chin. But somehow Brown held on and in the eleventh round he managed to let go a terrific right which rocked King back on his heels. The punch crashed home to the point of the champion's jaw and Brown leapt in after him with a fusillade of lefts and rights. But again King seemed happy to let Brown have his moment and as the challenger used up his precious reserves of energy, so King remained calm and collected. The twelfth round was a real cracker. Jackie Brown made one last desperate effort to take this fight and with it the British title. He punched with all his power, used every trick in his repertoire, and forced the champion into a position where he could only manage the occasional left of no real power. Then Brown swung in a left which landed suspiciously low and was followed by a right to the chin as the champion doubled up. Amid howls of protest, the referee stopped the fight and warned Brown. Nevertheless the champion was knocked back and the round went to Brown who ended it with a flurry of lefts and rights.

Johnny King now decided, in the interval between the twelfth and thirteenth rounds, to end the fight as quickly as possible. Brown was met with a left and then a right to the head which sent him back on to the ropes. Brown bounced off the hemp, did not gather his guard, and when he saw this, Johnny King wound up a right which he sent streaking towards the challenger's chin. Down went Brown, his head hitting the canvas with a dull thud, and that should have been the end. Incredibly the challenger somehow managed to beat the count, but once back on his feet he could not even find the will to gather up some form of defence. Johnny King was in again and sent another wicked right to the side of Brown's jaw. When Jackie Brown went down this time, he stayed down. The full count was a mere formality for King knew that he had retained his crown from the moment that right hit the challenger. Johnny King retained the British bantamweight title until 1947 when, his career interrupted by six years of war, he was knocked out in the seventh round of a title fight against Jackie Paterson in Manchester. A great British champion had been beaten by the advance of years.

JOE LOUIS v JAMES J. BRADDOCK
World Heavyweight Championship
22 June 1937

The mother of Joseph Louis Berrow, a black man born in Alabama on 13 May 1914, hoped that her son would become a violinist. In fact, young Joseph's chosen profession could not have been much further removed from that of a professional musician. He became a boxer . . . actually he became Joe Louis, one of the greatest and most colourful fighters that the ring has ever seen. The son of a cotton-picker in America's racially-prejudiced Deep South, Joe Louis's ability as boxer, and as a thoroughly decent human-being, over-came almost all the handicaps of his birth. As a well-respected world champion, Louis knew heights denied to most of his fellow black Americans. He held the world heavy-weight title for eleven years and defended it more times than any other champion. In the end he retired for the first time un-defeated, though, it must be said, after a couple of near things towards the end, and he was one of the greatest boxers of all time who did everything, and more, that could be expected of a world champion. Four of his world title fights are featured in this book, the first of them against James J. Braddock when Joe Louis won the crown for the first time. It was a great fight and one which just might have swung the other way if Braddock, to use his own words, 'had been smart enough . . . .'

Joe Louis's professional boxing career began immediately after Max Marek beat him in the 1934 finals of the American national amateur championships. There-after, managed by John Roxborough and Julian Black, Joe's rise to the top was steady and often spectacular. His first professional fight was against a boxer named Jack Krailken which he won, and for which he was paid the sum of \$40 (£10). A run of twenty-seven consecutive wins, all except four by knockouts, saw Louis beat such prominent fighters as Stanley Poreda, Charley Massera, Patsy Perroni, Natie Brown, Roy Lazer, Roscoe Toles and Hans Birkie. The defeat of Brown in Detroit, where Louis had earlier been working in the Ford factory, came on 28 March 1935 and marked a development in the future champion's career. After that, all his major fights were promoted by Mike Jacobs. It was Jacobs, together with Roxborough and Black, who guided Joe Louis sensibly towards the top rung of the ladder.

The quality of his opponents became higher and Joe Louis took them all. In successive bouts he knocked out Primo Carnera in six rounds — admittedly the Ambling Alp was on the decline having lost his title to Max Baer twelve months earlier — followed by a first round defeat of King Levinsky, a four-rounds hammering of Max Baer, who had just lost his title to Braddock; another four-rounds win, this time over Paolino Uzcudun, and then a first-round knockout against Charlie Retzlaff. Now people were talking of Joe Louis as the next heavyweight champion of the world, but in Louis's very next fight there was a sensation. Louis was matched with Max Schmeling, world champion in the early 1930s. The fight took place on 19 June 1936 in front of 40,000 fans at New York's Yankee Stadium. Louis was twenty-two years old, Schmeling near to thirty-one, and they staged one of the most amazing fights ever seen in New York. Louis, the Brown Bomber as he was now known, was expected to carry on his run and put Schmeling down and out, but the former

71

world champion had other ideas. He put Louis down in the fourth, and knocked him out in the twelfth. Joe Louis looked a sorry mess. His left eye was shut, the left side of his face badly swollen and his lips badly cut. In addition Louis had sprained both thumbs in a bout of wild punching and that fight must rank as Max Schmeling's greatest performance. That Louis later gave Schmeling a terrible beating in a return fight does not wipe out the memory of that night in 1936.

If justice had been done, Schmeling should have been the next challenger for Braddock's title. Louis, however, was backed by two astute managers and an even more astute promoter in Mike Jacobs, who had taken over where Tex Rickard left off. They ensured that Louis would be the next man to contest the world crown and a series of fights included a magnificent three-rounds 'execution' of another former world champion, Jack Sharkey. Next came Philadelphia's Al Ettore who was also beaten, though he lasted a little longer — halfway through round five! Quick defeats of Jorge Bresica (in three rounds), Eddie Simms (one) and Steve Ketchell (two) delighted Louis's handlers and his 'comeback' was going just as planned. the Brown Bomber was then matched with Bob Pastor of New York, who lasted ten rounds, mainly by backpedalling, and a return to the old ways with a knockout of Natie Brown paved the way for a shot at Braddock's title.

Almost a year to the day after that terrible beating at the hands of Max Schmeling, Joe Louis emerged into the Chicago White Sox baseball stadium to meet the Cinderella Man, James J. Braddock. Braddock's career up until then had been fascinating. He was born in New York in December 1905 and for a number of years he had fought as a light-heavyweight. His defeat of Max Baer for the world heavyweight title in June 1935 had been something of a sensation. Braddock had fought Tommy Loughran for the world light-heavyweight title in July 1929 and lost in fifteen rounds. There had then followed defeats by such men as Leo Lomski, Maxie

Rosenbloom, Yale Okun, Babe Hunt, Ernie Schaaf, Al Gainer, Tony Schucco, and Lou Scozza, who knocked him out. But this was a bleak time in the affairs of world heavyweight boxing. Talent was at a premium and Braddock came out of retirement to beat Corn Griffin on the same bill as Baer-Carnera. A fifteen-rounds win over Art Lasky, who was being groomed to have a shot at Baer's title, gained Braddock the chance and on 13 June 1935, at the Garden Bowl, Long Island, he gained the decision over Baer in a fight which went the full fifteen rounds, Braddock, despite his modest record up to his comeback, was too experienced a fighter for the champion who, true to form, astonished the crowd by clowning around.

After that surprise James J. Braddock, the last white man to hold the world heavyweight title until Rocky Marciano in 1952, did not defend his crown for two years. The Garden Corporation then had a contract with Braddock to defend against Max Schmeling, but Jacobs, the new supremo, who owned the Twentieth Century Club, which was a Garden rival, had an ace card in Joe Louis, the greatest boxing attraction in the United States.He offered Braddock a contract which the champion could not afford to turn down. It called for Braddock to receive a percentage of the gate receipts (the amount was fifty per cent and that alone netted the champion almost $300,000) and, if Braddock lost, he would receive ten per cent of Mike Jacobs's share in all future Louis championship fights. As Joe Louis went on to defend the crown more times than any other boxer and lasted at the top for more than a decade, that must rank as one of the shrewdest deals ever pulled off by a reigning champion. Schmeling protested, of course, but in boxing it is money which does all the talking and he was put on the sidelines. It was Joe Louis against James J. Braddock that everyone wanted to see.

The fact that since winning his title two years earlier, Braddock had had only one fight, a non-championship affair, and had endured a long absence from the ring, saw

James J. Braddock, the 'Cinderella Man'.

Joe Louis as 5-1 favourite a week before the fight at the Cominskey baseball park in one of the toughest quarters of Chicago. More than a thousand police were stationed in and around the stadium on that June evening in 1937, to guard against possible racial violence. In fact they were not needed even once and all the violence that night was confined to the ring. By the time the two boxers emerged from under the stands and headed towards that ring, the odds on Joe Louis had been halved due to reports that he had looked most unimpressive in training. There was one peculiar condition attached to the fight. The Illinois State Athletic Commission had a rule which stated that if a boxer was knocked out of the ring he would be allowed twenty seconds to regain his place. So it had to be agreed that the ten-seconds count would not be recognised in such an eventuality. There were some 55,000 fans, many of whom had arrived in Chicago on special trains and airliners, in the stadium as the challenger, Joe Louis, climbed into the ring at just before ten o'clock that evening. His big advantage was that he was eight years younger than his rival and had a slight weight superiority, though Braddock was an inch and a half taller and his reach was two inches longer. The referee was Chicago-based Tommy Hyams and after his last-minute instructions the bell went and the champion came out for his first defence of the title which he had won two years earlier.

Supporters of Joe Louis had an early shock when a right to the chin dropped the challenger in the opening round. There was one lesson of boxing that Joe Louis had not yet learned: to stay down and take advantage of the respite. Almost before the timekeeper could begin the count the challenger was up on his feet again. Braddock did not immediately follow up and the youngster — at five weeks past his twenty-third birthday he was about to become the youngest world heavyweight champion — was allowed to get away with his novice's mistake. In the second round Louis hammered in three rights to Braddock's head which opened a cut just over the champion's left eye. The challenger then took the third round and his supporters settled more easily into their seats. Their man was the favourite and it now looked as if he was about to prove the bookmakers correct.

The next two rounds caught Louis' supporters by surprise, however. In the fourth Braddock came right back and took it convincingly; and in the fifth the champion caught Louis with a devastating right plumb on the face which caused Louis's nose to spurt blood. Joe Louis fought back and in the sixth round, four punishing rights slammed into Braddock's head until the cut over his eye was reopened. This was the turning point of the fight, for although the Cinderella Man was on top, Louis saw the blood pumping from his opponent's eye and it somehow gave him the strength and confidence he needed. The champion tried hard for a knockout in the seventh, but the blood and swelling around his eye meant that he was hardly able to see and most of the haymakers were well wide of their intended target. As the round wore on, Braddock was having obvious difficulty in raising his arms which must have felt like lead. Nevertheless he held on and Joe Louis was having the greatest possible difficulty in dropping his man. But the champion was tiring and Joe Louis knew that he had plenty of time to get ahead on points, so feeble was Braddock's attempt to get back in the fight.

Braddock came out for the eighth and made another wild, desperate swing at his rival in a bid to end the fight with one blow. Louis saw the punch coming, swayed out of the way, and as Braddock's momentum caused his loss of balance, Joe Louis hammered in two short, sharp rights to the head. Braddock crashed to the ring unconscious. There were cuts over both eyes and his lip was severely torn. One eye was closed, the other badly swollen, and a severed artery brought forth the blood in spurts. Braddock was carried back to his corner and a bucket of water was thrown over him. He recovered, but he looked a dreadful mess. The crowd looked on in awe at Joe Louis, the first black world heavyweight champion since Jack Johnson had lost his crown to Jess Willard twenty-two years earlier. Apart from a nose-bleed Louis was hardly marked. Of that first-round knockdown he remarked, 'Sure it hurt, but then I always wanted to get up from a knockdown and win. I'll tell you this — that guy Braddock sure is a tough one. He's the gamest guy I ever met — and he can hit too!' Braddock allowed himself one more fight after that, beating Tommy Farr in ten rounds before retiring. He became an army captain during World War II but always rued that first-round knockdown over Joe Louis. He would say, 'You know, if I'd have been smart enough to follow up that punch then the result might have been very different. If only I'd been smart enough....'

JOE LOUIS v TOMMY FARR
—————————————— World Heavyweight Championship ——————————————
30 August 1937

There was no doubt in the mind of promoter Mike Jacobs that Joe Louis, the son of a black Alabama cotton worker, was a world-beater. Louis was one of the best all-round boxers that the ring had seen. He was a graceful mover, yet he possessed a cold and clinical aggression which destroyed so many fine heavyweights. If he lacked greatness in any single art, he more than compensated by being good enough at every one of them to become virtually unbeatable. He had a tremendous, devastating punch which capped all the good work which had gone before. So, Jacobs could feel well pleased with himself that he had apparently secured a monopoly over Joe Louis, and therefore a monopoly over the world heavyweight title which Louis had wrested from James J. Braddock and which the negro did not look like surrendering in a hurry.

But Jacobs had one problem. The fact that the former world champion Max Schmeling had beaten Louis and then been denied a shot at Braddock's title meant that the German was still a thorn in the promoter's side, a problem that would have to be resolved before Jacobs could feel truly confident that he had the world championship for himself. After Schmeling's defeat of Louis, the boxing authorities in New York recognised his right to challenge Braddock and even named the day on which the two should meet. Braddock, meanwhile, had been tempted by Jacobs's offer of a big payday. As we have seen in the previous chapter, he fought, and lost to, Joe Louis; but Schmeling was still regarded in some quarters as the rightful challenger; indeed, as the champion by some. On the date set for his fight with Braddock, Schmeling went down to the arena, was passed fit and weighed in, collected Braddock's forfeit, and went home with the rather dubious world heavyweight championship title which he had been awarded by default.

Now Jacobs's dilemma over what to do about Schmeling was compounded by a projected fight between the German and Tommy Farr, the former Tonypandy miner who held the British and British Empire heavyweight titles which he had taken from Ben Foord in March 1937. What was more, the German's claim to the world title had been recognised in Europe to where Schmeling had gone after his rebuff by Braddock, and the British Boxing Board of Control gave their official blessing to the fight between German and Welshman which the British promoter Sydney Hulls had billed as a world championship. Jacobs would ignore it at his peril. After all, although Farr was a virtual unknown, he had outpointed the former world champion Max Baer, admittedly a shadow of his old self, and knocked out Walter Neusal, undoubtedly the best German Heavyweight between the wars. More important still, if this fight did go ahead, the winner would have official recognition for his world title and this would lower the claims of Joe Louis in many people's eyes. The answer then would be to match Louis with the winner of the Farr-Schmeling fight, and that could conceivably mean that Mike Jacobs would be squeezed out of the reckoning, especially if Hulls was concerned. There was only one thing to do. He despatched his most trusted attorney to England armed with a contract for Farr to fight Louis in America for a fabulous purse. The lawyer did his job so well that Farr came back to the

*Joe Louis lands a left to the side of Tommy
Farr's head.*

States with him. Hulls was out in the cold and Jacobs had secured his world title fight. He had also secured, though he did not know it, one of the greatest such fights of all time.

Tommy Farr had discovered his talent for boxing during some light-hearted fisticuffs in his native Wales. He had been taken on board by a boxing booth promoter, touring Welsh mining villages. Success there had seen him enter the professional ring and at the age of nineteen he took the Welsh light-heavyweight title. Three years later he was Welsh heavyweight champion and that took him to the fight with Foord in which he took the British and Empire titles. Baer and Neusal followed and though there had been precious few Britons who had extended successive world heavyweight champions, it was felt in Britain that here was a man who might spring a few surprises. On the other side of the Atlantic, Farr was viewed with less respect and one writer even went so far as to describe his chances as 'about as good

as Shirley Temple's'. It was Louis's first defence and the American scribes thought that Farr would be a pushover.

Once Farr was installed in his training camp, however, opinions changed. The Welshman looked fast and fit and certainly capable of extending the world champion beyond a few rounds. Farr was a sharp fighter and his clever footwork and ability to duck and weave, coupled with a knockout punch, left no one in any doubt that Joe Louis was not going to enjoy the 'easy touch' which everyone had predicted for him. Certainly, Farr was supremely optimistic. He was always ready to tell newspaper reporters that, not only would he win, he would do it in style by knocking Louis out. The newspapers built up the fight until nearly 37,000 fans poured into the Yankee Stadium in New York, paying $265,753, of which the Welshman was reputed to have received $60,000. Yet for all Farr's impressive training stints, they still expected him to go the same way as thirty of Joe Louis's thirty-six professional opponents to date — by way of a knockout. They reckoned without the Welshman's fleetness of foot, and although Louis's straight left jab cut Farr early in the contest, the Welshman managed, by and large, to evade the champion's deadly right, getting in his own right to the head so easily and so often that Louis must have been thankful that Tommy Farr could not find a killer punch.

From the first bell Farr used every inch of that ring. He moved around, pausing only to land an occasional left, while Joe Louis kept on after his man and when he did get within the range the champion thudded out his left, prodding and punishing the Welshman who seemed quite happy to abandon defence and take the blows full on his face. The champion's punches were certainly not of the knockout variety, and yet they were still damaging. By the end of the third round Farr was cut under both eyes and blood streamed down his face. It was those cuts which caused Tommy Farr to adopt a more cautious approach for the next couple of rounds. He ducked and weaved in a bid to avoid the champion's punches and for a spell there were few punches landed. Then a straight right to the champion's jaw was minimised when Louis rolled his head and rode the punch. Louis countered with a two-fisted attack, but the Welshman stopped the champion in his tracks with a hard straight left. The Brown Bomber was momentarily shaken, but when Farr lunged again. Louis went inside the blow and countered with a right smack on Farr's face which sent the Welshman staggering into a corner.

But Tommy Farr was a long way from going down. He came back off the ropes and landed two long lefts, followed up with a right, and had Joe Louis retreating across the ring. Farr then drew back his right and grinned to see Louis jump back and bring up his guard. Farr did not land the punch but he had now confirmed that Louis still carried the painful memories of the rights he had suffered from Max Schmeling. The bell sounded to end the round before the Welsh-man could follow up, but he went to his corner knowing that Louis had hit him with his right — the punch that usually ended fights — and failed to down him; and he also knew that Joe Louis was still harbouring fears of an opponent's right. If only Tommy Farr could pack a knockout right, thought his manager.

Farr was off his stool and taking the fight to the champion as soon as the bell sounded. Before Louis had composed himself, Farr landed a crashing left on the champion's temple, and followed up that with a right which missed Louis's jaw by a whisker. Two wicked left hooks to the head rocked Louis back on his heels and Farr drove the coloured man before him. Louis then decided to counter-attack and for a full thirty seconds they stood toe-to-toe exchanging blows to the delight of the crowd who roared them on. But still it was Farr who forced the fight and once more he drove Louis back under a fusillade of lefts. Louis reached the ropes and tried a wild left hook which Farr ducked under before cracking Louis on the chin with a right. A furious two-handed attack from the Welshman followed and he took the round by a narrow margin. So the sixth round was Farr's, the fifth round had been halved, and Joe Louis and his handlers now knew that the Welshman from Tonypandy was anything but the pushover they had been promised. Urgent instructions were yelled into Louis's ear during the sixty-second break before the bell called the two boxers to resume their great fight.

Louis came out for the seventh round looking intent on wresting back the initiative in this fight. The champion hammered left after left into Farr's face, opening up the cuts and sending blood spilling down the Welshman's cheeks. But Tonypandy Tommy took them all without a murmur of complaint. Now, however, the pattern of the fight was different. Louis at no time gave Farr the opportunity to launch his own counter-offensive. A barrage of accurate punches kept Farr on the retreat, and when the Welshman tried to start up an attack on the champion's body, Louis responded with

Farr fights back and gives Louis one of the hardest fights of his career.

vision was now greatly impaired. Though Louis managed to land several good punches to Farr's head, the champion could not find the one which would send Tommy crashing to the canvas. Instead, Farr hammered home a left which raised an ugly lump over the champion's eye. Once more Farr received a standing ovation as he returned to his corner.

The tenth round saw a different picture emerge. Joe Louis decided to keep that machine-gun-like left pumping away from the start and it was a ploy which worked admirably. More cuts were opened up on Farr's face and it was now one mass of gore. Yet still the Welshman refused to give up. A particularly hard left hook to the jaw rocked him back, and Louis followed up immediately with a left and a right which forced Farr to take refuge in a clinch. Tommy hung on until the bell ended his immediate misery and it was Louis's round by a wide margin, the champion having now opened up a clear points lead over the gritty Welshman who had confounded his American critics. It is said that three hundred boxing writers were asked to choose their winner of this fight, and only one selected Tommy Farr.

His faith was rewarded in the next two rounds for Farr broke even in the eleventh round and actually took the twelfth by a small margin. One moment he had seemed a game but beaten man; the next he was summoning up superhuman reserves of energy to stagger the champion. His technique saw him outbox Joe Louis, yet sadly his efforts were by and large wasted. The terrible punishment which he had taken earlier now meant that when Farr did land those points-scoring punches, they lacked the power to hurt the champion and sap his energy. Equally, there were many punches which did not find their target, so weary were the challenger's arms at this stage in the proceedings. The fans really appreciated the gameness of the Welshman and they roared his every punch, but the thirteenth and fourteenth rounds were dominated by the champion. Again it was those dreadful cuts to Tommy Farr's eyes which cost him so

a series of left hooks which had Farr lurching back once more. The last of these punches landed just as the bell sounded and it visibly rocked Farr. But the Welshman had so much courage that he shook his head and managed a half-grin as he went back, somewhat unsteadily, to his stool. The eighth round found Farr in surprisingly fresh fettle. He walked straight through a barrage of blows from Louis and, to the champion's utter amazement, landed some powerful rights to his head. The roar of the crowd inspired Farr still further and he continued this form of attack with Joe Louis now completely out of his stride. Left after left then followed, interspersed by the occasional right, and it was Louis who was made to look the challenger, and not a very convincing one at that.

Farr had the eighth round to his credit and he added the ninth in similar fashion. His one real problem, though, was those injured eyes. Both were cut and swollen and his

much. Had he been able to see properly, then perhaps the Welshman might just have edged the verdict.

Nevertheless, he had taken Joe Louis all the way — and not many heavyweights had done that. The fifteenth and final round opened with Louis in the lead, but with the resolute challenger still there, so the result of the fight was still not clear-cut. Tommy Farr was off his stool and dancing around the middle of the ring even before the bell sounded. When it did, and Louis got to his feet, Farr was straight across to him and began a two-fisted attack. Louis was forced to respond and the two exchanged a furious barrage of blows — hooks, jabs and swings, all of which landed and hurt. They kept punching away and steadily Tommy Farr outfought the champion. Suddenly it was all the Welshman. He seemed oblivious to the nagging procession of straight lefts that Louis kept pumping in, and eventually he beat the champion back. Farr then flashed in a long left to the champion's chin and immediately followed it up with a right which caught him on the other side of his jaw. The crowd was now in an almost hysterical frenzy of excitement and Louis raised the temperature even further by fighting back, only to receive two more devastating rights to the head. Back went Louis on to the ropes and again Farr hammered him with lefts and rights. The champion hit back desperately, but still Farr came at him. It was one of the greatest last rounds in the history of world heavyweight title fights.

From first to last bell in this final three minutes, Tommy Farr, the man whose chances had been rated 'about as good as Shirley Temple's', never gave Joe Louis, the world champion, a moment's respite. At the end of it, the two men retired to their respective corners to a thunderous roar of acclaim from the crowd to await the verdict. It was Louis who got the nod and it was almost certainly the correct decision, for the champion had outscored his rival in the majority of rounds. Yet there were many who felt that Farr had done enough to win and there were more than a few boos amid the cheers for the winner. Even though Tommy Farr had lost, he had done so in a manner which gained British heavyweight boxing a new respect on that side of the Atlantic. Ever since Phil Scott's embarrassing defeat at the hands of Jack Sharkey, Britain had been known as the home of the 'horizontal heavyweights'. Now the sterling performance of a Welsh miner had changed all that. Joe Louis was still champion but he sure knew that he'd been in a fight.

BENNY LYNCH v PETER KANE
—————————————— World Flyweight Championship ——————————————
13 October 1937

Scottish professional boxing owes a great debt to one man; the promoter George Dingley. Born and bred to the business — he first boxed when still at school and turned to promoting when he realised that he would not reach the top inside the ring — Dingley staged many big fights in that country. But his greatest contributions were wound up together in that he discovered a boxer called Benny Lynch and took him from obscurity to international stardom, staged Scotland's first world championship bout, and put on the most thrilling flyweight fights ever staged in Britain. Indeed, when Benny Lynch met a young Liverpudlian called Peter Kane on an October evening at Shawfield Park in 1937, Dingley gave boxing one of its most classic contests.

George Dingley was always eager to discover new fighters. He set many on the road to the top, and then eagerly searched for others to depose them. So when he heard of a tough little Glaswegian newsboy called Benny Lynch who was apparently knocking over opponent after opponent in the Saturday evening boxing booths at local fairs, the promoter quite naturally wanted to see for himself. One look at Benny Lynch convinced Dingley that here he had a potential world-beater. He was soon talking to the boy and quickly had his signature on a contract. Before the ink had dried, Dingley had Lynch in the ring and he proved an instant success. Lynch soon became the area flyweight champion and that took him a step further along a road which was finally to settle the confusion which had reigned over the real identity of the world flyweight champion of the late 1930s. Ever since Pancho Villa died from blood poisoning from an infected tooth ten days after defending his world crown in July 1925, there had been arguments as to the champion. Frankie Genaro claimed the title until he was outpointed by Fidel LaBarba in August 1925. LaBarba defended his title against Elky Clark and then retired in 1927; then Corporal Izzy Schwartz outpointed Newsboy Brown and took the title. But only New York accepted Schwartz's claim and confusion reigned supreme.

The NBA meanwhile recognised Genaro, who outpointed Frenchy Berlanger in Toronto in February 1928, while Europe had their own 'world champion' when Emile Pladner scored a first-round knockout over Genaro in Paris in March the following year. There was yet another 'world champion' in Johnny Hill who outpointed Newsboy Brown in London in August 1928, and then beat Ernie Jarvis in Glasgow in March 1929. As if all this was not confusing enough, the New York authorities then recognised Midget Wolgast after he had outpointed Black Bill. Midget, with New York's vote under his belt, then boxed a draw with the NBA nominee Genaro to ensure that the business was far from settled. Genaro then went to Paris where he was knocked out in the second round by the French champion, Tunis-born Young Perez. The French authorities then claimed the world championship on behalf of their man and Perez had European support until a year later, in October 1932, when the Briton Jackie Brown stopped him in the thirteenth round in Manchester. Wolgast, the New York nominee, had by this time been outpointed by Small Montana for the American title, and matters were now coming to a head, for when Montana came to Europe he was about to set up the fight which would settle the argument once and for all.

On 9 September 1935, in Manchester, Benny Lynch, the pride of all Scotland, scored a dramatic win over Jackie Brown to claim for himself the world flyweight title. Offers for Lynch came flooding in from Europe and the United States, but the British Boxing Board of Control nominated Pat Palmer of London as the official challenger. Thirty-two thousand people crammed into Glasgow's Shawfield Park on 16 September 1936 to see their local hero smash the Londoner to the canvas in the eighth round. Palmer, after putting up the fight of his life, did not beat the count and Lynch was now generally recognised as the true world champion. But there was still one score to settle. The American title-holder, Small Montana, claimed the title too, after beating New York's man, Wolgast. This time Dingley stood aside, knowing that the fight between these two would best be staged in London, and on 19 January 1937, Benny Lynch gave the Filipino a boxing lesson. Lynch triumphed with a unanimous points decision and at long last there was absolutely no

argument about who was the flyweight champion of the world.

Now Dingley had to look around for new challengers for Benny Lynch's title. One star flashing across the sky was coming from the direction of Liverpool where a young blacksmith from Golborne, called Peter Kane, was pulling in the crowds at Liverpool Stadium. Kane was a natural scrapper, a boy with a punch like a mule and a fast and furious style which owed more to his instinctive flair than to any coaching manual. Kane had boxed since he was a schoolboy and visits to the local gymnasiums had enabled him to pick up a few elementary tips. Soon, the amateur circuit could offer him little in the way of stern opposition and the boy who was by now working in a local smithy where he further toughened himself up, turned professional just three months after his seventeenth birthday. On his first appearance at Liverpool Stadium, Kane stopped his opponent in the fifth round and from that moment was assured of success. The public loved his whirlwind style and he was sure to fill seats, which is all that any promoter really asks. He went to London where he

Kane takes a count in the very first round.

knocked out the Welsh flyweight champion, and then on to Paris where the top French flyweights all fell before his barrage. In two and a half years Kane fought on an average of once a month and very few of his opponents got beyond the fourth round.

Back in Britain, Peter Kane won the Northern Area flyweight title by stopping the holder, Phil Milligan, in eleven rounds. The Liverpudlian was now being talked of as the natural challenger for Lynch's world title as he was now matched against the Irish champion, Jim Warnock, in a bout to decide who should challenge the Scotsman. Now the Irishman had twice defeated Lynch on points, once in Belfast and once in Glasgow, but both contests had been at catchweight so Lynch still held the title. Peter Kane was not however over-impressed by Warnock's pedigree and inside four rounds he had boxed the Irishman into submission. Kane was now the undisputed challenger to Lynch, and indeed, this was a fight which everyone demanded: Lynch, the dour, machine-like Scotsman with the classic style, against Kane, the tough, gritty, uncomplicated Englishman whose whirlwind style would provide the perfect foil and set up what promised to be a great fight.

Dingley was not alone in wanting to promote this fight. Indeed, every other promoter in Britain wanted to put it on and he had his work cut out to retain the prize for himself. He set great store by the fact that he had a verbal agreement with Lynch that the champion's next defence would be under Dingley's wing in Scotland. But the Liverpool promoter held just as strong a hold on Kane, and Lynch soon found himself on the receiving end of a tempting offer to fight in the challenger's home city. To complicate matters, offers were also pouring in from the big London promoters. Dingley got Lynch to sign a contract giving the champion thirty-seven-and-a-half per cent of the receipts from Shawfield — Lynch signed mindful of the 32,000 who had seen him fight Palmer in London — and then the Glasgow promoter made a dash to Liverpool where he got Kane's signature in return for a £1,500 fee.

Meanwhile, a London promoter had cabled Lynch and offered him an even bigger sum than Dingley's contract. Lynch wanted to accept it, but when Dingley promptly guaranteed the champion £4,000, the London offer paled and the big fight was set for Shawfield Park on 13 October 1937.

No flyweight fight had so captured the imagination of the British boxing public since the days of Jimmy Wilde. The challenger was unbeaten in the ring, the champion stood as undisputed head of the world, and the two widely contrasting styles made it a natural sell-out. There were many, however, who wondered if it was really wise to match a nineteen-year-old with less than three years professional experience against a champion five years his senior and with seven years at the top behind him. There was the feeling that Kane was being sacrificed at the very onset of his career for the sake of lining the pockets of a promoter and champion with money. Yet this fight just had to take place. Despite his apparent lack of experience, Kane had done everything asked of him in arriving at this position. The fact that the public interest demanded such a fight was shown in the attendance. Over 33,000 people paid well over £12,500 to see it, and many more thousands were unable to gain admittance. Indeed, it was a minor miracle that those who had paid for ringside seats actually got to them, such was the incredible crush of bodies before the promotion got underway.

It was obvious from the very first bell that Benny Lynch was not thinking in terms of giving the punters much time for their money. Straightaway he went into the offensive and a left to the body and a right to the jaw found Kane rocking back into the ropes and down on to the canvas in a sitting position. That the challenger got up at the count of three, doubly confirmed his lack of experience, for he should never have left himself so wide open in the first few seconds of the fight, nor should he have been in such a hurry to rise from the canvas. Those who had said that the fight should not have been staged were quick to exchange knowing glances, for it looked as though Lynch was going to score a very quick win. But the champion did not move in for the kill and Kane fought back so well that when the round ended the honours were even.

The second round saw Kane now much more into his stride and he almost succeeded in dropping Lynch to the canvas when he swung in a right which was just a shade too high to do any real damage, though it did set the champion back. Both boxers landed heavy punches and the crowd were driven to their feet urging the Scotsman and the Liverpudlian on. Once, Kane slipped, but Lynch drew back and allowed his opponent to regain his full composure. That sort of sportsmanship was a hallmark of this fight. The round ended with both men still slugging away, though Kane perhaps had a slight edge and had certainly caused his more experienced opponent a few nasty moments. In the third round the Liverpudlian set up a two-fisted attack which drove Lynch into the ropes. Once he had his man there, Kane set upon him with a furious barrage. Lynch fought back with equal fury, though Kane still managed to land a magnificent right hook to the champion's jaw. By now the fight had taken on the more predictable pattern dictated by the contrasting styles of the two men. Benny Lynch boxed in

his usual cool, classy style, letting Kane use up much of his energy and, at the same time, wearing him down with a few well-chosen blows which went right to their target. Occasionally, Kane's onslaught would make him step back a pace or two, but for most of the time he stayed his ground and swapped punches.

So it went on until the ninth round when it was obvious that the Liverpool blacksmith was beginning to tire. Lynch handed out a lesson in the art of boxing and for a while it appeared that Kane would surely disappear under this clinical, aggressive display. Yet somehow the challenger seemed to draw strength from his predicament and he fought back. Just before the bell he launched into a volley of punches which culminated with a blow to the champion's jaw which sent Lynch staggering back. It was a tremendous right and it was as well for the title-holder that a minute's respite was at hand.

Kane was obviously encouraged by this and at the start of the tenth round he was back on the attack from the bell, forcing Lynch around the ring and punishing him with a two-fisted attack of ferocious power. Lynch was content to take things easy in this round and Kane took it by the slenderest of margins, though once again, when the champion did hit out he did so with more effect

Lynch looks on as Kane fails to beat the timekeeper's clock.

than the challenger. It was just that Peter Kane was allowed to do most of the attacking and who therefore scored the points. It was the same in the eleventh round but the crowd now had the feeling that Benny Lynch was in command of the situation, maybe he was taking a breather, maybe he was merely waiting for the challenger to run out of steam. In the twelfth round the answer became apparent.

Lynch was straight out of his corner and wading into Kane. A cracking left hook hammered Kane into the ropes and for a full sixty seconds he could do nothing but cover up as the champion smashed blow after blow into his body and to his head. At last Kane managed to wrest himself clear and regain the centre of the ring, only to find that, as he came forward to counter-attack, Lynch was also jumping forward on the offensive. The champion sent home a sweeping left hook and Kane crumpled on to the canvas. He was up at the count of three, another grave mistake, and only the bell saved him as he reeled around the ring, glassy-eyed and bleeding from cuts on the mouth and from the nose. It was a punch of tremendous power which had felled him and the challenger had actually added to its weight by meeting it as he came forward himself. The crowd applauded the Liverpudlian to his corner, for though they were intent on seeing the local man retain his title, they could not fail to be moved by the gameness of Peter Kane, the Liverpool smith.

The challenger came out for the thirteenth, looking to carry the fight to his opponent but his efforts were but weak and feeble, compared to the punishment that Lynch was about to inflict. The Scotsman let go a barrage of lefts and rights about which Kane could do nothing. Lynch dropped him with a left to the point of the chin, but, amazingly, the Liverpool man was up at seven. Lynch could hardly miss now. He moved in and let go another classic hook. It thudded into the side of Kane's jaw and once more the challenger went to the canvas, this time to be partly supported by the bottom rope. He hung over the hemp while the referee relayed

the count to him, but it was to no avail. there was now no way that Peter Kane would beat that count and as ten was called, Benny Lynch turned around and accepted the congratulations of his corner and of his home city crowd, for yet another magnificent victory. He was truly one of the great flyweights of all time.

Sadly, Benny Lynch was to meet an unhappy end. Set to meet the American Jackie Jurich in a title defence in 1938, Lynch failed to make the eight-stones limit and on the day of the fight weighed in at 8st 6lb 8oz. The fight went ahead, though obviously not for the title, and Lynch knocked Jurich out. It was the start of a slippery road for the ex-world champion — Peter Kane and Jackie Jurich now fought for the vacant title — and Lynch was reduced to boxing in the fairground booths where he started his days. He was too fond of the bottle and died in 1946, aged just thirty-three years old. Kane, meanwhile, had his world title, outpointing Jurich at Liverpool Stadium on 22 September 1938 — a fight, incidentally, which cost Kane the little finger of his right hand which was amputated after the bout. After that Kane did not defend the title until June 1943 when he fought against another Scotsman, Jackie Paterson. It was five years after he had won the title and Kane had great difficulty in making the weight. The fight lasted just sixty-one seconds, which was how long it took Paterson to knock down his man and become the first southpaw winner of the world flyweight title. The 22-year-old Paterson was unlucky to find himself in the shadow of Lynch, who was Scotland's real hero, but on that rain-soaked evening in Glasgow he did the former champion proud. How sad, though, that Lynch and Kane — the men who gave Glasgow what referee W. Barrington Dalby described as 'the greatest fight I've ever seen' — should both lose their way in that city. Kane fought back as a bantamweight and became European champion. Lynch was dragged from the gutters of a city which, for one glorious night in 1938, had belonged to him.

JOE LOUIS v MAX SCHMELING
World Heavyweight Championship
22 June 1938

In 1938, the German Max Schmeling, heavyweight champion of the world from 1930-2, was still smarting over the way he had been sidestepped when James J. Braddock, lured by the rustle of dollar bills, broke his contract and fought Joe Louis instead of the former champion. The result was that Louis became the second black man to hold the title and Schmeling had only a 'phantom' title, awarded to him through Braddock's default. Since that day Louis had proved himself to be no overnight wonder with three title defences; the great battle with Welshman Tommy Farr, a three-rounds knockout over Nathan Mann in New York in February 1938, and a victory over Harry Thomas in Chicago two months later when the challenger failed to beat the count in the fifth round. But there was still the shadow of Max Schmeling, the man who had given Joe Louis the only beating of his professional career and who had done so in such convincing manner that the black man's face was barely recognisable by the end of the fight. So the German had to be given the chance of which he still felt cheated: another attempt at the title, this time against Louis the champion.

The fight was set for 22 June 1938, less than three months after Louis's successful defence against Thomas, and it was to be staged at the Yankee Stadium, home of the New York Yankees baseball club. Seldom can there have been a fight with such ramifications. There were so many factors involved; not least the fact that Joe Louis was bent on avenging that desperate defeat of two years earlier. But there were also issues which transcended the parochialism of the boxing world. In 1938 the world was heading towards a war which would encompass almost the whole globe. Again Germany would be regarded as the aggressor. Max Schmeling was a German, a member of the 'Master Race' fighting against an 'inferior' Negro. The Louis-Schmeling fight symbolised the fight between good and evil, between freedom and oppression, between right and wrong.

The German propaganda machine had not been slow in building up Max Schmeling as the world's great white hope who would surely smash down the inferior upstart with the coffee-coloured skin. Two years earlier the Nazis had used the Olympic Games, held in Berlin, to advertise their own unsavoury philosophies, only then it was black American athletes like Jesse Owens and Cornelius Johnson, the first man to be 'snubbed' by Hitler, despite what legend says, who exploded the myth of Ayran supremacy. Yet, make no mistake, there were plenty of American citizens who were ready to applaud a German victory. Racial bigotry was still rife, even in the north of that country, in 1938; and in the Deep South there were plenty of red-necks, some who even donned the sinister hooded cloaks of the Ku Klux Klan, who were aching for a repeat of the first Louis-Schmeling fight. All they wanted was to see the nigger meet his dues once more. In his book, *Joe Louis: My Life* (1978), the champion told how members of the American Nazi party visited his training camp daily: '. . . they'd come up to my camp day after day with swastikas on their arms . . . they watched me train and sat around laughing like jackasses.'

This was a fight, then, which held the whole city of New York in its grip. Everyone was talking about it and it was impossible to take a cab ride, or to go into a bar, without being drawn into conversation about the big fight. Louis was, of course, the favourite. He was eight years younger than the 32-year-old German, and though the challenger was far more experienced — he had been boxing professionally for fifteen years — there were statistics to show that despite this he was a vulnerable fighter. True, he could land a knockout punch and no less than thirty-five of his sixty-four bouts had been won inside the distance. To counter that he had suffered seven defeats and been held to a draw on five occasions, so he was far from infallible. Joe Louis on the other hand had knocked out thirty-two men in thirty-nine fights and had been beaten only once — by the German — as well as having successfully defended his title three times in his first year as heavyweight king.

The German had always complained about low punches in that first fight and this added further fuel to the flames which threatened to engulf this world championship bout. Schmeling led a spartan life and it is said that he had never touched tobacco or alcohol. His training routine was a rigid affair and he was every inch an athlete, the Nazis' idea of the 'master' Aryan, all of which made the fact that his manager, Joe Jacobs, and the promoter Mike Jacobs (no relation), were both Jewish all that more ironic. The way to the stadium was choked with traffic and with pedestrians as just over 70,000 people fought their way through the turnstiles. Louis was the favourite of course — the odds at this time were 9-5 — but that did not stop Adolf Hitler sending Schmeling a telegram which was addressed to 'The New Heavyweight Champion of the World'. Since his defeat of Louis some twenty-four months earlier, Schmeling had fought three times. In December 1937 he scored an eighth-round knockout over Harry Thomas in New York, beat the South African-born former British champion, Ben Foord, in Hamburg the following month, and in April that year knocked out Steve Dudas in the fifth round of their fight, also in Hamburg. Thus, the man born Maximillian

Adolph Otto Siegfried Schmeling, was as ready as ever he would be for this bid to regain his world title.

The night was hot and clammy, a typical New York June evening, and the atmosphere in the Yankee Stadium was electric as, surprisingly, Louis, the champion, came into the ring first, although the German was close on his heels. The weigh-in had recorded that the champion was 14st 2lb 12oz, the challenger 13st 11lb, and so Louis had kept his weight advantage. The last time that these two had met in the ring had resulted in Joe Louis being hammered unmercifully. Two years later, the world had moved even nearer to a new Dark Age; it was the year of the German moves into Czechoslovakia and the Munich agreement. Schmeling's victory was even more important to the Nazis than it had been in 1936, for they never lost an opportunity to capitalise on any kind of German success. It may seem strange to us today, even though sport and politics are still inexorably woven, that so much store was set by this confrontation by Negro and Aryan. Yet it was against just such a background that the fight took place.

The bell rang — for the only time in this fight as it turned out — and Joe Louis was straight out of his corner and on his toes, looking for the German who had come to put him in his place. Then there was an unusual pause, perhaps because Schmeling appeared not to have heard the bell, and then the champion put in two hard straight lefts. The challenger's head was rocked back and as he blinked at the power of the black man's blows, Louis was at him again, this time with a combination of left hooks and right crosses which again staggered the German. It was already quite obvious that this fight was not going to go the distance, though no one could have imagined how short a course it would run. After that first barrage of punches Schmeling was already in terrible trouble. His legs were splayed apart; indeed it was probably only that flat-footed stance which kept him upright, and Louis came forward again to meet the only punch that the German managed to land, a right which

The Brown Bomber
has Schmeling in
trouble on the ropes.

grazed Louis's chin before passing harmlessly over the champion's right shoulder.
There was an incredible din from the 70,000
spectators as Louis hammered away at the
helpless figure of Schmeling who was now
tangled up in the ropes, unable to get up,
unable to fall down. It took the quick-
wittedness of referee Arthur Donovan to
retrieve a bizarre situation. Donovan got
between them and began a count, though in
those days before the standing count it was a
debatable action and excused on humani-
tarian grounds only.

The champion was still entitled to land his
punches and this he did with Schmeling still
trapped between the ropes and now twisted
round until only his back was presented to
Joe Louis. Louis did not mind, he cared only
about avenging his humiliation at the hands
of this German. He rained down blows upon

Schmeling, each one packed with venom.
One sledgehammer of a right crashed into
the German's body and above the roar of
70,000 people came an awful, ear-piercing
scream. The punch had broken one of
Schmeling's spinal vertebrae. Perhaps it
was the pain, perhaps the shock, but as the
count reached three, Schmeling somehow
extracated himself from the hemp, only to
walk straight into a vicious right hook
which lifted his feet clean off the floor.
Glassy-eyed and doubtless not knowing
what he was doing, Schmeling was up at
three; Louis was waiting for him and another
unerring right sent the German crashing to
the canvas again. Amazingly, he got up at
two, but Louis meant to finish the job this
time. Two left hooks and the customary
right follow-up put the challenger down
again.

Joe Louis exacts revenge from Max Schmeling and drops the German to record a 124-seconds win.

Arthur Donovan bent over the prostrate German, screaming the count into his ear above the din — as if it mattered, for there was absolutely no way that Schmeling could get back on his feet this time. As the count proceeded, the towel came flying through the ropes at the German's corner, followed by the German's trainer and friend, Max Machon. It was over, thank God. Joe Louis, the Brown Bomber, had just staged his own special brand of blitzkreig on the German. It was the end of Schmeling as a world con-tender, though he did win the European heavyweight title by knocking out Adolf Heuser in Stuttgart not long before the outbreak of war. In March 1941 Schmeling relinquished that title after injuries sustained while serving as a paratrooper on the island of Crete, though he did try a comeback in 1947. He had been out of the ring for eight years and it was seventeen years since he had first won the world title by default over Jack Sharkey in New York. Schmeling met the little-known Werner Vollmer in Frankfurt on 28 September 1947 and knocked him out in the seventh round, then followed this, three months later, by outpointing another 'nobody' in Hamburg. He went on to meet Walter Neusal in Hamburg, fourteen years after he had outpointed that boxer over eight rounds. This time it was Neusal's turn for victory, on points over ten rounds, and after two more fights — one win, one defeat — Schmeling was ready to call it a day.

The German is thus best remembered for two fights of contrasting fortunes against Joe Louis, a man whom he later befriended despite those bloody battles. Louis was paid $349,288.40 for that return fight which lasted just 124 seconds. That gave him a net return of $2,832 per second for the second-fastest knockout in the history of the world heavyweight championship.

ERIC BOON v ALBERT DANAHAR
Lightweight Championship of Britain
23 February 1939

The work that Peter Kane did in the Liverpool smithy helped to toughen him up to the point where he eventually won the flyweight championship of the world. Before Kane there was another blacksmith, the legendary Bob Fitzsimmons, whose hammer punch took the world heavyweight title towards the end of the last century. In the late 1930s there was yet another champion boxer whose work at the forge had helped him to develop a knockout blow. Eric Boon's work at his father's smithy at Chatteris in Cambridgeshire, developed his muscles and even as a schoolboy Boon was feared in local boys' competition for the weight of that KO delivery. It was not long before his prowess as a KO specialist attracted the attention of the London rings and a trial at Hackney's Devonshire Club, where Jack Solomons's patrons enjoyed Sunday morning kippers with their boxing. This resulted in the boy from Cambridgeshire impressing with his free-fighting style. Boon was invited back the following Sunday and he accepted, though he did not like to mention that he could not afford the train fare. Instead he cycled over seventy miles, propped his bicycle outside the club, won his fight, and then promptly cycled seventy miles back home again.

That episode in the life of Eric Boon who had not long passed his sixteenth birthday, illustrates just what dedication and resolve to become a champion he possessed. Solomons was impressed with the boy and soon found him a trainer who would channel his youthful exuberance towards a more technical approach to the fight game. At the same time the promoter found him a string of opponents, opponents who were picked for their ability to test the youngster. Boon met and beat them all, many of them falling to one-round knockouts from the sledgehammer punch of the kid from Chatteris. A narrowly-won points victory over the reigning British lightweight champion Jimmy Walsh confirmed Boon's pedigree, though the fight was not for the title.

Boon never had an opportunity to fight Walsh for the title because Dave Crowley took it from him at Liverpool in June 1938, defeating the champion over fifteen rounds. Boon, however, was not too impressed with the new champion and soon issued a challenge. The British Boxing Board of Control recognised the Cambridgeshire boy's right to a shot at the title and when Sydney Hulls agreed to stage the match at the Harringay Arena, all was set. There were many, however, who felt that Boon would not last overlong with the champion. The Chatteris boy had relatively little experience, whereas the new British champion had fought many fine boxers and although he did not possess the challenger's punching power, he was a clever boxer whose science must surely outdo Boon. Indeed, for eleven rounds of their title fight Crowley gave Eric Boon a lesson in the art of boxing, closing one of the youngster's eyes with incessant left jabs and generally making Boon look the novice everyone thought he was. But in that eleventh round Boon caught Crowley a terrific blow in the solar-plexus. It was the punch which altered the course of this fight. It sent Crowley gasping to the canvas and two rounds later a similar blow ended the fight and Eric Boon was the new British lightweight champion. He was still two weeks short of his nineteenth birthday.

While Eric Boon was setting the boxing world alight with his devastating punching ability, a new star was winging his way into the limelight. The 1937 ABA lightweight championship had been won in brilliant fashion by Albert Danahar, a youngster from Bethnal Green who was a year older than Eric Boon. Danahar's fine form in the amateur ranks had persuaded him to turn professional and in his first nine months as a paid fighter he scored fourteen victories, most of them well within the distance. Danahar had been 'adopted' by the National Sporting Club and his success was due less to any explosive punching quality than to a superb technique, the highlight of which was a classic left hand. With that near-perfect left, Danahar would seek out his opponent before laying on him the right which almost always ended the fight in a knockdown. Danahar's ability to make the grade became obvious in his fourth fight as a professional when he faced Jim Cameron, a Scottish lightweight of considerably greater experience. Cameron put Danahar down for an eight count and the Londoner was decidedly groggy when he resumed his stance. The Scotsman failed to catch him again, however, and it was Danahar who landed the next knockdown punch, a right which exploded on the point of Cameron's jaw and ended the fight.

So London had two favourite lightweights. There was the fast and furious Eric Boon, pride of the fanatical fans at Harringay; and Albert Danahar, the classy stylist whose supporters at the more sedate National Sporting Club were equally convinced that their man was the best. Naturally, the only way to resolve the matter was for the two to meet in the ring and such a prospect was a promoter's dream. Sydney Hulls, with Jack Solomons, secured Boon's signature for a title defence against Danahar. The challenger was equally loyal to the National Sporting Club which had given him his chance and he wanted its matchmaker, Jack Harding, to have first chance. So the situation arose where Hulls had the champion and Harringay, but no challenger; Harding had the challenger and Earls Court, but no champion. The matter was at deadlock when a wealthy sportsman offered to finance a fight in private at London's Grosvenor Hotel. The proposal was for an eight-rounds fight at the lightweight limit of 9st 9lb, shortly after midnight on 20 November 1938. The fighters signed their contracts but there was such an uproar, both in the sporting press and throughout boxing in general, because people felt that this fight belonged to them, not to a privileged few wealthy people sitting in the comfort of a London hotel.

Danahar gets through a fine straight left to Boon's face.

As quickly as it was suggested the 'secret' fight was called off when both Boon and Danahar stated that they had reconsidered and that the fight should be seen by as many boxing fans as possible. Hulls now reached an agreement with the National Sporting Club and the fight was fixed for Harringay Arena on the evening of 23 February 1939. The arena held some 12,000 people and a week before the fight those tickets had all been sold with twice as many people bitterly disappointed, for remember, this was in the days before mass television and the chance to see a title fight 'live' was a rare thing and one which conferred a certain amount of status on the lucky ticket-holders. It was those ticket-holders who had literally to fight their way into the stadium on that raw winter's night not long before the outbreak of war. Danahar was a good inch taller than the champion but when the two men entered the ring it was the challenger who looked the more apprehensive of the two. Boon appeared fit and strong while the Bethnal Green boy appeared to have had some trouble in making the weight and he looked pale and tired.

The first round of this title fight found the challenger doing almost all the scoring, jabbing out his almost flawless left into Boon's face as the champion looked for an opening to get in an early left hook. Boon's men were not unduly worried, however, for the champion looked to be taking this opening three minutes as a feeler. The second round was somewhat different. First, Danahar brought up a swelling under Boon's left eye with a stylish right; then an equally classy right uppercut stopped the champion in his tracks. Finally, Boon got through and landed several heavy punches to the body before Danahar managed to clinch, then wriggle free and land a left to the champion's face. The fight was now beginning to hot up and in the third round Boon managed to let the challenger have a series of crashing hooks to the body, but only at the cost of absorbing several lefts to the face. At the end of the fourth round, Boon's eye was closed up tight and as Danahar proceeded to deliver

text-book blows, it appeared that Boon's reign as champion would be a very short one.

Eric Boon had been in a similar position when he met Crowley, but he now suffered several other disadvantages as well. He was smaller than his opponent, gave away inches in the reach, and found that Danahar was boxing so clinically and tightly that there was little room for the champion to get back into the fight. A change of tactic was needed and Boon responded to the challenge by altering his stance so that his injured eye did not present so open a target. The champion coupled this with the opening of a furious attack on Danahar in the hope of landing the one devastating blow which would alter the course of the fight as he had done against Crowley. But when the eighth round opened, Boon was still way behind on points and had suffered some considerable punishment. Then came the moment for which the champion had been waiting. As they came out of a clinch, Danahar hesitated for a split second and left his jaw exposed. Boon saw his chance and let go a fizzer of a right which carried the champion's full weight with it. The blow hammered home on Danahar's jaw and his legs buckled. But he did not go down and out, simply down. He gained one knee as the referee continued the count and then at eight he was up. Boon came in again and this time Danahar went down for a seven count. He then managed to stay out of reach until the bell rescued him.

In the ninth round Boon was again into the attack, but this time Danahar was quite content to get into the clinch and hang on while he recovered his strength. The referee admonished the Londoner, who then caused a shock by catching Boon with a right to the chin which saw the champion sit on the bottom rope and take a short count. As he lifted himself off the hemp, Danahar's eagerness to follow up ended with him striking Boon before he was properly ready. The crowd booed and Boon responded with another bout of furious punching. The bell sounded with both men hammering away at each other and during the respite, the referee went over to Danahar's corner to remind him

91

Eric Boon (left) during his fight with Dave Crowley at Harringay in 1938.

of the consequences should his over-eagerness result in another incident like the previous one.

This was indeed a classic fight. In the tenth round the Londoner once more gained the upper hand. He had regained most of his composure, recovered from his earlier beating, and was now giving the crowd, and Boon, a boxing lesson. The Bethnal Green boy boxed himself out of danger and then scored with several clean punches, while those blows of Boon's which did land were not anywhere near as strong as the crowd had come to expect from the man with the blacksmith's hammer blow. Clearly, Boon would have to find that killer punch from somewhere and towards the end of the eleventh round he did. There was less than a minute to go when Boon at last got to grips with the speedy Danahar. A left hook from the champion jolted back Danahar's jaw and sent him staggering into the ropes. Only the ropes saved him from immediate defeat and

the bell went before Boon could finish the job. That punch had knocked all the fight out of Danahar, just as Crowley had all the stuffing knocked out of him, and it was amazing that the challenger got through the twelfth round without being knocked down. Time and again Boon hammered home a left hook against Danahar's jaw, but the Bethnal Green battler simply refused to go down. Then Boon, whose left eye was in a terrible mess, changed tactics again and caught Danahar with a tremendous right to the chin. This time he went down and it was nine before he could stagger back to his feet. Boon dropped him again, again he took a nine count, and then Boon allowed him to fall into a clinch and hang on until the bell.

During the minute's rest that elapsed there was considerable discussion among those at the ringside as to whether Albert Danahar would bother to come out for the thirteenth round, so badly beaten had he been in the preceding three minutes. He did, however, and he tried some desperate measures to ward off his opponent. But three times in that unlucky-for-Danahar thirteenth round, Boon dropped the challenger to the resin — and three times he struggled back on to his feet after taking lengthy counts. Each time he rose to walk into another battery of punches and when the round ended it was considered amazing that this lion-hearted fighter had not been counted out. There was now the possibility that, if he could stay the distance for these last two rounds, Danahar might incredibly win on the strength of his early lead, but Eric Boon soon banished those thoughts from the mind. Danahar was hardly off his stool when Boon was across the ring and delivering a crushing right swing which landed smack on the challenger's jaw. Danahar wheeled round and collapsed in a heap on the canvas, making no move at all for the first few seconds of the count. Then he managed to get himself on all fours, and finally on to two feet as the referee signalled nine. He stood there, arms by his side, totally defenceless, as Boon came roaring in again to deliver what would surely be the last punch of this epic boxing match. But the referee would not allow it and the fight was over. Eric Boon retained his title against a courageous, and skilful, let it be said, opponent in British boxing's first publicly televised bout.

The following Monday, the two men met again at the National Sporting Club where Eric Boon presented Albert Danahar a silver cigarette box as a token of his great esteem for the game loser. Ten months later Boon fought Dave Crowley for the second time and beat him to win the Lonsdale Belt outright in a record eleven months and twenty-four days. Boon's next defence was not until 1944, when Ronnie James knocked him out in the tenth round at Cardiff, but the war had by then interfered greatly with Boon's boxing, though he was still only twenty-five years old. Of all his fights, though, Eric Boon's greatest memory had to be of that epic bout with a fine boxer, Albert Danahar.

HENRY ARMSTRONG v ERNIE RODERICK
_____ World Welterweight Championship _____
25 May 1939

Henry Armstrong was a unique boxer. A black American who was born in St. Louis, Missouri, in December 1913, Armstrong held three world titles. True, Bob Fitzsimmons had also achieved that feat, but Henry, the man they called Homicide Hank, or the Human Buzz Saw, held them *simultaneously*. His professional career started in 1931 and six years later he took his first world crown by knocking out Petey Sarron in Madison Square Garden, dropping Sarron, who had never even been knocked down before, never mind knocked out, in the sixth round of their title bout. In fact, there were several claimants to the world featherweight title during this era and the previous year Armstrong had outpointed Mike Belloise in Los Angeles in a fight which was also claimed to be for the title. Armstrong should then have tried for the lightweight title held by Lou Ambers, for the new featherweight champion was having great difficulty in maintaining the weight limit in that division, but Ambers's manager put his foot down and objected, no doubt aware of the probable consequences. So Armstrong went up a division and challenged Barney Ross, one of the toughest welterweight champions of all time.

The challenge was accepted and they met on 31 May 1938. People thought that Armstrong would be no match for the tough New York Jew. Armstrong was way below the weight and trained for the fight by drinking great quantities of beer, but though he gave away well over half a stone, Armstrong hammered Ross around the ring for fifteen rounds and took his second world title on points. Armstrong's very next contest, just two and a half months later, was for Amber's lightweight crown, for the champion could

not avoid Homicide Hank any longer. Again, everybody thought that the Human Buzz Saw had met his match. But Ambers, the Herkimer Hurricane, was beaten, though he did give Armstrong the toughest fight of his life. Armstrong was warned for low blows, needed twenty-two stitches in a cut lip, also he cut his left eye, but, for all that, won by outpointing the champion. So Armstrong held three world titles at one and the same time and he finished that year by successfully defending his welterweight title against Ceferino Garcia and Al Manfredo, and then relinquished his featherweight title.

Armstrong's style was reminiscent of the great Jack (Kid) Berg, although Henry had one great asset which the London fighter never enjoyed. Armstrong's speed was allied to a devastating knockout punch. Also he could apparently absorb punishment without any real ill effects. All this made him a great champion, three times over, and a natural box office attraction. His later slide into drunkenness and still later reform as a Baptist minister is worth a story of its own, but here we can only concentrate on his wonderful boxing ability. For a man of his size he hit with amazing power and it has been said that he had the torso of a welterweight on the legs of a featherweight. Yes, speed, strength and courage marked down Henry Armstrong as an exceptional athlete. Between 1931 and 1945 he fought 175 men, won on 144 occasions, ninety-seven times by a KO, and lost just nineteen bouts, two of them by a knockout. Where as many boxers with a heavy punch could not always catch their men, Armstrong's speed and agility meant that not many men could run away from him in the ring. He wore them down, found them and destroyed them. There seemed to be no ultimate escape from the Human Buzz Saw.

In the first three months of 1939 Armstrong defended his welterweight title no less than four times against Baby Arizmendi (beaten on points), Bobby Pacho (fourth round KO), Lew Feldman (first round KO), and Davey Day (twelfth round KO), the last three fights all happening within a twenty-seven-day span. Then, with all America's best hopes put away, Armstrong set sail for England to see what the British champion could do. That champion was Ernest Roderick, a Merseysider who had just won the British welterweight crown by knocking out the Scotsman, Jake Kilrain in the seventh round of their fight at Liverpool Stadium. Roderick had been an amateur for several years and he was twenty-five when he met Kilrain. In 1931 he had asked the Liverpool promoter Johnny Best for a trial and in his first year as a professional went unbeaten in the lightweight ranks. He was befriended by Nel Tarleton, the fine British featherweight, and went to Australia with him, though on the trip Roderick, by now nineteen, was unwell and did not enjoy the experience. Back in England things changed for the better. Roderick moved up the welterweight ranks until he was the main challenger, won the title, and married Tarleton's sister into the bargain.

At about the time Ernie Roderick won the British title, his mentor Johnny Best was asked to take over matchmaking at the Harringay Arena. It was not long before Best was thinking in terms of a world title fight for his protegé and with the arrival of Henry Armstrong in England the fight was set. It had taken a fairly big purse to induce Armstrong to come over the Atlantic, even if he could find no one of real class left to fight in the United States. Ten thousand pounds was mentioned and this is not far off the mark. Certainly, it was a huge guarantee for the black champion, but if Best and Harringay wanted that title fight for the British boy, then that was what they would have to pay. The problem was that not many people in London felt that the world champion could fail to win. And for that reason the attendance was poor. Ticket sales were very slow and in the end only 5,000 people were in the stadium. Best could not help but reflect that, had the fight been in Liverpool, the attendance would have been much greater. There is nothing to beat putting a fighter in front of his hometown fans.

Best's troubles did not end there. The Americans wanted a neutral referee (at one stage Georges Carpentier was mentioned) but they had to settle for Wilfred Smith, that fine British official. Then the visitors were worried that the length of bandage allowed in British rings would not be sufficient to protect their fighter. On this point the British gave way and Armstrong was allowed his extra yard or so, with Roderick also enjoying a mite more protection. The faithful 5,000 who did pay to watch the fight were to be rewarded with a magnificent bout worthy of many times that number of spectators. Ernie Roderick was about to succeed where most men had failed and go the distance with this triple world champion. Surprisingly, the American came into the ring one blur of animation. Not for him the ploy of conserving energy until the very last moment. In the dressing room he had indulged in a furious spell of shadow boxing; out in the ring he continued to bob and weave, while the British challenger chose a more leisurely approach to the pre-fight formalities. At last all the talking was over, only the action remained. Wilfred Smith bade both men to their corners and the bell clanged its call to arms.

It was Ernie Roderick who took the lead in that first round. Around and around the champion he went, flashing out straight left followed by straight left. The black man did well to evade a looping right hand, then two more rights got home and at the end of the three minutes the Liverpudlian was a clear leader. The fans cheered him and his corner welcomed him back with open arms, full of praise for their boy's efforts against this fearsome opponent. But their joy was a

Ernie Roderick lands a left but Hurricane Hank is already swinging over a right.

short-lived affair. From the first bell of that second round Roderick was hammered by a man intent of saving his honour. Although the Briton was more than ten pounds heavier than the champion there was little he could do against a barrage of hooks, uppercuts, short-armed jabs and straight lefts. Almost everywhere on the legal target of Roderick's body felt the pounding of those leather-wrapped hammerheads. Into the bargain Armstrong was too quick on his feet, too nimble around the ring, to allow Roderick to land any blows of consequence. For the best part of that second round the Briton was either chasing shadows, or else fastened up against the ropes trying to ward off the champion's blows. Round three was much the same, though Armstrong was punching even faster now and had he found the killer blow at that point then poor Roderick would have been felled there and then. As it was, a short right which thudded under Roderick's heart sent him ashen-faced, and the two left hooks which thundered into his jaw immediately afterwards did not improve his complexion. Yet just before the end of the round Roderick cracked in two good lefts to the champion's jaw which raised the fans'

hopes a little, though they did not appear to bother the American.

At the start of the fourth round Armstrong again received a heavy blow to the chin, but it did not stop him from carrying out his avowed intent. He hammered Roderick's body with punch after punch, not aiming at any particular spot, but landing wherever he saw an opening. The ferocity and variety of the onslaught gave the Briton little chance to combat it and all Roderick could do in retaliation was to complain that the champion's head had caught him. It might have been that bobbing head which caused the cut over Roderick's right eye in the fifth round, which at one stage was bleeding so badly that the fans feared a stoppage. But Ernie was allowed to continue, though the pounding he took swelled the eye so that he could not see properly. The Briton weathered the storm and got in one or two telling punches of his own, though Armstrong was still clearly in charge.

This is the way the fight continued for the next few rounds with Armstrong on top and dealing out so much punishment that the crowd began to wonder just how much poor Roderick could absorb before he had to admit defeat. In the seventh round the Briton came off the ropes after a particularly severe assault from the champion and fought back with tremendous courage. When the bell went the challenger did not hear it and it was left to Smith to pull him off the American. That was one of the few things the home fans had to cheer until round eleven when Armstrong appeared to slip down a gear for a while. It allowed Roderick to go on the offensive and he took the round with several excellent lefts which landed on their target on the champion's torso and hurt him. But Roderick was so tired and he could not find the one punch that would have perhaps earned him a sensational victory. The twelfth round found the American back on top and a wicked hook to the jaw sent Roderick's legs rocking and buckling, though he managed to retain his ground.

Round thirteen found both men resolved to slug it out to the last and for almost the

96

whole three minutes they had the crowd on their feet, yelling and cheering them on as they stood square-on, toe-to-toe, exchanging barrage after barrage of punches, lefts and rights, hooks and straight-armed thrusts, until it seemed that one of them, most probably Roderick, would drop. But they were still standing when the bell sounded. The last two rounds belonged to Armstrong. He took them both with a wonderful display of boxing, landing punch after punch, scoring point after point, and then slipping away so deftly from anything that Roderick still had left to throw. The bell went and the crowd knew the verdict. Armstrong retained his championship and was presented with a gold trophy to mark his twenty-four carat status as one of the truly great champions of world boxing.

Armstrong lost his lightweight title later that year, to Lou Ambers who reclaimed it after fifteen rounds in New York. But also in 1939 he successfully defended his welterweight title no less than eleven times, and was to do so a further seven times in 1940 before Fritzie Zivic won a points decision in New York on 4 October that year. Roderick held his British title until 1948, and also took the middleweight crown in 1945. Between them they had given Harringay a night to remember.

JOE LOUIS v TONY GALENTO
World Heavyweight Championship
28 June 1939

By the middle of 1939 Joe Louis was well on his way to becoming one of the greatest world heavyweight champions of all time. Since his 'grudge' return with Max Schmeling had ended in such humiliating defeat for the German, Louis had defended his crown twice within the first four months of 1939 and on each occasion the challenger did not get past the first round. It was the start of what became known as the 'Bum of the Month' competition, when Louis defended his title against a host of challengers, all of whom met a sticky end, though the real once-a-month defence was from December 1940 until June 1941. Even back in 1939, however, Louis was not afraid to lay his title on the line. In January that year he defeated John Henry Lewis when the referee stopped the fight in the first round; and in April that year he scored a first-round knockout over Jack Roper.

Then came Tony Galento, Two-Ton Tony, the Beer Barrel Palooka as he liked to be known. On the face of it, it is difficult to imagine how a man like Galento was ever allowed to fight for the richest prize in sport, as indeed the presence of some other challengers over the years has caused a great deal of head scratching. Let me explain: Tony Galento was a little fat man who owned a bar in Orange, New Jersey, and whose appearance can best be summed up by Joe Louis himself who, on setting eyes upon this latest challenger for the first time, was heard to comment, 'He's a saloon keeper alright — and he looks as if he's had a drink with every single one of his customers!' Galento stood only 5ft 9in tall, and weighed sixteen and a half stones. He was balding and his beer belly flopped over the rim of his

shorts to make him one of the most unlikely challengers of all time. So, how had he got a fight with the world champion. To begin with, Louis was fast running out of challengers to keep his career going. When Lewis, the former world light-heavyweight champion, and Roper were halted within the first three minutes of their title shots against Joe, then the promoters began to get a little desperate for new blood.

Even so, just how did Two-Ton Tony get his chance? The answer is by a combination of well-orchestrated publicity on his part and the fact that there was no-one else immediately available in the United States. The publicity side centered around Galento's own bizarre figure and training routine. He seemed to do most of his serious training with booze and huge cigars. Once he went out on a training run with some of his sparring partners, only it was the partners who were doing all the sweating and pounding the roads while Two-Ton Tony lay back in the luxury of a limousine and puffed on an even bigger cigar! If that was not a publicity man's dream then such a dream has never been answered. Of course there was a more serious side to Galento's boxing career. He was only twenty-nine and yet he had been through the mill 103 times as a professional, though he had lost twenty of those fights. One thing which captured the public's imagination, however, was that he had never been knocked out, though he had succumbed to cut eyes on a couple of occasions. He was also, shall we say, an uncomplicated fighter. His observance of the finer points of the rules left something to be desired and there was the famous case of his fight with the Chilean Arturo Godoy, on the same night that Louis won the title from Braddock incidentally, when after the first round the referee retired to a neutral corner and let them get on with it, his orders and pleas for a clean fight having been totally disregarded. Galento lost that six-rounder, presumably on the basis that after Godoy took the first round the referee gave up trying to score.

There was Galento's repeated insistence that, no matter who he was fighting that night, 'I'll moider da bum!' It was the same with the champion: 'Who? Oh, Joe Louis — I'll moider da bum!' There is a story, perhaps apocryphal, that one reporter, tired of receiving the same answer to questions about leading heavyweights, ventured to inquire Tony Galento's opinion of William Shakespeare. Apparently Mr Galento thought that perhaps Shakespeare, of whom he had never heard, might be some European heavyweight and he declared that he would 'moider dat bum too!' Is it any wonder then, that despite his limitations as a boxer, more than 35,000 people went to the Yankee Stadium on 28 June 1939 to see Joe Louis, the bronze god of American and world heavyweight boxing, take on the Beer Barrel Palooka who had threatened to 'moider' him.

The fun started even before a blow had been thrown. When referee Arthur Donovan called the two men together to give them their final instructions, Galento was more concerned with what he claimed was too much grease on the champion's face. Two-

Ton Tony insisted on wiping his gloves across Joe Louis's face and through his hair. Louis was, not unnaturally, incensed and said as much when he returned to his corner. It made him mad, and that is the last thing that a boxer wants to feel when the bell clangs and he steps out of his corner at the commencement of a fight.

As Galento stepped out at the beginning of this fight, he began to wind up the one punch that he knew. It was telegraphed from the first moment, yet poor Joe Louis seems to have been the only man in 35,000 who did not read it. The left hook, not a particularly wicked punch by world title fight standards, slammed home on to Joe's right cheek. Had it been on the chin, then strangely it would have caused the champion less of a problem. But the cheeks were Joe Louis's weak spots and the blow injured him. He fought back all right, but Galento kept prodding in lefts to the champion's face and when the opening round ended, Louis's cheek was red and lumpy from the pounding it had received. Galento was also damaged. Almost on the bell Joe Louis had swung over a left hook which exploded on Two-Ton Tony's mouth, smashed his lips back against his teeth, and opened up a nasty cut on the upper lip. Blood pumped out of the wound and the sight of it did much to settle Joe Louis down as he made his way to his stool.

It was obvious that Joe Louis had recaptured his composure during the second round. Though Galento continued to swing those lefts and rights, Louis was in complete command. His footwork dazzled the challenger and his punches went home like guided missiles of the future, stabbing into Galento and hurting him. Galento tried to avoid them but his footwork was that of a lumbering ox and, try as he did, he could not get out of the way. Blood from a cut above the challenger's right eye now mixed itself with that still pumping from his lip. Then Louis struck. A right and a left hook were followed by another left. . . and Galento was down.

A rather bemused Joe Louis finds himself on the canvas while an equally surprised Tony Galento looks down at him.

Many had forecast that this fight would not get beyond the second round and it now appeared that they were right. Galento crunched into the canvas, his eyes staring glassily into space, his legs devoid of any strength. Donovan began to relay the count to the prostrate challenger and Louis retired to a neutral corner to await the call that would confirm he was still world champion. Somehow, though, Galento managed to get to his feet. He looked ashen-faced and could surely have not withstood the barrage which Louis then launched on him. The crowd would never find out because the bell sounded and ended the second round. Most people now felt that the end was a formality. Not Tony Galento. He shrugged off the damage as best he could and came out for the third round looking to take the fight to the champion once more, employing, as usual, his swinging hooks as the main weapon of offence.

The fight was now being held at close quarters and, inevitably, Louis's extra height meant that from time to time Galento's head clashed with his own. The Beer Barrel Palooka was employing few, if any, of the dubious tactics for which he was well-known, though it must be said that Galento was never a 'dirty' fighter in the true sense of the word. It was just that he was a natural rough and tough scrapper who thought that the majority of the rules of boxing were an unnecessary intrusion on a man's sport. It was certainly through no illegal blow that Galento caused a sensation in this round. He swung a left hook at Joe Louis and the champion, instead of going inside the punch, chose instead to draw back; at the same time Joe somehow managed to get his legs crossed and that took him off balance. When Galento's next swing landed (and do not forget that despite his squat build he was thirty-three pounds heavier than Louis) the champion could not help but fall backwards and land ignominiously on the canvas with his pride probably hurting a good deal more than the cheek on which the punch had landed. Louis got up and Galento missed the immediate chance to follow up his shock

blow. Instead it was the champion who boxed his way out of trouble, sending left after left smashing home into the podgy face of the challenger. The round ended with Joe Louis again doing all the scoring and with little need of instruction as he waited for the fourth round to open.

That fourth and, as it turned out, last round was all Joe Louis. From the bell he came towards Galento intent on finishing off the fat little guy who had just become only the third man to drop him in his professional career. Galento was on the receiving end from the start and although he took his punishment like the rough, raw hero he was, he could not fight back. Punch after punch thudded home until Galento's face was barely recognisable. A left hook from the champion ripped an ugly tear in his already gaping lip and blood spurted forth, splashing the champion and those closest to the ringside, as well as giving the challenger a sticky, sweet taste in his parched mouth. The eyebrows were also bleeding badly and the pain had taken all the strength from Galento's body. What punches he did throw were but powder-puff attempts which the champion scorned contemptuously, not even bothering to evade them, but simply getting on with the destruction in hand.

Tony Galento was now nothing more than a human punch bag. His fat quivered as Joe Louis delivered each one of his earth-moving punches. Galento simply took each one and then prepared himself for the next... and the next... and the next. The end came with no particular punch to be credited for ending the butchery. Galento simply caved in under the weight of the punishment. He went down like a rubber dummy with a fast puncture, the last few dregs of strength spilling from him until he finished up on his knees, leaning against the ropes with his back half-turned away from the champion. Arthur Donovan had seen enough, too much in fact, and he ended the challenger's immediate agony. Joe Louis was still the world champion and the fevered work in Galento's corner now was simply to get him into a good enough shape to get him out of the ring. Back in the dressing

The incredible character 'Two-Ton' Tony Galento.

room Two-Ton Tony still had much to endure. His eyes, lips, even his tongue, needed stitches, though playing his tough-guy role to the last, Galento refused even a local anaesthetic while the doctor scwed his face back together again.

Galento went straight back to his New Jersey bar, one of the gamest losers in the history of the world heavyweight championship. His boxing days were not over, however. Less than three months after that terrible beating at the hands of Joe Louis, he scored a fourteen-rounds win over Lou Nova, who had beaten Tommy Farr and who was therefore no 'bum'. The Galento-Nova fight has been described as one of the dirtiest of all time and so Two-Ton Tony was obviously back fighting in the way he loved best, but that was the last of his good days. In his next fight Max Baer beat him so badly that the referee was forced to stop the fight in the eighth round. But Tony Galento was nothing if not game. His next fight was against Buddy Baer, bigger brother of the former world champion. He went one better than his 'little' brother and stopped Galento in seven. Galento had a two-year lay-off and then came back to the ring in 1943 with six knockout wins over 'no-hopers', one of whom was actually a professional wrestler who fought under the splendid title of the Golden Terror of Chatanooga. In Galento's 113th fight he scored his last win, a three-round KO over a boxer named Jack Suzek in Kansas. Even then this colourful character was not finished with the ring and he took up wrestling, two of his contests being against Jack Doyle, the equally colourful Irish boxer. It was an inglorious end for Galento; in the second bout in Dublin, both he and Doyle fell out of the ring and Tony cracked his head on the floor and was knocked out. Better to remember him for the night he surprised Joe Louis, when that great world champion was at his greatest, but still found himself on the canvas. Just for a few seconds the Beer Barrel Palooka came near to 'moidering da bum'.

FREDDIE MILLS v LEN HARVEY
British and British Empire
Light-Heavyweight Championship
20 June 1942

There have been plenty of tough boxers whose grounding was in the tough East End of London, or the docklands of Liverpool, or the grim Gorbals area of Glasgow. But Bournemouth. . .? That genteel English South Coast seaside resort hardly seems the place to breed the sort of boy tough enough to put on the gloves and go to the top in the world of professional boxing. Yet such a boy was born there and learned the first rudiments of the noble art in that balmy town, then in Hampshire now in Dorset, and he did go on to become a world champion. Freddie Mills, a local milkman who boxed in the fairground booths in his spare time, was that boxer. His rise to fame was confirmed on a June evening in wartime London when 40,000 fight fans went to Tottenham Hotspur's White Hart Lane soccer ground to see Mills win the light-heavyweight titles from another of Britain's finest boxers. The night that heralded the arrival of Freddie Mills also saw the curtain brought down on the great career of Len Harvey who, though he did not realise it at the time, was fighting his last of over 400 professional bouts.

Freddie Mills was born in Bournemouth on 26 June 1919, and he might never have turned his youthful energies to boxing, but for the fact that a local man called Jack Turner took to hiring a dance hall in that town and staging boxing shows. By the time Mills was sixteen he was a regular favourite on Turner's modest bills. Boxing in Bournemouth was well-established, young Freddie's elder brother also boxed, and when the youngster came home with a silver cup, the prize from a novices' competition, it was natural that his enthusiasm should be fired still further. Soon he faced the problem which confronts all up-and-coming boxers; there were too few local men who could stay the distance with him and Freddie was forced to ply his fists further afield, following the booths which were attached to local fairs in those days. As the fairs went further afield Freddie found that his job in the dairy was interfering with his fighting, so he did the only thing he felt was possible and turned professional, glad, no doubt, to be rid of his mundane milkman's job anyway.

Freddie found plenty of work in the booths during the summer, but in the autumn, when the fairs broke up, he returned to Bournemouth to face the fact that he was out of work. No matter. Jack Turner realised that in this young middleweight he had a potential box-office winner and soon he was filling his Bournemouth hall with those people who wanted to see the local lad fight against some of the best middleweights that London and the provinces could send. Most of them were well beaten, but it was still a rarity to see Freddie Mills box outside the Bournemouth area, for he was still only a local attraction and, indeed, he was to fight in almost all parts of the country before he was at last allowed into a London ring.

While the formative years of Freddie Mills's boxing career were speeding by, the world was sliding into war and when the inevitable happened and German panzers went into action against Polish cavalry in 1939, it was not long before Freddie Mills and thousands of young men like him found themselves called up into the service of King and Country. Boxing had to be put to one side; there were other people to be given bloody noses now. Mills's boxing career was brought to a sudden halt and it was a year before he was able to obtain one or two fights in provincial towns and cities. One of them created a shock when young Mills outpointed the British middleweight champion Jock McAvoy in Liverpool. But it did not lead Freddie to a title because boxing, like most sport at that time, was dead. It was August 1940, the Spitfire and Hurricane pilots of Fighter Command were grabbing all the headlines during the Battle of Britain, and the country was braced to withstand what seemed an inevitable German invasion. So the fact that a young unknown boxer had beaten a British champion over the distance, while it might have been a talking point in normal times, was hardly likely to set the country alight now. Mills did not have another fight for eight months, though boxing was obviously on his mind and he wrote to Gilbert Odd, then editing a boxing paper, and asked if Mr Odd could get him a fight in London. Unfortunately, the editor's own call to arms was imminent, but before he went he did have time to send the letter on to an almost unknown Irishman, John Muldoon, who, despite serving as an LAC in the Royal Air Force, was still finding the time to promote boxing shows at the Royal Albert Hall. Five months later Mills made his London debut and did well enough to stop Tommy Martin in five rounds. He also did well enough to persuade Ted Broadribb to take him under his wing, and had moved out of the middleweight bracket to tackle some of the best heavies around.

Defeats over such notable heavyweights as Jim Wilde, Jack London and Tom Reddington earned him another crack at Jock McAvoy in a fight which was billed as a final eliminator for an attempt at Len Harvey's light-heavyweight titles. Freddie Mills already had the confidence of a points win over the middleweight champion. Now he converted that into a sensational first-round KO, staggering McAvoy with his first punch of the fight and finishing the matter well within the first three minutes.

That victory brought Freddie Mills into the ring against Len Harvey. Harvey held the British and Empire titles at both heavy-weight and light-heavyweight, and the British also considered him to be the world light-heavyweight champion. They had never recognised the men put up by the Americans for John Henry Lewis's vacant title: Tiger Jack Fox and Melio Bettina, Billy Conn, Anton Christoforidis and Gus Lesnevich. Britain's claims that both Len Harvey and Jock McAvoy had given Lewis a run for his money, both having stayed fifteen rounds in world title fights with him, received much support in Europe. So when Harvey and McAvoy met in July 1939 in another version of the world title, it was Harvey's points victory which gave him the crown. Indeed, until Mills met Lesnevich in 1946 there were many claimants for the world light-heavyweight title. So Mills's fight with Len Harvey in June 1942 was reckoned, in Britain at least, to be for the light-heavyweight titles of Britain, the British Empire, and the world, though we shall consider it to be only for the British and Empire titles because of the considerable confusion.

Muldoon had often dreamed of staging a world title fight and despite the dubious nature of Harvey's claim, that was what he felt he had now obtained. Harvey had promised him sometime earlier that if it was at all possible his next title defence would be under the Irishman's promotion and when Harvey agreed to fight, the champion wanted Mills who he now saw as the logical challenger. Muldoon had little difficulty in persuading Broadribb to let Mills fight for the titles, but there was a problem for both boxers in that they were serving in the RAF. Mills had expected to be allowed a crack at Harvey sometime, but not until after the war. When the fight was announced for 28 June 1942, both men had little more than a week to prepare. Both had to use up valuable leave, Mills training in the garden of a pub at Feltham, Middlesex; Harvey at Taplow near Maidenhead.

Muldoon's greatest fear was that the weather would be unkind for his first 'world' title fight. But the day dawned fair and when Len Harvey, RAF pilot officer, climbed into the ring to meet Freddie Mills, RAF sergeant,

Mills has Harvey on the ropes at Tottenham Hotspur's football ground and a great career is about to end.

at White Hart Lane at just after seven o'clock that evening, the skies were blue and the sun still evident on an English midsummer's day. The ring was erected in the middle of the famous pitch where generations of Tottenham Hotspur teams had entertained their fans. Where Jimmy Dimmock, Jimmy Seed and Arthur Grimsdell had weaved their magic patterns in the lilywhite shirts between the wars, now heroes from a different sport were about to show their skills. Seats were set on the pitch and then spread away and into the more conventional accommodation of the football ground. They held a crowd, the size of which Tottenham Hotspur would be glad to have any Saturday, and when the first boxer appeared in the ring (it was dark, snub-nosed Freddie Mills who made the first entrance) the fans, starved of top-class sport of any kind, greeted him with deafening cheers. The champion was met with a similar wall of sound which rose to a crescendo as he immediately walked over to Mills's corner and gave the challenger a little pat on the back and a pleasant grin. Then

back to his stool where his trainer and friend Wally May, who had looked after Len's interests in so many big fights, began to put the gloves on the champion. Harvey looked a little tense, the grin had disappeared and he fiddled nervously with the gloves.

In the other corner Mills looked so confident it was difficult to imagine that he was fighting the biggest fight of his life. He was so relaxed that he might well have been waiting to take part in a six-rounder back at Jack Turner's Bournemouth dance hall promotion. But, as the preliminaries dragged on, Mills, too, began to show signs of tension and there was no smile on his face either when the bell signalled the start of the first round. They came out fighting and Len Harvey straightaway tried a sharp straight left to Mills's nose. The Bournemouth boy evaded the blow and retaliated with several wild swings. Harvey covered up and this first round passed quietly enough, both boxers content for the most part to test out the other's armour. Remember that Len Harvey was within a week of his thirty-fifth birthday and had not been in the ring for a serious contest for three years. There were no conclusions to be drawn and Cornishman and Hampshire lad returned to their stools hardly having broken sweat.

This fight looked to be going on for quite some time, thought the more knowledgeable in the crowd. Yet within half a minute of the second round Freddie Mills, ex-milkman and fairground boxer, had the crowd on their feet and Len Harvey on his knees. Mills saw a chink in Harvey's armour and unleashed a tremendous left hook which exploded right on the point of the champion's jaw. Down went Harvey and referee Eugene Henderson took up the count. Harvey struggled to one knee and still it looked as though he would not beat the count. 'Six, seven, eight. . .', Henderson was still relaying the count from the timekeeper as Harvey stared glassy-eyed towards the challenger's corner. One can always tell when a punch *really* hurts and the blow which Mills had landed on Harvey was just such a punch. Then, in one superhuman effort, Harvey managed to get back on to both feet with only hundredths of a second between him and a knockout.

Mills now had the light of victory in his eyes. He knew that the championship titles were there for the taking and he went hell-for-leather after them. Arms swinging like piston rods he tore in Len Harvey again and in the face of all this, the champion had absolutely no defence. He could not even get his hands high enough to protect himself and when Mills swung a right to the head and landed it on the right cheekbone, down the champion went again. As he leaned back towards the rope for support, sitting on the middle hemp which he flattened against the bottom rope to make an unsteady seat, the champion of Britain and the Empire — and, some claimed, the world — disappeared from view. He fell backwards out of the ring and landed on the press table from where he fell onto the grass of Spurs' pitch. Freddie Mills could hardly believe his eyes. The referee took up the count and down on the ground there was an almighty drama being enacted. Those who could see witnessed Len Harvey surrounded by people, some wondering whether to help him, others warning that any bid to do so would result in his certain disqualification. The count continued and those who could not see, just waited for Harvey's head to reappear above the level of the canvas. Just as ten was called, Harvey's dazed countenance did indeed appear, but it was far too late. Unlike Dempsey against Firpo no one had given him a helpful shove back into the ring and Freddie Mills was the new champion.

Harvey certainly did not realise that it was all over as he climbed back into the ring, knocked out for the first time in his long and wonderful career. It took him all his time to drag one foot behind the other as he made his way to Mills's corner where the new champion was drinking in the atmosphere. It was a long way from the fairgrounds of Bournemouth where he had fought after a long day on the milk round. Harvey now realised that he had been shorn of his crown and stretched out his hands to congratulate the new light-heavyweight king. Even in defeat, Len Harvey was a gentleman. Then he turned and received the condolences of his wife who had been none too keen on his returning to the ring after so long an absence. It took him some time to accept that his boxing days were over and he did not announce his retirement until some six months later. For Freddie Mills there were even greater days ahead.

NEL TARLETON v AL PHILLIPS
British and British Empire
Featherweight Championship
23 February 1945

There have been few finer featherweights than Nelson Tarleton — 'Nel' on the boxing bills and 'Nella' to the fight fans of his native Liverpool. Though he never quite reached the same heights as 'Peerless Jim' Driscoll, Nel Tarleton was good enough to fight twice for the world title, and good enough to win two Lonsdale belts outright. He was a stylish boxer with great finesse and textbook skill, a man who possessed the most exquisitely executed defence and, at long range, one of the best boxers in the world. Like Driscoll he never suffered the indignity of being knocked out, and like Driscoll he retired an undefeated champion. Yet on a February night in 1945, at Manchester's Belle Vue stadium, he was pushed all the way by a tough little Londoner, a boy called Al Phillips, known as the Aldgate Tiger and who was so much Tarleton's junior that his ring career had not started until 1939, five years after Tarleton first fought for the world title.

Nel Tarleton was born in Liverpool on 14 February 1906 and from his schooldays he knew that he wanted to be a professional boxer. His progress through the amateur ranks was assured and a month before his twentieth birthday Tarleton signed professional forms and, naturally, his start in the paid ranks came at the Liverpool Stadium, where his obvious talent as a skilled boxer soon made him a firm favourite with the Merseyside fans. Within a few months Tarleton was impressive in fifteen-round bouts with some of the country's leading bantamweights and by the end of his first year as a professional he made his first trip to London where he was unlucky to drop the decision to Alf (Kid) Pattenden who was emerging as a

serious challenger for the British title. A long and successful run at Liverpool was followed by a second trip to London, this time to meet the bantamweight champion Johnny Brown at Premierland. Again Tarleton was unsuccessful, but his third trip to the capital saw him outpoint featherweight championship challenger Billy Hindley at the National Sporting Club. A few months later Tarleton won the nine-stones Northern Counties title by beating Dom Volante, and that put him in the top bracket.

Since his defeat by Johnny Brown, Nel Tarleton had strung together thirty-three successive victories, yet the path for a crack at the British featherweight title was not clear and in October 1929, his manager took him off to the United States where he had eight fights lined up. Tarleton lost two of them, and although he scored a fine win over Archie Bell, the man who had such a great fight with Teddy Baldock in Britain, the Americans did not seem over-enthusiastic about the featherweight from Liverpool, though they could not disguise their admiration for his scientific boxing. Tarleton's trip was not in vain however, and upon his return he went straight into a British featherweight title fight with Johnny Cuthbert. On 6 November 1930 they boxed a draw at Liverpool.

Eleven months later, on 1 October 1931, Tarleton had another chance and 30,000 people were at Anfield football ground to see him win the title in brilliant fashion, tearing Cuthbert's defence to ribbons with a murderous left hand. In fact, the win came almost exclusively through that left, and it was not until after the contest that Tarleton revealed that he had fought for most of it with an injured right hand. During the next twelve months Tarleton fought nine times, including a defeat of the reigning British lightweight champion Al Foreman, at catchweight, and a draw with the world bantamweight champion Al Brown. After this more than useful build-up Tarleton was ready to defend his British title and when he did put it on the line he received the shock of his life. At Liverpool, on 10 November 1932, Seaman Tom Watson, a strong young man from Newcastle, beat Tarleton on points and it was Watson, not Tarleton, who then went to America to meet Kid Chocolate for the world title fight. Watson lost on points while Tarleton was left to reflect on what might have been. Instead of a title shot, the Liverpudlian was left to embark on a trip to Australia with Ernie Roderick, the man who became his brother-in-law. Nel won one, drew one and lost one of his three fights and both men were thankful to return home. Upon his return Tarleton found that Watson was ready to give him a return fight and Nel took back his British title on points at Liverpool in 1934. While all this was happening, the hard-hitting American southpaw Freddie Miller had taken the NBA version of the world title (Kid Chocolate was the New York State Athletic Commission's nominee) and he agreed to fight Tarleton for

that title while he was in Britain. Miller won over fifteen gruelling rounds at Liverpool in September 1934, two months after Tarleton had regained his British title.

Tarleton finished the year on a high note however. In December he faced Dave Crowley in a defence of the British title and won his first Lonsdale Belt outright with a superb exhibition at the newly-opened Wembley Pool. The Earl of Lonsdale himself put the belt around Tarleton's waist after the Merseysider's points victory. The next two years saw Tarleton busily engaged. In June 1935 he had a second chance at Miller's world title but again went down over fifteen rounds at Liverpool. Then he faced the British bantamweight champion Johnny King — against whom he had dropped a decision before his second fight with Miller, and that gave King what he thought was the right to fight for the featherweight title. King was allowed a twelve-rounds fight with Tarleton (a non-championship fight of course) and held the champion to a draw. When they met again, at Liverpool in May 1936, it was for the title and Tarleton won easily over the distance. Four months later Tarleton was the ex-champion once more when Jimmy McGrory, the tenacious Scot, took the title from him on points at Liverpool.

Nel Tarleton then announced his retire-

Nel Tarleton bows on the ropes as Al Phillips wades into him.

ment and he surprised no one by the decision, for, after all, he had twice lost his title. Equally, though, Nella surprised no one by his decision to make a comeback. He was out of the ring for five months, came back for two fights, one of which he lost, and then had an eight-months lay-off which was followed by infrequent appearances until 1940 when the Liverpool promoter Johnny Best asked him to fight the new featherweight champion Johnny Cusick for the British and Empire titles. Cusick had taken the title from Spider Jim Kelly in June 1939 and eight months later he was defending it against Tarleton at Liverpool. Ring-rusty though he might have been, Nel Tarleton responded magnificently and at the end of fifteen rounds became British featherweight champion for the third time. A second notch on his second Lonsdale Belt came when he outpointed Dunkirk hero Tom Smith in November 1940, once more in Tarleton's home city, and it was a victory which underlined that Nel's superior skill was no match for youthful endeavour. Smith might have been awarded a rematch, for he had performed well, but service in the armed forces came first, though Smith did outpoint the champion in a subsequent catchweight contest. The next four years saw Tarleton fight fourteen times, but by the beginning of 1945 he was on the point of retiring for good.

There was, however, one young man who felt that he ought to have a crack at Tarleton's British title. Al Phillips, the boy they called the Aldgate Tiger, was fourteen years younger than the champion and his ring career was still but a dream in his eye the night that Liverpool's boxing fans hurled clods of earth into the ring when they felt that Tarleton had been cheated out of a points decision in his second fight with Freddie Miller. Phillips was one of a family of nine, six brothers and two sisters, and was a good all-round sportsman as a youth. He boxed as an amateur, joined the Merchant Navy for a spell, and then came out to fight professionally with a travelling fairground booth in the West Country. In that show were Freddie Mills and Gipsy Daniels, and it

was Daniels, the former British light-heavyweight champion, who taught Phillips so much. When war broke out Phillips found himself back at sea, this time in the Royal Navy, where he endured a hair-raising time before being shore-based at Liverpool where the promoter there, and in Blackpool, found him some work in the ring. In 1942 he went back to his native London to win six fights in a row and it was his non-stop style which made his name, particularly at the Queensberry Club where he fought many times.

Eventually he won a place in the eliminating competition to find a challenger for Tarleton. First, the Aldgate Tiger disposed of Jim Brady at Bristol on points, then scored a first-round win over George Pook at the Queensberry Club. The defeat of Pook came only two days after beating Tommy Davies on points at Leicester and it put Phillips in the ring with the fancied Welshman, Len Davies, for the final eliminator. The Welshman ruled himself out in the sixth round for an alleged infringement of the rules and suddenly promoters in both London and Liverpool were anxiously bidding to stage the fight between Al Phillips and Nel Tarleton. In the end a compromise was reached and the Northern Sportsmen's Charity Committee staged the fight at Belle Vue, Manchester. Both fighters brought hundreds of supporters, though Tarleton's men were better served geographically and travel was still difficult with the war in Europe, and the Far East for that matter, still to be won.

It was an intriguing match, for here was a challenger who, on paper, never stood a chance of getting within a mile of Tarleton's title. Yet the champion was now in his fortieth year, while young Phillips was in his prime. It might well be, thought the fans lucky enough to be travelling to Manchester, that the Londoner's youth and dash might be more than a match for the wiles of the Liverpool man who, while he was several classes ahead of Phillips when it came to scientific boxing, was still fourteen years older and consequently slower on his legs.

There were 7,000 fans in the stadium when Phillips, as expected, took the fight to the champion from the first bell. They saw the Aldgate Tiger snapping ferociously at Tarleton with a bevy of swinging lefts; and they saw the champion back-pedal slowly but surely, evading almost everything and occasionally scoring with straight lefts which caught Phillips smack on the face. Phillips never once stopped moving forward in that opening round, even when Tarleton landed him on the face, and it was obvious that the champion was quite happy to let the younger man expend as much energy as he liked. In the second round Phillips made another great charge at Tarleton and this time Nella buckled his opponent's knees with a perfectly-timed right. At the end of that round Phillips returned to his stool having failed to catch Tarleton with anything of note, despite those cavalry charges. In addition the challenger was cut under the eye, though his corner quickly stemmed the trickle of blood. The third and fourth rounds followed the same course with Phillips charging forward and Tarleton picking him off with lefts of grace and beauty, but it was in the fifth round that the crowd had a first glimpse of the drama to follow. One of Phillips's wild swings crunched the champion on to the ropes and the Londoner was on to him in a flash, raining down a fury of blows until it seemed that the Liverpudlian must go down. But Tarleton fought free and resumed a sally of his own, several good one-twos thudding home to Phillips's head and sending him back to his corner dizzy from the attack.

Tarleton took the sixth round by a narrow margin, thanks to some good long-range boxing, but it was the challenger who had the seventh round, though if Phillips had landed even half the blows he swung then, he would have secured a much bigger lead. Rounds eight and nine saw Tarleton keep the challenger at long range where he could do less damage and it was now evident that Phillips had slowed down appreciably. Swing as he might, the Londoner was always a target for those nagging lefts from Tarleton.

It was the tenth round which set the stadium alive to the possibility of a sensation. Phillips knew he was now well behind on points and he decided to do something about it. He hammered his way through Tarleton's defence and sent a right crashing on to the champion's jaw. It both hurt and shocked Nel and he staggered into the ropes to be hit by four more fearsome rights and then a cracking left cross. Nella could only cover up and wait for the bell. It came as Phillips was hammering blows down on the half-turned back of the champion and the Londoners who had made their way to Manchester began to think that it was worth all the time and money.

The eleventh round saw Phillips chase Tarleton all around the ring, though by now the champion had recovered his composure and was able to once more keep the challenger at long range. The points went into the champion's bag at the end of that round, and at the beginning of the next it was Tarleton who came out fighting with a superb straight into the challenger's face, followed with an equally fine right to the jaw which dropped Phillips momentarily. He was up in a flash, before a count could be started, but from that moment he was in deep trouble and his legs buckled and wobbled. Then he began to shake his right leg and Tarleton saw that his man was troubled with cramp. He was after the Londoner in a flash and for the remainder of that round, and for the whole of the last three, the challenger was on the retreat, limping around the ring while Nel Tarleton scored as many points as he pleased. It was a grim task and Phillips stuck to it well, his mouth bleeding, his leg paining him, and his arms aching. When the bell ended the fight everyone knew that Nel Tarleton's vast experience had proved too much for the Aldgate Tiger. Phillips later took the Empire and European titles, but for Tarleton it was time to retire with his second Lonsdale Belt won outright, and he did it with only one lung!

GUS LESNEVICH v FREDDIE MILLS
World Light-Heavyweight Championship
14 May 1946

At the end of World War II there were two men who claimed to be the light-heavyweight champion of the world. The American, Gus Lesnevich, had reached one version of the title by way of a competition between the nominees of the National Boxing Association and the New York State Athletic Commission. While the Briton, Freddie Mills, was regarded as champion on his side of the Atlantic after beating Len Harvey, the man whose 1939 victory over Jock McAvoy was alleged to make him the champion. There was only one way to decide the issue and that was to pit Lesnevich and Mills together so that, for the first time in almost a decade, the world would have an undisputed light-heavyweight title-holder. The result was a fight of which promoter Jack Solomons later said, 'Quite honestly, I'm rather doubtful about being remembered as the man who promoted it.' It was, according to Solomons, 'the most savage fight I've ever seen.'

We have already seen, in the chapter on the Mills-Harvey fight, how Freddie Mills came to be British, Empire and 'world' champion. Lesnevich had been a star in the amateur ranks, winning the coveted Golden Gloves tournament as a middleweight and then turning professional and for two years fought the best in the country without getting a shot at the actual champion. Gus then went to Australia where he was an outstanding success and when he returned he found himself a light-heavyweight and matched against Billy Conn, one of the classiest light-heavyweights around at that time and a man who had recently assumed the world title after outpointing Melio Bettina. It was here that the world title became confused. Bettina and Tiger Jack Fox were the survivors of an elimination contest to find John Henry Lewis's successor and Bettina had stopped Fox in the ninth round at the Garden in February 1939. After Conn beat Bettina he was matched with Lesnevich and after a terrific struggle in New York, Conn emerged a close points winner.

Seven months later they were rematched and after another gruelling encounter, Conn again emerged the winner. Then Conn relinquished the title to seek a match with the heavyweight champion Joe Louis, who stopped him twice, in 1941 and 1946. With Conn's retirement from the light-heavyweight ranks another elimination was started. After a series of preliminary fights, the New York State Athletic Commission and the NBA named their men and in January 1941, the Greek Anton Christoforidis met Melio Bettina in Cleveland. The Greek won the decision and the right to meet Lesnevich. The fight was staged the following May at Madison Square Garden and Gus became the 'American world champion' by winning on points. The war meant that European boxing was generally inactive, though as far as Britain was concerned, of course, Harvey and McAvoy had fought for the 'real' title and in 1942 Mills was to take that from Harvey. To confirm his status, Lesnevich twice fought and beat New York's leading contender, Tami Mauriello, before entering the service of Uncle Sam in the US Coastguard. He remained inactive until the end of 1945 when he received an honourable discharge and resumed his boxing career in 1946 with a New Year KO of Joe Kahut who was put down and out in the first round of their fight in Seattle; a month later he forced Lee Oma to retire with eye trouble in the fourth round of their fight in New York.

Mills, too, had little real competitive boxing during the war. After winning the titles from Harvey he spent two years boxing mainly as an RAF PT instructor, though in that time he did manage to fit in four professional fights. Then, with Harvey having relinquished the British and Empire heavyweight titles, Mills was matched with sixteen-stones Jack London for the vacant championships. London won on points in September 1944 to become the new British title-holder and Mills, after stopping Ken Shaw, the Scottish champion, was posted to India where he remained until the Spring of 1946. Mills had been out of the ring for almost a year and had spent that time in a country whose inhospitable climate is hardly conducive to serious preparation for a world title fight. Yet within a short space of time, this was exactly what Freddie Mills faced.

It was about this time that Jack Solomons was establishing himself as Britain's leading promoter. Solomons had staged the Jack London - Bruce Woodcock fight in July 1945 when Woodcock knocked out London in the

Mills puts Lesnevich on the defensive in 1946.

sixth round to become the new British champion. He had started years before in Hackney when, with others, he converted a dance hall into the Devonshire Club. At first the venture was not a success and sponsors dropped out. But the far-sighted Jack Solomons soldiered on and was rewarded when the place eventually became popular. He went on from here to stage shows at the Royal Albert Hall and at the end of the war, with that venue and Harringay Arena among those under his control, he staged Woodcock - London at White Hart Lane and after that the sky was the limit. Woodcock's British title gave Solomons the drawing card he wanted, but to pit the Doncaster man against Joe Louis was out of the question, especially since the world champion was due in the ring for a second battle with Billy Conn. Besides, Woodcock, though a fine British champion, did not have the credentials to fight a man such as Joe Louis.

Solomons lowered his sights slightly and they fell upon Gus Lesnevich. The promoter flew to New York and found Lesnevich in Stillman's gym in New York where he persuaded the champion to meet Woodcock in a catchweight contest in London. The deal was clinched, but when Solomons returned home he found that a snag had developed on Woodcock's side and the fight was off. So here was Jack Solomons with the world light-heavyweight champion coming to his doorstep and no one to fight him. At this point Freddie Mills returned from India and the picture changed dramatically. What a fight that would be, mused Solomons, Mills against Lesnevich in a bout which would give the world its first undisputed world light-heavyweight champion since John Henry Lewis abdicated the title in January 1939, just three months after his last successful title defence against Al Gainer. Mills was raring to go and went straight into training; the sum of £12,000 tempted the American and then Solomons set about building a bill around this world title fight so that he could fill Harringay Arena.

Gus Lesnevich, at thirty-one, was four years older than Freddie Mills and while 111 both men had been largely inactive in the sport during the war, the American had an added disadvantage in that he came into this fight with an injured eye. Yet he was far more experienced than the Briton, even if Mills had been ten years in the fight game. All these factors added up to a potentially great fight underlined when, two weeks before it was due to take place, there was not a single ticket left for sale. Eleven thousand wedged themselves in Harringay Arena and they naturally reserved their biggest cheers for Freddie Mills, former milkman and the man who was first bitten by the excitement of the ring while still a schoolboy watching the fairground booth shows in his native Bournemouth. Indeed, when Mills climbed into the ring ahead of the champion that evening the rafters fairly shook with the thunderous applause. From the end of the war until the 1950's British sport was assured of huge attendances. Soccer and cricket both enjoyed a boom the like of which neither sport has seen since, and boxing too, claimed huge audiences. People had been starved of sport during the war and the month previous to the fight had seen the first peacetime FA Cup Final for seven years. It was against this kind of electric atmosphere that Freddie Mills met Gus Lesnevich.

The first round was a big disappointment for British hopes. Mills came out looking to create mayhem with his left; instead he found himself walking into a barrage of lefts from the champion. It was halfway through the opening round before Mills could land a punch, and then only at the cost of taking three straight lefts in return. Whenever the challenger moved forwards, the champion moved back and then came in with those lefts. The second round started with Mills attacking strongly and he got in several good one-twos to Lesnevich's midriff. But the American's greater experience told and Lesnevich came back with a magnificent right to the chin, followed by another right which sent Mills down to the canvas. Mills took a count of six and then got to his feet only to meet another right to the chin which dumped him back on the floor for one more six count.

Gus was in no mood to hang this fight out any longer than was absolutely necessary and yet another right put Mills down, this time for eight. Up he got once more, but this time his knees were bent and his arms hung loosely by his side. Lesnevich wheeled in again with a two-handed attack which sent the Englishman down for the fourth time in this round. It seemed all over, for there seemed to be no way for Mills to beat the count. The referee had signalled nine when the bell rang out and Lesnevich turned to his corner, robbed by one second of finishing the fight there and then. Mills managed to get back to his corner and there was general consternation in the champion's corner. Those nearest to his stool saw that an ugly cut had been opened up over the American's left eye.

By the time the third round bell sounded, Mills had made a remarkable recovery and Lesnevich was so surprised that he allowed Freddie to get to close quarters and hammer him to the body and then to the chin. Though Freddie was still open to the champion's left it did not keep him at bay and he moved Lesnevich around the ring. He managed to land hooks and uppercuts which damaged the champion whose eye, in particular, was a sorry mess. The fourth round saw Lesnevich dash straight into the attack in the hope of cracking Freddie Mills with a right, but it was the challenger who scored with his right and then had Gus beating a hasty retreat in the face of a heavy two-handed attack. Straight lefts from Mills worsened still further the champion's eye and took their toll on his body. The British champion was now completely recovered after his terrible second-round beating, and with the American also prepared to give no quarter, the crowd were treated to some tremendous rallies as the boxers slugged it out toe-to-toe.

The subsequent rounds were all full of action. Clinches were at a premium and the fighters elected instead to stand face-on and punch it out. Lesnevich's left eye was now completely closed and his nose had been broken from a punch by Mills. The damage meant that Gus had to keep moving away

Two years later and Mills is about to become the world champion by gaining his revenge over Lesnevich.

from Mills whenever he could and the challenger found himself having to follow Lesnevich around the ring to get in his punches. Mills did this, relentlessly boring away and prepared to take any amount of punishment in return so that he could land his own salvoes. Mills's complete abandonment of defence meant that Lesnevich could score quite easily with his left. At the end of the ninth round Mills was clearly the stronger boxer and was perhaps slightly ahead on points. Into the bargain, Lesnevich's eye was now so badly swollen that there was the distinct possibility that the referee might stop the fight in the Englishman's favour. Certainly, if the fight continued in this way, Gus's chances of staying the full fifteen rounds would diminish further with each passing minute.

When they came up for the tenth round this was clearly in Gus Lesnevich's mind, for he stormed after Mills and, for the first time since the second round, the champion had the challenger on the retreat. But Freddie Mills was not the sort of man to be on the retreat for long. He came back once more and that rush proved to be his undoing. His guard was never sound at the best of times and he left his jaw exposed to the champion's right. Lesnevich caught sight of Freddie's chin and unleashed a straight right of ferocious power. It crashed home with such force that it carried the challenger from the middle of the ring and sent him hurtling into the ropes. As Mills bounced off the hemp, Lesnevich was on him again and a perfectly-judged right to the jaw sent Mills down. At the count of eight he got to his feet, though he was now operating purely on instinct. Lesnevich knew that he had to finish the fight now. To let Mills recover again, as he had after the second-round beating, would be a grave mistake, and one which Lesnevich did not make. He sent in one, two, three successive rights to the chin. Any one of them would have dropped lesser men and the last dropped Freddie Mills. Yet at the count of four he was up again, oblivious to the fact that Lesnevich was closing yet again. The champion hammered another right into defenceless Freddie's jaw and down he went. Referee Eugene Henderson began the count but then realised that it was a formality and that Mills could not continue. He waved the champion back to his corner. The fight was over.

There is no doubt that Henderson acted correctly, though afterwards the arguments raged because it was revealed that there were only four seconds of the round remaining. Therefore Mills could not have been counted out and after a minute's rest... who knows? But Henderson did not know there were only four seconds left. What he did know was that Mills was a sadly beaten man and that was all that mattered. In those circumstances, time is academic, life is more important. Gus Lesnevich was still the champion, this time the undisputed champion, of the world, but Freddie Mills had contributed as much to one of the greatest ring battles ever seen.

Boxing had not seen the last of Freddie Mills. Three weeks after his terrible beating at the hands of Lesnevich, and only seventeen days after Bruce Woodcock's fifth-round knockout by Tami Mauriello, the two Britons met in a non-title fight which Woodcock won on points. In November 1946, Mills, still only a light-heavyweight remember, was matched against the huge American Joe Baksi and was hammered into defeat by the man who, a few months later, broke Woodcock's jaw and stopped him in seven rounds. In 1947, however, Mills took the European light-heavyweight title by stopping Belgium's Paul Goffaux in four rounds in London and then defended it the following year when he scored a second-round KO over Spain's Paco Bueno. It was in July of that year, on the eve of the 1948 London Olympics, that Mills at last gained an undisputed hold on the world title. He met Lesnevich at the White City and this time outpointed the American to become the first Briton since Bob Fitzsimmons half a century earlier to hold the title. When referee Teddy Waltham held up his hand, Freddie Mills rewarded the fans who regarded him as a great favourite. Mills was a fine fighter, yet as a cruiserweight he was expected to do the impossible against heavier men. In the summer of 1949 he was matched against Woodcock for the British heavyweight crown, only to be knocked out in the fourteenth round. It was that defeat which may have 'softened him up' for his world title defence against America's Joey Maxim in January 1950. Maxim knocked out three of Mills's teeth as he KO'ed the British champion in the tenth round. At thirty, Freddie Mills retired, still undefeated British, British Empire and European light-heavyweight champion, and went into a career in showbusiness. In 1965 he was found shot dead with a gun by his side and a coroner's jury ruled that he had taken his own life. There were others who claimed it was murder and Freddie Mills was, in death as in life, surrounded by controversy. But he was a great champion.

TONY ZALE v ROCKY GRAZIANO
_____ World Middleweight Championship _____
27 September 1946

Everybody loves a good fight. No matter how delightful an exhibition is staged by two scientific exponents of the boxing art, there is nothing to raise the temperature and the roof like a good old-fashioned slugging match where the fighters ask for and offer no quarter, where blow is traded for blow, and where everyone knows that the fight is never going to last the distance. Even the purists have to admit to that, and when such a bout is staged between two boxers of championship calibre, then the spectacle is even more appreciated. Such a fight took place in New York City's Yankee Stadium in the Fall of 1946 when the world middleweight champion, Tony Zale, defended his crown against a tough New Yorker from the East Side, Rocky Graziano. Indeed, it was the first of three such fights between these men and it was one of the most bloody ever seen, described by one newspaperman as 'a throwback to the days of bareknuckle fighting'.

The world middleweight title had been in some confusion until Zale claimed it in 1941. When Mickey Walker, the Toy Bulldog, gave up the title in 1931 to concentrate on the light heavyweight class, it opened the door for several claimants, including Gorilla Jones, Marcel Thil and Ben Jeby among others. Zale, whose real name was Anthony Florian Zaleski and whose parents were Polish immigrants who had settled in Gary, Indiana, took a circuitous route to the title. He was next-youngest in a family of seven and needed to be tough to stand up to the rigours of shift work in the neighbouring steel mills. His leisure time was spent in the local YMCA gymnasium and it was here that he became interested in boxing and where he

became one of the outstanding amateurs of the day. In the annual Golden Gloves interstate tournament, Zale made what was in effect the Chicago team and in 1934 boxed in Madison Square Garden where seven years later he was to win the world title. He did not win the amateur championship, however, being outpointed in the middleweight final, and after that Zale decided to turn professional.

Yet his entry into the paid ranks was far from spectacular. He found it hard going from the start and after two years and several disappointing defeats he decided to quit after one especially bitter pill when he was knocked out. Zale went back to the steel works, but his love of boxing was still there and he could always be found at the ringside, when he was not working, watching someone else box. Zale could not stay away for ever and a year after his retirement he was back in the ring. This time the young Pole made steady, if not spectacular progress and the natural free-hitting style which he exploited soon came to the notice of a team of Chicago managers who persuaded him to join their stable. A defeat at the hands of Jimmie Clark, who caught Zale with a first-minute 'sucker' punch, was overcome by two subsequent defeats of Clark inside the distance and then, out of the blue, Zale was offered a fight with Al Hostak, a heavy-punching Czech from Seattle who was recognised by the National Boxing Association as the world middleweight champion. It was a ten-rounds nontitle fight in Chicago and looked to be a tough assignment, for none other than Jack Dempsey had described Horstak as the heaviest middleweight puncher since Stanley Ketchel.

It did not take Zale long to find out

whether Dempsey was correct. In the first round he was laid on the canvas by a full-blooded left hook to the jaw and then hammered with a barrage of punches until the bell rescued him. Zale weathered some heavy punching for the next four rounds until the champion tired and then powered his way to a points win in the second half of the fight. That win earned Zale a championship fight later in the year and in July 1940, in the champion's home town of Seattle, Zale knocked out Hostak in the thirteenth round. He defended his version of the title twice, knocking out Steve Mamakos in fourteen rounds and Hostak in two, and then, as NBA world champion, he was offered the chance to meet the New York champion, Billy Soose. Before the fight could be arranged, however, Soose outgrew the class and Georgie Abrams, who had defeated Soose on three occasions, was put up instead. When Zale won a fifteen-rounds decision at Madison Square Garden on 28 November 1941, the world had its first undisputed middleweight champion for a decade.

Unfortunately, Zale's elevation to the top of the heap came about a week before Pearl Harbour and America's entry into World War II. Zale, now aged twenty-seven, joined the US Navy and the world title, which had waited for so long to be sorted out, was put into cold storage for four years. Zale was demobbed at the end of 1945 and looked to pick up the pieces of his once-thriving boxing career. There were naturally renewed doubts about the champion's rights to the title, as so much had passed since he had won it outright, and he was called upon to defend it against a 23-year-old called Rocky Graziano, whose real name Thomas Rocco Barbella (he boxed under his maternal grandfather's name) and who was a product of the tough East Side of New York City. That tough background inevitably got Rocky into trouble with the police and one officer is reported to have said of him: 'Ten years from now, he'll be in Death House at Sing Sing'. But it was organized boxing which saved Rocky from his vicious environment. He started fighting in 1942,

though many fight managers soon shied away from the wild twenty-year-old. Eventually, one man, Irving Cohen, himself a mild sort of a man, gained his confidence and took him under his wing until the US Army claimed his services.

Twelve months later, Graziano was back on Cohen's doorstep, hinting that the army had discharged him, but omitting to say that it was because he had gone AWOL. Boxers were scarce in New York around that time and Cohen had no problems in getting Graziano into the ring. Standing 5ft 7in, he was a middleweight who packed a terrific punch in his right hand and in 1943-4 he took part in thirty-eight bouts and won twenty by a knockout. The only opponent he disliked was Harold Green who could dodge Graziano's rights and stab him with his left. Twice Green got up from the canvas to beat Rocky by this method and although Rocky was twice the loser, the fact that both fights were held at the Garden put him in the spotlight. In 1945 he scored five sensational KOs at that great venue: they were served out to Al Davies, Freddie Cochrane (twice), Billy Arnold and, at last, Harold Green. In early 1946 Rocky scored a two-rounds win over Marty Sevo, the man who took the welterweight title from Cochrane. Rocky's win over Sevo was so emphatic that the champion retired. Next to Joe Louis, Rocky Graziano was the best crowd-puller in America and that crowd insisted that he meet Tony Zale.

Zale got back into trim with a series of warm-up fights and then the fight with Rocky Graziano was set for the Yankee Stadium on 27 September 1946. Nearly 40,000 people paid over a quarter of a million dollars to see it: and how they were rewarded. From the very first bell they were treated to one of the most bloodthirsty fights that New York had ever seen. Zale was in his thirty-second year and was giving eight years to his challenger. Moreover, Zale had been out of the ring for four years whereas Rocky had been in constant action. No wonder then, that Rocky was 7-2 favourite as they went into action. It was Graziano

Rocky Graziano sits befuddled and bemused after being dumped on the canvas by Tony Zale.

his own. A lightning right caught Zale full on the chin and as the champion staggered back, the challenger followed up with three more. Zale tottered, the crowd screamed and roared, Rocky buckled the champion's legs even more with another right to the chin — and then the bell sounded to end a sensational first round. The second round found Zale meeting his man with two straight lefts which left Rocky floundering with his swings. That was the start of a furious barrage from the champion; straight lefts, uppercuts and right crosses all made their mark and yet Rocky took them all and inched gradually closer, despite Zale's bid to box him off. Then the challenger let loose a succession of head punches which thudded home, drawing blood from Zale's nose. The crowd loved it and Zale fought back until both men were in the centre of the ring trading punch for punch.

It was Zale who broke away, only to come back with a series of short little jabs and sweeping hooks. But Rocky managed to get within firing range once more and three crunching rights hammered high into Zale's head, followed by another smack on the jaw. It sent the champion crashing across the ring, his head hanging over the edge of the canvas and his mouth agape and bleeding badly. He clawed at the rope, but showed no real sign of getting up and it was the bell which saved him. Rocky did not hear the bell in all the uproar and wanted to go after his man again. Eventually the end of the round was signalled to him and he stood and glowered as Zale made his unsteady way back to the safety of his corner.

Rocky Graziano's blood was up. He came out of his corner for the third round looking for all the world like a demented animal. Zale was battered all around the ring as Rocky delivered punch after punch to the champion's head. Then the champion halted the New Yorker's approach with a right to the face. It was only a temporary stay of punishment, however, and back came Graziano again, crashing Zale's head from side to side. Zale was forced on to the ropes, fought back and set up another of those fierce exchanges that all boxing crowds love. If only Graziano

who made the early running, though it was the champion who appeared to be getting home the most telling punches when he did score. After some heavy body punching, both men switched to the head and then Zale returned to the body and landed two cracking punches into Rocky's rib cage. They called Zale 'The Man of Steel', and he needed to be made of such stern metal in the next few minutes. A straight left from Rocky brought up a lump on the champion's nose, then followed with another to the cheek which inflamed the taut skin. Zale responded with a sizzling left hook and Graziano found himself on his back, more surprised than hurt perhaps and certainly able to get up at four.

He did so, only to walk straight into a series of head punches which culminated in a right uppercut that almost parted head from neck before Zale again switched his attack to the body. Only Rocky's great fitness saved him from a KO here and he weathered the storm to cause a sensation of

had steadied himself at this point, he might well have had the champion down again. Instead he continued to swing wildly and the bell ended round three with Tony Zale still standing and fighting back.

The interval enabled the champion to recover enough to be governor in the opening stages of round four. He outboxed Rocky and seemed to be getting on top when the challenger opened up again. He crowded into Zale and threw a right to the chin, a left to the nose which sent blood pouring down the champion's chin, and then two hands slammed into Zale's ribs. Zale took them all and then returned fire with a barrage to the challenger's midriff. The bell went to end another grand stand-up fight between these two, Rocky slamming punches to the body, Zale sending his man dizzy with a salvo of lefts and rights to the head. The champion won the round and was well satisfied as he sat down heavily on his stool.

The fifth round was to prove even more sensational than what had gone before, however. Zale started it with a hook to the head, Rocky retaliated with a right to the ribs, perhaps landing a shade low, and for the first ninety seconds of the round it continued like that. Towards the middle of the three minutes both men appeared to be taking a breather as the pace had been tremendous, and then Zale ended the brief respite with two powerful blows into the challenger's stomach. That sent Rocky wild with fury. A tremendous right smashed Zale full in the face, to be followed by a left hook to the jaw that rocked the champion back. Then Rocky noticed that Zale was not using his right; it transpired later that the champion had broken his right thumb when mishitting on Graziano's head. For the rest of that round Rocky administered one of the biggest beatings any boxer has ever had to face. At the end of the round people marvelled at the fact that Tony Zale was still standing. For a full minute and a half he had to endure a terrible hammering and it would have been no surprise if the towel had come in there and then.

In the champion's corner, ice-packs, cold water, smelling salts and pummelling hands prepared Zale for what would surely be the last round. When they came up for that sixth round Graziano looked so fresh; Zale had nothing except his guts and instinct to keep his tired body going. It was enough. After taking two lefts to the face the champion was met full in the face by a tremendous right and then received two rights which crashed home under his heart. Another vicious right to the body further hurt the champion and then he did something extraordinarily brave, even by the standards of this fight. He gritted his teeth, tried hard to forget that he had just broken his thumb, and sent a right into the oncoming challenger's solar plexus. It was a blow of stunning power and spun Rocky around like a top. In a flash Zale was firing in a left hook to the New Yorker's temple which dropped him to the canvas in a sitting position. He shot out a left hand and tried to grab hold of the rope but his legs were not responding. By the time he was on his feet, the referee had counted him out and battered, bleeding Tony Zale was still champion of the world.

Even then Rocky did not accept that the fight was over and he had to be wrestled to his corner by his seconds. It was one of the greatest middleweight fights of all time and, of course, there had to be a rematch. In July 1947, Graziano, with one eye closed and the other cut, hammered Zale so hard in the sixth round in Chicago Stadium that the referee had to stop the fight. It was a fight watched by a then record indoor attendance of 18,547, who paid over $200,000 for the privilege of seeing Graziano, this time, pull the fight out of the jaws of defeat, just as Zale had done the first time. In June 1948 these two met for the third and final time. The fight was staged in Newark, New Jersey, and it lived up to the other two. In the third round, Zale sent in a long left which KO'd Graziano in one of the most dramatic knockout incidents of all time. Zale thus became the first man to regain the world middleweight crown since Ketchel in 1908.

Three months later, a Frenchman called Marcel Cerdan took the title when Zale was unable to come out for the twelfth round in Jersey City's Roosevelt Stadium. But Zale had already proved himself one of the greatest champions of all time. In eighty-eight professional fights he won seventy — forty-six by the KO — lost twelve, drew two and was himself stopped four times. Rocky Graziano's career went on until 1952, by which time he had fought eighty-three times as a pro, winning sixty-seven fights, fifty-two by the knockout. He was once suspended by the New York State Athletic Commission for allegedly failing to report a bribe to throw a fight. Subsequently he was told to forget the whole thing, for it appeared that his early criminal record had made him a convenient fall guy. He had made every effort to lead a decent life and most people knew it. With Tony Zale he gave boxing three world championship fights to remember.

JOE LOUIS v JERSEY JOE WALCOTT
World Heavyweight Championship
5 December 1947

Just occasionally the result of a world title fight causes controversy. We have seen three such examples already in this book: did Jack Johnson, the first black heavyweight champion, deliberately lie down against Jess Willard, shielding his eyes from the sun as he did so? Would Jack Dempsey have got back into the ring against Luis Angel Firpo, had he not been given a more-than-helpful shove? Would Gene Tunney have beaten the infamous 'Long Count', if Dempsey had retired immediately to a corner? They are all fascinating imponderables of sport about which arguments still rage. Another highly controversial decision came when Joe Louis met Jersey Joe Walcott for the world title in December 1947, only on this occasion it was the result of a points decision which caused all the furore. Even today there are still plenty of people who saw that fight and who are convinced that the Brown Bomber lost his title that night in Madison Square Garden, and that Jersey Joe would have been more than justified in coining that old sporting cliché, 'I wuz robbed!'

Joe Louis was the great pre-war champion. He had defended his title against anyone who cared to have a shot at it during the early part of the 1940s — his famous 'Bum of the Month' competition seeing them all off — but since 1942, when he knocked out Abe Simon in six rounds in New York on 27 March that year, the champion had fought only twice. Over four years in the US Army had taken up much of his time and only in 1946 did Joe Louis get back into the ring for some serious boxing. In that year he fought a return bout with Billy Conn, the man KO'd in thirteen rounds in 1941, and this time delivered the

knockout punch in the eighth round of their New York fight of 19 June. Then three months later Louis met Tami Mauriello and thrashed him to the canvas in the first round of their title fight, also in New York. So the Brown Bomber, or the Tan Killer as he was also known, was still undisputed heavyweight champion of the world. There were, however, question marks against him. The Conn fight had been a slow, disjointed affair; and Mauriello had staggered Louis with a right that sent him crashing into the ropes in the opening seconds of their fight.

It was clear that the advance of years and his long army service had taken much of the edge from the once-great champion who was in his thirty-fourth year when his next title defence came towards the end of the following year. Louis's opponent this time was Joe Walcott, born Arnold Raymond Cream from Camden, New Jersey, who fought under the name of Jersey Joe Walcott. Walcott was actually a few months older than Louis and his life up to that point had hardly been a bed of roses. He had made several attempts at a professional boxing career, only to have the stuffing knocked out of him by a succession of unscrupulous managers. He was now on the dole, trying to support a wife and six children, after a series of menial jobs had failed one after the other. He had managed to maintain his ideal heavyweight's physique — six feet tall and almost fourteen stones in weight. In addition, while Joe Louis had been lacking match practice in the army, Jersey Joe had been active in the ring and in the three years before he met Louis he had enjoyed no less than twenty-two fights, losing three, two of which he later avenged.

So, with no other obvious challenger for Joe Louis's title, up stepped Jersey Joe for his shot. The fight was not expected to draw a large crowd and for that reason it was staged at the Garden and not at the Yankee Stadium. The bookmakers were so confident of Louis easily seeing off this ageing challenger their odds on the champion were 1-10, hardly generous considering that, despite his pre-war greatness, Louis had been relatively inactive for so long. Walcott on the other hand, though he was by no means a leading heavyweight of the day, had been around for upwards of eighteen years and the records showed that his first paid fight had been at the age of fifteen, four years before Joe Louis made his entry into the professional ranks. Moreover, some of his defeated opponents had been of high calibre. There had been Joe Baksi, the man who earlier that year had broken Bruce Woodcock's jaw; and Joey Maxim who was to take the world light-heavyweight title from Britain's Freddie Mills in 1950. When one considers that, in almost six years, Joe Louis had been required to fight less than nine rounds of competitive boxing, the fans' complacency was perhaps ill-judged.

One thing was for certain. American boxing desperately needed a 'good, clean fight', a wholesome bout of boxing that would redeem much of the sport's tarnished image in the United States. For it was around this time that Jake La Motta, Bull of Bronx,

Joe Louis spars before his fight with Jersey Joe Walcott in 1947.

121

threw a fight and was suspended for seven months and fined, just one incident of many which illustrated the way that much of boxing was being conducted in the States. A lot of 'bad money' was invested in the game, gangsters were known to have involvement and some controlling interests, and the sport certainly had its shady, seedy side. Boxing was glad, then, to have fine, upstanding Joe Louis, the man who was undoubtedly above all that. Some 18,000 people were at Madison Square Garden on that December evening in 1947 (they paid over $216,000), when the usual pomp and ceremony that precedes a world heavyweight title fight got underway. There was the introduction of other star boxers — Gus Lesnevich, the world light-heavyweight champion, and Arturo Godoy who, with Tommy Farr the other, was only the second man to have gone fifteen rounds with Louis. The choice of referee was, on the face of it, somewhat strange in that the official, Ruby Goldstein, the former lightweight boxer known as the Jewel of the Ghetto, was a friend of the champion. But Goldstein was also one of the finest referees around at that time and he commanded a great deal of respect from all boxers, champions and no-hopers alike.

The fight opened with Louis, heavier and taller, adopting his old and much-loved technique of manoeuvering his man into a position where he could stab out his left hand until the opening was there for his right to finish the job. In the second minute of that opening round it looked as if Louis had, indeed, finished the job. A right to Jersey Joe's chin sent the challenger's jaw askew and his mouth gaping from the force of the blow. Before the war, when he was at his prime, Louis would not have let his man escape from such a position. A flurry of punches would have put him down and that would have been that. But this was an older, rustier champion. Walcott had the luxury of a split second to recover and it was enough to allow the challenger to fight back. In he came at Louis with left hooks and jabs. Then it happened! A short right to the champion's

jaw put Louis down. The champ was up at two, driven back to fight by damaged pride as much as anything, and it showed when he swung across a series of wild rights. Walcott was composed through the hail of punches and he crashed another right to Louis's jaw. The champion went into the ropes and the bell ended a sensational first round.

Walcott had taken the first round and he then took the second to confirm that this fight was not going to be over in the first quarter with Louis claiming another easy victory, as so many people had prophesied. A defeat for Joe Louis would have been one of the biggest boxing sensations of the age, infallible as had the champion become in people's eyes. Yet Jersey Joe Walcott, the poor black man who had known only too often what it was like to have an empty belly and not be able to feed the wife and kids, was well on the road to such a sensation. The third round found Louis still trying to catch the challenger, who continued his tactics of retreating, then weaving inside to score with that unexpected counter-punch that surprised Joe Louis every time it was landed.

It was a difficult time for the champion and for the first time in anyone's memory Louis seemed unable to work out what to do next. He was baffled by the challenger's back-pedalling and swift countering. What happened next surprised him even more. Louis threw a left which swished through thin air as the challenger danced away once more. Then Walcott countered again, this time with a right-hander of immense power. It cannoned into the champion's jaw, knocking it sideways and momentarily out of line with the rest of his head, and Joe Louis was down. As with the first knockdown, his pride was undoubtedly hurt, only this time there was little prospect of him leaping straight to his feet. He managed to get to his feet at seven, and then only after some considerable difficulty, and from then on Walcott was in the box seat. Always it was the same, retreat, bob, weave, counter, retreat... and so on. It was defensive boxing, of course, but it was winding Joe Louis up and the legs of the champion were doing an

Joe Louis is put down by Jersey Joe Walcott –
but Louis still got the decision.

enormous amount of work in following the challenger around the ring while scoring precious few punches for all that effort. In cost-effectiveness, Joe Louis's work rate was on the low-paying side. The eighth round came and went in much the same fashion, and so did much of the ninth. Everytime Joe Louis got into position to land a punch and make a real fight of it, Jersey Joe danced away and the champion was left standing there with no one in front of him.

Then, in the last minute of that ninth round, Louis at last managed to get Walcott bottled up against the ropes. There was no avenue of escape this time, no way in which the challenger could jink away to frustrate the Brown Bomber. Jersey Joe had to stand there and fight, or be knocked senseless like so many of Louis's opponents before him. Jersey Joe chose to fight . . . and fight he did. When the bell went, Walcott had survived a full minute of pounding and stayed on his feet, a fact which made the assembled experts look at each other and ask silently if Joe Louis's big punch had gone for ever. He'd had his man at his mercy and was still unable to deliver the final blow. There was not much change for Louis out of the tenth

round, and even when the champion managed to land a wicked right, the punch which he had been searching for all the fight, Walcott took it and then dished out some of his own fire.

The thirteenth round saw Walcott on the canvas, but he had only slipped and, eager to prove it, he was soon up and slamming a left which buried itself in the champion's face and sent him reeling backwards. The fourteenth round went to the champion who, for the first time in the fight, caught up with Walcott and punched him around the ring until the bell halted the proceedings. Then the final round: Louis went after Jersey Joe, determined to floor him. Walcott had obviously decided to keep running, and who could blame him? For he surely felt that he had done enough to win the fight on points and was certainly not going to repeat Billy Conn's mistake and open himself up to a Joe Louis sledgehammer at such a late stage. Walcott knew that, if it came to a slugging match, then he was no match for Louis. The bell ended the fight with Jersey Joe and his seconds well pleased with the way that the final round had gone. All that now remained was for the decision to be announced, for under New York rules the referee was supported by two judges and they scored the fight by the number of rounds, not points, that had in their opinion been won.

Joe Louis was actually on his way out of the ring before the result was announced and he had to be shepherded back by his handlers. Then came a hush. The announcer, Harry Balogh, came to the centre of the ring and told everyone that judge Frank Forbes had marked Louis the winner with eight rounds to six and one even. Then Ruby Goldstein's decision was announced. It was seven for Walcott, six for Louis, and two even. All now rested on the verdict of the other judge, Marty Monroe. You could have heard the proverbial pin drop: 'Judge Marty Monroe', intoned Balogh, 'nine rounds for Louis . . .' That was enough to lift the roof. No one heard the rest of the announcement — six rounds for Walcott and none even, as it happened — for it was academic. Joe Louis had retained his world heavyweight title. The noise of the spectators was not, however, that of adulation for the champion. The vast majority were incensed, for they thought that Jersey Joe Walcott had done more than enough to win. It was a highly debatable decision, certainly, but perhaps Walcott had only himself to blame for his backpedalling tactics, for no man had ever won a world title without attacking outright.

Of course, everyone demanded a rematch and it took place, this time at the Yankee Stadium, on 25 June 1948, when 42,657 people saw Louis win in more emphatic style, though for a long time he was hardly more impressive than the first fight. Then Walcott forgot the lessons of Billy Conn and decided to slug his way to victory, though who could blame him when he had been criticised for not making more of a fight of their first meeting? In the eleventh round Walcott, clearly on top, and having dropped Louis in the third round, got caught on the ropes. This time he did not box, or dance, his way clear. Louis hammered into him with a flurry of blows and Jersey Joe went to pieces. He had tried to swap blows and walked right into three magnificent straight lefts and

then a right. More blows pounded in and there was not really a KO punch. Walcott just slid to the floor under the barrage and was counted out.

Walcott duly and decisively beaten, Joe Louis then announced his retirement, unbeaten in twenty-six title bouts. If only he had stayed in retirement! Two years later, Ezzard Charles was the new champion, having taken up the vacant crown when the NBA asked him and Walcott to meet in Chicago. Charles won on points but only the NBA recognised him as New York and the Europeans did not. To prove his worth, Charles was then obliged to fight Gus Lesnevich (beaten when the referee stopped the fight in round seven), and Pat Valentino (KO'd in eight). New York came over when Charles stopped Freddie Beshore in fourteen rounds and then the man from Cincinnati found the Brown Bomber opposing him. In pre-war days Charles would not have lasted three rounds with Joe Louis. But now the old champ was forced to fight again for tax reasons. Slow and creaking, Joe was outpointed with ease. A sad end to a great champion, but there was more ignominy to come. Still Joe Louis could not afford to retire and two months later he was back in the ring. Eight wins against boxers who could largely be described as no-hopers, apart from a sixth-round KO over Lee Savold, the man recognised, by the British Board at least, as world champion, were followed by a fight against a young rising star called Rocky Marciano. On 26 October 1951, 37-year-old Joe Louis was hammered to the canvas in eight rounds by an almost apologetic Marciano who came into the Brown Bomber's dressing room afterwards and said, 'Joe, I'm sorry'. The referee that night was Ruby Goldstein, the great friend of Louis who had given Walcott the decision on the night that Jersey Joe thought he was robbed. Joe Louis grossed well over four and a half million dollars from his fights. It was sad that the need to pay the IRS a million dollars in back taxes did not allow him to retire as champion as everyone would have wished.

JERSEY JOE WALCOTT v ROCKY MARCIANO
World Heavyweight Championship
23 September 1952

One of the biggest boxing surprises of the post-war period was the night in Pittsburgh in July 1951 when Jersey Joe Walcott knocked out Ezzard Charles to become the oldest man to win the world heavyweight title. At the time of his KO win over 1-6 favourite Charles, Jersey Joe was reckoned to be thirty-seven years old, though later estimates added anything up to four years to that figure. Charles, after his defeat of Louis in the former champion's sad comeback, had beaten Nick Barone, Lee Oma, Jersey Joe (who he outpointed), and the tough Joey Maxim, before accepting a rematch with Walcott in what was their third title fight. This time Walcott delivered the goods and became the oldest challenger to take the title, beating the record of Cornishman Bob Fitzsimmons in 1897. Walcott then successfully defended his title against Charles, outpointing the ex-champion eleven months later in Philadelphia. Three months later Jersey Joe was in the ring to defend the title once more, this time against the man christened Rocco Marchegiano, but known through his ring career as Rocky Marciano. Jersey Joe was that night to be hit by what those who saw it claimed was 'the hardest punch of all time'.

Since 1937, when Joe Louis became only the second black man ever to win the title, every heavyweight champion of the world had been of negro origin; Louis himself, Charles and Walcott. Now, just as forty years before the world had looked for a 'white hope' capable of beating Jack Johnson, the fascinating question was being asked again: was there a white man good enough to win what, for the previous fifteen years, had become a total preserve of the black man?

Such a man emerged in the shape of Marciano the son of an Italian immigrant who had come to the United States in 1916. Marchegiano senior soon found himself in the US Army and it was the next world war which involved Rocky, so that it was 1947 before he had his first professional fight, and by then he was almost twenty-four.

The Brockton Blockbuster, which was Marciano's other nickname apart from, inevitably, The Rock, had set a staggering pace as a paid fighter by the time he earned the chance to fight for the world heavyweight title in 1952. Up to September that year he had fought forty-two times, and won every one of them. Moreover, thirty-seven of them had been by the knockout, and twenty-five had not got beyond the third round. His elevation to the national stage had come with his defeat of Louis, even if the Brown Bomber was over the hill, and what delighted the punters more than anything was that tremendous right hand of his, the devastating punch which Marciano himself called 'Suzy-Q'. Under the astute guidance of his trainer, Charlie Goldman, Rocky Marciano began preparations for the biggest fight of his life. He was by no means the biggest of heavyweights, standing a shade over 5ft 10in tall and with a short reach to match. Goldman had, however, taught him more than a few tricks to compensate for this lack of height and he went into his training camp full of confidence. Walcott, by some, reckoned to be thirty-nine years old, gave ten years to his opponent but was equally happy about the outcome of the fight. He told reporters that he could not agree with the odds which made the challenger the firm favourite, and pointed to the fact that he had

125

been in the professional fight game for well over twenty years compared to Marciano's five. It was going to be, claimed Jersey Joe, the easiest fight that any champion had ever enjoyed.

When the two men climbed into the ring that night, the champion's physical advantages were there for all to see. At fourteen stones he was twelve pounds heavier than Marciano, stood three inches taller, and had a reach of six inches more. Perhaps they remembered that twenty-six years before, to the very day, Gene Tunney had wrested from Jack Dempsey the world heavyweight title in this same arena before a record crowd of 120,757 people. This latest title fight attracted fewer than one-third of that number to the Municipal Stadium in Philadelphia where the cool night air made those in dinner jackets wish they had brought a top coat with them. Yet even though the fight attracted far less spectators (the fight was being screened in cinemas across the length and breadth of the United States) there was still that same electric atmosphere which

Rocky Marciano has ageing champion Jersey Joe Walcott in desperate trouble.

126

surrounds any world heavyweight title fight. There was the usual parade of champions, the excitement as show business stars, including Frank Sinatra, made their way to their seats, and all the razmatazz of a big fight night in America.

That first round was all action from start to finish. There was no feeling the temperature, no dipping the toe in the water. Before the echoes of the bell had died away the two men were into a close-quarters scrap, locked together and slugging in short little jabs which did not look much but which undoubtedly hurt. Then the champion got home a hard left to Marciano's middle section, followed by rights and lefts to his head. A right and then a left hook threatened to push Marciano's nose through the back of his head and he dropped for a count of three, with blood smearing his upper lip, not because it was cut but because that punch had opened up the blood vessels in the challenger's nose. It was the first time in his career, amateur or professional, that Rocky Marciano had felt what it was like to hit the canvas, and he did not like it one little bit. Jersey Joe did not make the mistake that Joe Louis had made during their first title fight. He gave Marciano no time to recover but was on the challenger in a flash, pumping in rights and lefts. Marciano's great strength got him through to the bell and although Walcott won the round, Rocky had fought back well enough to shake the champion with two punches to the face before the bell sounded.

The fans warmed to this fight and they were already on the edges of their seats when round two opened, eagerly anticipating developments. Walcott took the second round, though again Marciano was able to slam a left to the champion's head in the last few seconds. The Italian-American had largely ignored Jersey Joe's punching and conducted his own brand of attacking boxing, moving forward all the time and landing a few of the many hooks and swinging punches which he let fly. Walcott opened round three by cracking Marciano with a wicked left to the chin and the challenger

Walcott is smashed to defeat by the fighting machine that is Marciano - The Rock.

blinked hard. Jersey Joe was doing all the real boxing, showing up Marciano's limited style for what it was. At the bell they were exchanging punch for punch, though Joe's legs, ten years older than the challenger's, were still spry enough to float him out of trouble. Jersey Joe had taken the first three rounds and the way Marciano came out for the fourth suggested that the challenger had been ordered to get in straight away before Walcott had time to settle into his stride.

But Walcott again took the round, though he could not now fail to be impressed by

It's all over! Walcott is counted out and Marciano is the new champion.

Rocky Marciano's resilience under fire. In the fifth round Marciano landed a left under Walcott's heart which brought a grimace to the face of the champion. Blood trickled from his mouth as another left from Marciano landed on his face, but Walcott levelled the round with a right to the body and a left to the head which sent a shudder through Marciano's entire body, travelling down his legs and making them wobbly around the knees. The sixth round was Marciano's, though he took it only at the expense of a cut on the forehead from which blood pumped to mingle with that which was still trickling from his nose. It was blood and sweat which now flowed into Marciano's eyes, making him blink and lift a glove to wipe them clean for a second or two. The round ended on a high note for the challenger and he had now forced Jersey Joe to trade punch for punch and to abandon his graceful progress around the ring, skipping lightly out of trouble. Now the progress of the fight began to tip this way and that. Walcott came back to his more familiar style and took the next two rounds. But the ninth went to Marciano who once more forced Walcott to stand and fight; he did so in the tenth as well and took that in the same way. It was by now a tough, brawling fight with not an inch given by either man.

By the end of the tenth round Walcott was looking his age and the scales began to tip in the challenger's favour. Jersey Joe, while losing the previous round, had scored some points himself and there was little in it. But the longer the fight went, the better it was for the younger man and in the tenth he sensed that he was getting on top and that Walcott was running out of steam. The blood flowed in the eleventh round. Jersey Joe had cuts to his left eye and cheek; Marciano had a cut near his right eye which looked bad and which was causing him problems. Round twelve saw still more blood from these injuries; though now both men were slowing

up and Marciano, in particular, seemed less able to get to grips with the champion. Jersey Joe hammered him with the occasional flurry and when the round ended Walcott was in a commanding lead. All the champion had to do in order to retain his title was to stay on his feet for the remaining nine minutes of this fight. In fact, however, he managed to do that for less than one minute.

Marciano came out looking a terrible mess. His scalp was split, lips were swollen to twice their normal size, his right eye was badly cut and his left eye had closed completely. For twelve rounds he had taken everything that Jersey Joe Walcott cared to throw at him and, although he had taken some of the honours himself, he was still far short of winning this fight if it went the distance. Forty-four seconds into the thirteenth round Rocky Marciano let go Suzy-Q. To say he hit Walcott with a short, powerful right is like saying that someone dropped a bomb on Hiroshima. It was the most telling blow ever thrown in a professional fight. Jersey Joe never saw it coming, for surely, Marciano's hand came through faster than any human eye could capture. It exploded on Jersey Joe's jaw and wrenched his head back with such force that it is a wonder it did not snap his neck. Walcott was unconscious even before he hit the resin. Sight and sound meant nothing to the champion who was paralysed by what one ringside witness described as 'the hardest punch of all time'. Referee Charles Daggert went through the formality of the count and then the ring was invaded by hundreds of fans from Marciano's hometown of Brockton. Rocky was the first white heavyweight world champion since Braddock lost his crown to Louis in June 1937. He had achieved it, not with ring craft, but with sheer courage and one sledgehammer blow which knocked the hopes of America's black boxers into oblivion for the next four years.

ROCKY MARCIANO v EZZARD CHARLES
―――――――――――― World Heavyweight Championship ――――――――――――
17 June 1954

After beating Joe Louis in 1951, Rocky Marciano earned his shot at Jersey Joe Walcott's title with impressive wins over Lee Savold, Gino Buonvino, Bernie Reynolds and Harry Matthews. After taking the title from Walcott in 1952, The Rock defended it six times, letting Jersey Joe have first bite in Chicago in May 1953. That fight was a fiasco and lasted less than two and a half minutes. Marciano hit Jersey Joe with a left hook, followed it with a right to the jaw and Walcott sat on the canvas and appeared to be musing over the fact that he had been knocked down, when the referee counted him out. That he then scrambled to his feet and, upon hearing the boos of the crowd,

One of the biggest surprises of 1951 was Jersey Joe Walcott's KO of Ezzard Charles on 18 July

complained that he had beaten the count, did him no credit at all. It was a blessing that he did not fight again and a pity that he did not take his manager's advice and retire after that first defeat by Marciano. Four months later, Marciano allowed Roland La Starza to fight him for the title and removed him in the eleventh round of their fight in New York. So Rocky had confirmed his status with two emphatic victories, but in June 1954 he came up against the former champion Ezzard Charles in the Yankee Stadium. What followed was one of the most savage of all the gruelling battles staged for the world heavyweight championship.

Charles, of course, had taken the vacant title when Joe Louis first retired. His early life had been spent in Georgia, hardly an easy place in which to be a black man in those days, and his amateur boxing career saw him undefeated in forty-odd fights. Charles turned professional at the age of eighteen and within three years he could have fought Tony Zale for the middleweight title, had the champion not been otherwise engaged in the US Navy. After his own service for Uncle Sam, Charles fought his way to within challenging distance of Gus Lesnevich's light-heavyweight crown, but Gus managed to stay out of Charles's way until Ezzard moved into the heavyweight division and, after some impressive victories over people like Joe Baksi and Elmer Ray, found his way clear to challenge the world title.

The way in which Ezzard Charles won that title, and later lost it to Jersey Joe Walcott, have already been chronicled in previous chapters. Now, in mid-1954, the man they called the Cincinnati Cobra was given the opportunity to become the first man to regain the title and so return it to black domination once more. Charles had already had one opportunity to win back the world crown when he allowed himself to be outpointed by Walcott in June 1952, and for the next two years he was not considered worthy of another chance, though he had fourteen fights and won eleven of them. Then, out of the blue, came the chance to

fight Marciano. His defeat of Louis when the champion of old was forced back into the ring to help pay his taxes had made Charles an unpopular man in both black and white circles. If, however, he could beat Rocky Marciano and regain the title for his colour . . . well, that would make him, in black America at least, the most popular fighter since the great Joe.

Though he was only two years older than Marciano, Charles was a boxer of infinitely greater experience. His boxing career had started in the amateur ranks eighteen years previously and in 103 professional fights he had emerged victorious ninety-two times. He was by no means an assured box office success, however. Though he possessed a combination of boxing skills which were good enough to take him to the top, he was never an exciting fighter and seemed almost reluctant to hammer his man when he had him in trouble, a fact which may date back to the awful day in 1948 when he scored a tenth-round KO over Sam Baroudi who died immediately afterwards. It was not Ezzard Charles's fault, of course, and even the unfortunate opponent's family were at pains to express their sympathy almost as much for Charles as for their dear departed Sam. It was a terrible experience for Ezzard though, and, as he was not a naturally aggressive fighter in the first place (that is to say he did not possess the 'killer' instinct of so many of his trade) it further eroded his determination to crucify a man who was already his inferior. Having said all that, there were plenty of fighters who *did* feel an Ezzard Charles KO punch and in his career he won nearly sixty bouts inside the distance, such fighters as Elmer 'Violent' Ray, Archie Moore and Anton Christoforidis feeling the sleep-inducing qualities of a Charles punch. Yet, when he met Marciano, Ezzard had no reputation for being a big puncher.

The fight still attracted 47,585 people to the Yankee Stadium and they paid over half a million dollars through the gate. Added to that were radio and television rights as the fight was screened coast-to-coast, and film rights brought the turnover for the fight into

Blood streams from Marciano's eye as he distorts Charles's face with a right.

the million dollar bracket. Those lucky enough to have tickets and not have to rely on the second-hand atmosphere of celluloid were treated to the usual pre-fight spectacular. There were the champions, past and present, the film stars, the singers, the politicians, the oil barons, the industrialists, and the gangsters one supposes, all the extras in a supporting cast of thousands, though when the bell went, all attention was focused on the two men, one white, one black, under the arc lights of the ring.

Charles, who was expected to be heavier than the champion, scaled 13st 3$^1/_2$lbs, two pounds lighter than Rocky Marciano, but in the first round, though Rocky inevitably struck the first blow, it was the challenger who made all the running and took the round with a series of uppercuts and his familiarly ponderous left. Already Marciano's face showed signs of wear and in the second round Charles 'improved' on that, bringing blood from the champion's nose. But it was Marciano's round by a fraction. He shook Charles with a left hook to the jaw, and while the challenger was still wincing, thudded home two rights to his sleek black body. The third round went to Charles, though again Marciano plundered the challenger's strength with some hooks and uppercuts, some of which landed, many of which, however, did

not. Marciano's uglier side showed in this round. His head and elbows did a lot of rough work at close quarters and Charles was fortunate on one occasion to evade an uppercut which, if it had landed, might well have parted his head from his body. Marciano's left eye was opened up in the fourth round, a cut above it spilling blood so that the champion was operating for much of the round with only one eye to see what Charles planned for him next. Charles warmed to his task and flicked out again and again at that cut, hoping that he could worsen it to the point where the referee might have to intervene.

The Cincinnati Cobra came out for the fifth, looking to inflict still more damage on Rocky's eye, but he reckoned without Marciano's incredible staying power. Marciano's seconds had done a good job on the cut in the interval and now the champion managed to keep Charles at bay for much of the next three minutes, so much so that he took the round. Rocky increased that advantage in the seventh round. He was on the offensive from the first bell and when he saw the chance to land his first big right of the fight he did so. It landed fair and square on Ezzard's jaw, and he tottered back and almost lost his balance as both feet could not retreat fast enough to maintain his centre of gravity. In the seventh round Marciano, with blood now pouring unabated from that left eye, cracked Charles again, rocking him back once more with a right, which this time was followed by a tremendous left, to the jaw. But Charles did not go down and he then surprised Rocky with a right and a left, probably edging the round with some useful close-quarters boxing.

Round eight saw Charles's right eye cut, but with Rocky's left eye now streaming with blood too, it seemed almost academic. It was a particularly bruising three minutes. Marciano jostled in again with head and elbows and did enough to win the round. The ninth saw Charles hammered by a left hook to the jaw, though he did get in two of his own to the champion's chin, and again the champion took the round. Rocky was fighting for his undefeated record like he had never fought before. He was the man doing all the scoring and a succession of rights left Ezzard gasping.

Rocky might have, indeed should have, finished the fight in the next round. He had Ezzard Charles at his mercy, his legs wobbling, his arms so tired that he could hardly raise them. But the champion lost his head. He hammered punch after punch at the black man in a desperate bid to finish him off; and every one missed. Marciano instead found only fresh air, and yet instead of flailing those punches, all he really had to do was take careful aim just once, and it would have all been over. As it was, the bell saved Charles who staggered back to his corner relieved and somewhat amazed that he had been allowed to get off the hook. Whatever had happened to Suzy-Q?

The eleventh round again saw Marciano fail to deliver that punch, though Charles was hardly in a fit condition to avoid it had it been posted. Round twelve saw the champion bring blood spurting from Charles's mouth; and round thirteen again had Ezzard absorbing so much punishment that his face presented a gruesome picture, all cuts, bruises and swellings and the best possible advertisement for the anti-boxing lobby. Yet somehow the challenger managed to win

the penultimate round, thanks to a series of punches which again turned the carefully patched-up skin above Marciano's left eye into raw meat. Two left hooks caught the champion by surprise at the start of the last round but then Marciano got to work and for the rest of that round he smashed punch after punch into Charles's body. For the first time he jammed Charles against the ropes and from then until the end of the contest, hammered him so hard that when the bell went there was an audible sigh of relief from the huge crowd. Marciano was still the champion, winning the decision like this: referee Ruby Goldstein, eight rounds to Marciano, five to Charles and two even; judge Harold Barnes eight to Marciano, six to Charles and one even; judge Arthur Aidala nine to Marciano, five to Charles and one even.

Ezzard Charles had given Rocky Marciano one of his most difficult fights and in the end it was the champion's youth which was the deciding factor. It was certainly one of the most savage, all-action title fights ever seen. Three months to the night after that scrap, Ezzard Charles was in the ring against Marciano for the rematch. Again there was plenty of action but this time the fight did not get beyond the eighth round. At that point Marciano hit him with that famous KO punch and down and out went Charles, though not before he had caused the champion a real scare by opening up a serious cut on his nose in the previous round. Perhaps if Marciano had not then landed a quick knockout, the fight might not have been allowed to proceed much longer, so bad was that gash. Ezzard Charles's career dipped alarmingly after that. He fought a further twenty-three times and lost thirteen of them. His last fight was a points defeat by Alvin Green in Oklahoma City in September 1959, though, sad to record, British fans saw the sight of the former world champion being disqualified against Dick Richardson in October 1956. Ezzard Charles died of multiple sclerosis on 27 May 1975, six weeks before his fifty-fourth birthday.

ROCKY MARCIANO v ARCHIE MOORE
_____ World Heavyweight Championship _____
21 September 1955

Rocky Marciano had the perfect record in his all-too-short career of forty-nine professional fights and forty-nine straight wins. Gene Tunney was the only other heavyweight world title holder to retire undefeated; he and Marciano were the only ones to stay retired with their records unblemished. Like Tunney, Rocky Marciano was a wise man who knew when enough was enough, though that is not to say that he could not have fought on and retained his crown for some time, had he wanted too. After his second defeat of Ezzard Charles, though, Rocky had taken nine rounds to dispose of Don Cockell in San Francisco: the first Briton to fight for boxing's ultimate prize since Tommy Farr met Joe Louis in 1937. It disappointed the champion that this British and British Empire champion had taken so long to go, though in the end the fight was won easily and its effect on Cockell was so great that he retired soon afterwards. Then there was the fight with Archie Moore, probably the greatest light-heavyweight of all time. That came four months after the Cockell fight, and although Rocky once more emerged victorious, he suffered the ignominy of being knocked down for only the second time in a competitive fight. Old-timer Moore pushed the champion hard in the Yankee Stadium and Rocky's last fight was probably one of his most difficult. It was also one of the best of world heavyweight title fights.

Archie Moore had been boxing since 1936 and this fight, his first for the world heavyweight title, did not take place until he was forty-one, so he would have easily beaten Jersey Joe Walcott's record of being the oldest man to win the title. Archie Moore had

been boxing for eighteen months as a professional before he tasted his first defeat against a boxer called Johnny Romero. He fought in towns and cities, big and small, across the length and breadth of America, and in Australia, suffering illness at times in his career, but never letting that stop his quest for a world title, the chance of which eluded him until 1952.

In consecutive years 1946-8 Moore was beaten by Ezzard Charles, outpointed on the first two occasions and then stopped inside eight rounds. Moore kept going and at the end of 1952 he was allowed a shot at the world light-heavyweight title. Just eight days before Christmas Day that year, he met Joey Maxim in St Louis. Maxim had wrested the title from Freddie Mills in January 1950 and Archie Moore took it from him. Maxim had successfully defended it against Bob Murphy in New York over the distance, and against Sugar Ray Robinson, world welterweight champion from 1946 to 1950 and then middleweight champion. Robinson, pound for pound probably the greatest of all postwar boxers, was well ahead by the thirteenth round but was then overcome by the excessive heat in the Yankee Stadium and retired. Archie was a clear winner in Maxim's next defence and he allowed the ex-champion to have the first two chances at it, defeating him on points on both occasions. Before he met Marciano for the heavyweight crown, Moore had two more defences for his light-heavyweight title, beating Harold Johnson in New York, KO'ing his opponent in the fourteenth round, and then he stopped Carl Olson, the middleweight champion, in the third round in June 1955.

Almost exactly three months later Archie

Moore was stepping into the ring looking to become the oldest man ever to win the heavyweight title. The fight was set up after a big publicity campaign aimed at matching the holders of the heavyweight and cruiserweight crowns. Three Toledo men, none of whom had any financial stake in Moore, set about planning his assault on the premier title. Five hundred sports writers were bombarded with publicity material and there was even a 'wanted' poster showing Marciano's picture and signed by Archie Moore, the 'sheriff'. It worked and eventually the champion agreed to meet Moore on 20 September 1955; the fight was actually put back a day because a hurricane was boiling up in the area. Archie Moore, also known as The Mongoose, had fought no less than 183 bouts up to this day and he had lost twenty-one of them, though only one in the last six years. One hundred and thirteen of his victories had been by knockouts up to then, and over fifty of his opponents had failed to make it past the third round. That was a pretty impressive record and Marciano knew it. In fact he had been in full-time training for nearly three months to prepare for this, his sixth defence of the world title.

Archie Moore's head shudders as Marciano lands a right.

Jack Dempsey was there that night, as were Joe Louis, Max Baer and Jim Braddock, all men who had won boxing's supreme prize. There were champions and past champions from other weights as well, the usual glitter of showbusiness stars, and everyone else from millionaires to stevedores. They were all in their seats as the bell sounded and this most intriguing of world heavyweight title fights got underway. The first round was fought at close quarters and when the three minutes were up it was impossible to separate the two men on points. There had been much in-fighting, both men had scored with short-arm punches, and although it was Moore who managed to do most of the clinching, he got in enough shots to earn a fair division of the spoils.

In the second round he almost won the fight. Rocky Marciano came out and went into action at once, lashing lefts and rights at the challenger. Moore let fly just one punch, a right cross, which threw the champion clean off his feet. In most cases it would have ended the fight because there have been few men in the history of boxing who could take such a punch and then beat the count. Marciano was one of those few and he was

up at four. Then Archie Moore was the victim of a cruel stroke of fate. Had this not been a title fight then there would have been a mandatory standing count of eight, but this did not apply to a fight for the world crown. Sadly for Moore, referee Harry Kessler momentarily forgot and while Marciano, who also appeared to think that he was entitled to that standing count, waited, Kessler jumped in and for a vital couple of seconds prevented Moore from doing what he was perfectly entitled to do: go in and crack Marciano again. It is open to debate whether Archie Moore could have finished the fight then; what is certain is that he was prevented from trying. When he did get to grips with the champion, Moore hammered home another right to the jaw and Marciano looked groggy; when further punches were landed on the champion's nose it began to bleed; and Moore finished the round, winning it convincingly, with an uppercut which made Rocky wince as it buried itself under his chin.

Marciano seemed to forget about the pain of the second round when he came out for the third. Lefts and rights to face and body won the champion the round, even though Moore did hurt him with another right cross to the jaw. But Moore was in more pain than the champion and Marciano slipped into top gear in the fourth round. They traded punches all right, but Moore was short-changed by four-to-one and Marciano permitted himself a smile as he went back to the corner. Moore, however, took the fifth round when his punching proved more accurate than that of the champion. Marciano hammered away in fine style, but many of his blows fell short and it was the cruiserweight champion who scored more often, picking his spot and then delivering the goods. He had kept his head where Marciano had perhaps lost his a little, thinking that he could smash his way to victory without further ado.

They were about even now, but in the sixth round Rocky Marciano changed the course of the fight. He caught Moore with a left and a right to the chin which dumped the challenger on the canvas. Moore stayed down for five, but when he got up he found that Marciano had trapped him against the ropes. It was the last place on earth that a boxer wanted to find himself when this unarmed fighting machine that was Rocky Marciano was on the loose. One says 'unarmed' and yet in his leather-cloaked fists, Rocky had all the armour he needed. Another fearsome crack to the chin from that right hand and Archie Moore was down again, this time rising only as the referee signalled the eight seconds. Moore lasted out the round and after a brief visit from the medical officer he was out for round seven. Marciano dictated the fight now, choosing exactly where in the ring it should take place. He dropped Moore again, though the challenger was able to get up at only three this time, and brushed aside Moore's now feeble attempts to fight back. The eighth round signalled the near end to the fight. Moore tried every trick he had learned in almost two decades of boxing, but against such sheer strength as Marciano possessed it was all but useless. There was no place to hide, no way to avoid the punishing hands. For the last minute Moore was subjected to a barrage of punches and six seconds before the bell he was floored again. When the end of the round came it was academic to wonder if Archie might have made it to his feet in time. The next round was to settle any arguments about that.

Once more the medical officer checked on Moore's condition before allowing the fight to proceed. The first time had been no more than a cursory glance, the second was a much more serious enquiry. It took Marciano just seventy-nine seconds of the ninth round to put Archie Moore down for the fifth time. It had taken Don Cockell nine rounds to succumb to Rocky Marciano and Archie Moore went in the same number of rounds. After one minute and nineteen seconds he sank to his knees in his own corner and strung his right hand across the bottom rope as Kessler counted him out while Rocky Marciano wandered almost unconcernedly to his stool. It was a left hook, not the

Moore is a pathetic sight as he goes down for the final count. Marciano strolls back to his corner, the job done well.

fearsome right, which delivered the final blow. It left Moore looking blankly towards the retreating figure of the champion. Rocky Marciano had fought his last fight.

Rocky announced his retirement and stuck to it. He was a warm and generous man, despite those who said the contrary, and it was a tragedy when his life was cut short by a plane crash in Iowa on 31 August 1969, just before his forty-sixth birthday. Archie Moore carried on. With Marciano gone, Floyd Patterson and Tommy (Hurricane) Jackson fought an eliminator which Patterson won. Moore then fought Patterson on 30 November 1956 in Chicago and was knocked out in the fifth round and Patterson at twenty years and ten months became the youngest man to win the title, so the fight would have produced a record either way with Moore the oldest to have won it. Incredibly, Archie Moore kept on fighting until he was nearly fifty. After he had defended his cruiser-weight title against Yolande Pompey in London in June 1956, he fought Patterson for the heavyweight title. On 8 July 1957 the NBA and New York declared his light-heavyweight title vacant through his in-activity. Harold Johnson and Tony Anthony were ordered to fight for it, but the authorities later relented and on 20 September that year, Moore met Anthony in Los Angeles and stopped him in seven rounds after a terrible beating. Moore defended it three more times but by February 1961 the NBA named Harold Johnson the new champion after he KO'd Jess Bowdry in nine rounds. Archie Moore boxed yet another title

defence, outpointing the Italian Giulio Rinaldi in New York on 10 June 1961, now aged forty-seven. In February the following year Moore lost the recognition of the New York State Athletic Commission and when Johnson, the 34-year-old from Philadelphia, outpointed Doug Jones in that city on 12 May that year, he received universal recognition as Archie Moore's successor. It should perhaps be said that Moore beat Johnson four times out of five between 1949 and 1954, but it was not unreasonable that he was now shorn of his championship, for he could not now make the light-heavyweight limit. Yet still he would not hang up his gloves and two heavyweight victories in 1962 actually saw him listed sixth in the world in the *Ring* magazine ratings. On 15 November 1962, Archie Moore met a young boxer then called Cassius Clay, and was knocked out in the fourth round of their Los Angeles fight. Clay was but four fights away from winning the world title from Sonny Liston. Archie went on for still a little longer and on 15 March 1963 he knocked out a boxer called Mike Di-Biase in Phoenix, Arizona in his 228th fight. It was his 140th KO win and he was nine months short of his fiftieth birthday. Then this remarkable boxer called it a day, mindful perhaps of the day that he almost dented Rocky Marciano's perfect record. Rocky might have eventually won that last fight with apparent ease. But for a few seconds in that second round in the Yankee Stadium, Archie Moore stood poised to win another great fight.

FLOYD PATTERSON v INGEMAR JOHANSSON
World Heavyweight Championship
26 June 1959

Sweden is not a country noted for its boxing and in 1959 there were perhaps a dozen or so professionals from that country. Yet on a rainy June evening that year, one of them, a 4-1 shot named Ingemar Johansson, shocked boxing circles rigid by becoming only the fourth non-American since the days of bare-knuckle fighting to win the heavyweight championship of the world. Before some 18,000 fight fans, Johansson, from Gothenburg, arrived regarded as something of a joke and went away leaving none of them laughing as he delivered a right hand of such immense power that it ended the American domination of the world heavyweight crown. On the receiving end of that punch, called the Hammer of Thor, was Floyd Patterson. In one of the most sensational fights of all time, the title was taken out of the States for the first time since 1934 when Primo Carnera's reign came to an end. The giant Italian who lost his title to Max Baer was also regarded as something of a joke in his day. Perhaps he was, but there was no doubting that this latest non-American challenger was a real boxer, a real champion whose powerful punching took everyone, including of course, the vanquished champion Patterson, very much by surprise.

Patterson's world title came with the resignation of Rocky Marciano. The former Olympic middleweight champion — he took that title in Helsinki in 1952 — hailed from North Carolina. A month after returning from the Olympics he turned professional and as a now quick-moving heavyweight with a useful punch, he had lost only one fight, a highly-debatable points reverse against Joey Maxim, prior to meeting Archie Moore for the vacant world title in November

1956. Moore was the favourite but the young Patterson put him away in five rounds to become the youngest man to win the title. A left hook finished the job in the Chicago Stadium, though Patterson was already well ahead on points. Floyd Patterson won the world heavyweight title at a time when for 'political' reasons wound around the International Boxing Club, big-time boxing in general in the States, and the heavyweight title in particular was going through a pretty grim time.

Formed in 1949, the IBC was to control all big boxing in the United States until 1960, and even then it took a Supreme Court judgement to break its stranglehold on the sport. Patterson's manager, Brooklyn-based Gus D'Amato, refused to allow Patterson to meet many of the challengers put forward by the IBC, resisting its attempts to take control of his boy. The principle was a laudable one, but the result was that Patterson was forced to avoid all the really good challengers and instead accept fights with second-raters. His first four title defences can only be described as 'mismatches'. First there was Tommy (Hurricane) Jackson, who had been beaten by the champion thirteen months earlier in an eliminator to decide who should fight Moore. Jackson was an illiterate — they called him 'The Animal' — and the only justification for his being allowed to fight for the title was that the previous Patterson-Jackson fight had gone to the man who was to become champion only by a split decision. On 29 July 1957, at the New York Polo Grounds, Patterson underlined the fact that this was nonsense by smashing Jackson all around the ring until Ruby Goldstein was forced to intercede in the tenth round. The

137

fight was staged by a New York dressmaker called Emil Lence and was the first independently-staged heavyweight title fight for several years.

Then came the most farcical fight of all. Patterson met the Olympic champion, Peter Rademacher, who took that title in Melbourne in 1956. In what was his professional debut, Rademacher was allowed to challenge for the world title, though there was a storm of protest from many quarters, and although he managed to put Patterson on the canvas for a count of four in the second round, he was himself downed six times before being knocked out in the sixth round. That fight took place in Seattle, just three weeks after Patterson's defeat of Jackson. A year then passed and on 18 August 1958, Patterson defended his title once more, this time against an unknown Texan called Roy Harris from the intriguingly-named town of Cut and Shoot. Harris was a colourful

Ingemar Johansson was the shock champion from Sweden.

character; he was then unbeaten in twenty-two professional fights and apparently used to go in for alligator wrestling, though a year's military service had halted his battles both in the ring and in the swamp. The fight took place in Los Angeles and after Harris managed to floor Patterson in the second round he was beaten so badly that he was unable to come out for the thirteenth round.

These so-called title defences were now verging on the ludicrous, but Patterson and D'Amato had not yet ended the comedy. They arranged to meet Brian London, who had just been beaten for the British title by Henry Cooper, in, of all places, Indianapolis. The British Boxing Board of Control quite rightly refused to sanction such a fight but London went ahead with it anyway and was not surprisingly KO'd in the eleventh round. So far, the boxers assembled to challenge Floyd Patterson for his world title had not amounted to very much, but there was a fight looming on the horizon against the Swedish and European heavyweight champion, Ingemar Johansson. While that prospect did not look all that much more exacting than some of Patterson's previous fights, the man from Waco, North Carolina was soon to learn of his error.

Ingemar Johansson had won the International Golden Gloves in 1951 before going on to compete in the 1952 Olympic Games. While Patterson was winning the middleweight title in those Games, the Swede was competing as a heavyweight. In his fight with the giant American black fighter Ed Sanders, the Swede was disqualified for 'not trying'. The fight was reduced to a farce as the giant American followed the Swede around the ring. It was the final of the heavyweight competition and Johansson was branded a coward for his failure to make a fight of it. Yet less than a year later he had lifted the Scandanavian heavyweight title as a professional. Thereafter, he proved himself to be a man with a considerable punch. Twenty-two wins in a row included fourteen by the knockout including, on 30 September 1956, a thirteenth-round KO of the Italian Franco Cavicchi in Bologna, a

Round three and Patterson bites the resin once more as the Swede moves in for the kill.

victory which gave Johansson the European title. The British boxers Peter Bates and Joe Bygraves had both been beaten by the Swede, who KO'd poor Bates in two rounds and broke his jaw into the bargain, and now Henry Cooper was lined up to meet Johansson in Stockholm. This was not 'Our 'Enery' of later years and the British fighter was utterly humiliated in five rounds. The following year, Johansson defended his European title against the British champion Joe Erskine and forced Erskine to retire in the thirteenth round of their fight in Gothenburg. A fourth-round KO of Heinz Neuhaus followed in that same city and then Johansson scored his most important win to date. On 14 September 1958, again in Gothenburg, he knocked out the American Eddie Machen in the first round. Machen was a leading contender for the world title but within two minutes and sixteen seconds, the Swede had jumped the queue.

With Machen disposed of, and the other leading American contender Zora Folley also out of the way for the moment, the logical contender for Patterson's crown was not from within the United States, but from the unlikely boxing country of Sweden. D'Amato was now forced to realise that his champion must fight someone of greater note than the likes of Rademacher, the willing amateur, Harris, the alligator-wrestling Texan, or the brawling Britisher, Brian London. Ingemar Johansson trained for the fight which was now the inevitable result of his removal of all the European and American challengers, at Grossingers, the Catskill Mountain resort where Rocky Marciano had once prepared for his title fights. For Marciano there was only a spartan existence and a gruelling training schedule. For Johansson the accommodation had to be more luxurious and whereas Rocky had seen precious little of his wife when training, the Swede an entourage consisting of his attractive girlfriend, Brigit Lundgren, his parents, sister, brother, doctor and trainer. Where Rocky spent most of his time at Grossingers either sparring or pounding the roads, Johansson seemed more at home beside the swimming pool or playing golf. He explained away this unusual routine to reporters thus: 'If I train too hard I use up all my energy. Better to save it for the real thing'.

The real thing was set for 26 June 1959. In fact it should have been staged the previous evening but a torrential rainstorm ruled it out. As it was, the attendance was a disappointing 18,215, the weather no doubt keeping away many more thousands, and the Yankee Stadium lacked something of its usual electric atmosphere for a world title fight. The first two rounds also lacked much drama. The Swede weighed in at spot on fourteen stones, exactly a stone heavier than the champion who was just over two years younger, and both men looked nervous under the glare of the lamps which sent steam rising from the damp, sweaty bodies of the fighters. Right away in the distance there was an occasional rumble of thunder. When the fight got underway, however, there was precious little thunder and lightning in the ring. For two-thirds of that opening round it was difficult to spot a punch of any kind. The efforts which were made consisted only of little 'touches', with both boxers content to amble around the ring and flick out the very occasional pat. Eventually Patterson tried a right hand which found its way high to the head of the challenger and then the bell clanged and the gladiators went back to their respective corners. An even round and one which had hardly stirred the crowd from their popcorn and hotdogs.

The second round gave no one any real hope of action, either. Johansson tickled Patterson with a succession of flicking lefts which, while they seemed to be annoying the champion, did nothing to hurt him. As the round proceeded the champion began to get a little irked at the apparent reluctance of the Swede to fight. He said as much in his book *Victory Over Myself* (Pelham Books 1962):

'. . . There were people in the ball park who paid one hundred dollars for a seat at ringside and some of them were already beginning to boo because there just wasn't any action in the fight. I could understand their dissatisfaction. It seemed a boring fight to me and the burden was on me to make it more interesting.' At the end of that second round Patterson, who admitted later that he was almost as angry with himself as with Johansson, threw a scowl at the challenger as he moved to his corner.

There can seldom have been a round such as the third round of this fight, coming as it did in direct contrast to the yawn which had gone before. Patterson came out and was again met by that irritating left of Johansson's which was doing no damage, but which was preventing him from making a fight of it. The champion bobbed his head down in an attempt to escape the maddening left. As he did so, Johansson sent in another left, only this time it was made of steel, not marshmallow. A stunning hook slammed into the champion's face and jerked him up; it was followed by a right which turned Patterson's facial features into something resembling a reflection in a fairground hall of funny mirrors. Only Floyd Patterson was not laughing. He was down on the canvas and fighting desperately to regain his feet and cling on to his crown. He made it at nine and then turned away from the challenger, wandering back glassy-eyed to his opponent's corner. Johansson followed him and dropped him again for another nine, again with the deadly Hammer of Thor right hand. Up again, and down again went Patterson, this time for the count of six and with blood splashing from his nose. The fourth time the champion went down again saw him back on his feet at six, only to fall again almost without help from Johansson. Another obliging right landed the champion on the canvas for the sixth time, and when his body hit the resin a seventh, referee Ruby Goldstein considered that enough was enough. The Hammer of Thor had caused one of the biggest shocks in post-war boxing.

FLOYD PATTERSON v INGEMAR JOHANSSON
World Heavyweight Championship
13 March 1961

By the 1960s, boxing had undergone some fundamental changes. In London Jack Solomons's wonderful era as a promoter was over and a new king, Harry Levene, was set to hold the stage. Boxing had moved into the space age and British fight fans who could stay awake were now able to wander into a West End cinema in the small hours of the morning to see live action of world title fights being staged, at that very moment, on the far side of the Atlantic, thanks to Jarvis Astaire's far-reaching business acumen. In the United States, the stranglehold of the International Boxing Club was broken for good. Men like Jim Norris were found guilty of infringing the US anti-trust laws and they were forced to sell their shares in Madison Square Garden, while the shady figure of hoodlum Frank Carbo was removed from boxing. Carbo, found guilty of extortion and conspiracy, began a twenty-five year prison sentence and boxing's air is all the cleaner for it. Also in the United States, Floyd Patterson, the youngest man ever to win the world heavyweight title was now the first man to regain it.

The Swinging Sixties were just six months old when Patterson faced Ingemar Johansson at the New York Polo Grounds. It was a year since the Swede took the title so sensationally and he had not bothered to defend it since. 'They never come back' is one of boxing's oldest clichés, but on 20 June 1960, Floyd Patterson *did* come back. From the beginning of the fight a heavier, remodelled Patterson took the fight to the champion. Johansson, who had spent the last twelve months modelling and looking at film scripts, was attacked with a barrage of two-handed punches from the former champion. In the fifth round Patterson landed a left hook that flattened Johansson and the Swede made it up again at nine. The Scandanavian then managed to avoid Patterson for a full minute, but Floyd would not be outdone. Another one-two barrage was followed by that lethal left hook and this time Johansson cracked his head on the canvas for good measure and was counted out. It was his first professional defeat.

Patterson's knockout of Johansson was a frightening experience for those who saw it. The punch which delivered the KO was one of the hardest left hooks ever seen, Johansson's unconsciousness lasted far longer than was healthy, and when his left leg began to twitch and quiver, there were many at the ringside who began to fear the very worst. But Ingemar Johansson happily recovered and with the championship back in Patterson's grasp it seemed that there ought to be a deciding fight between the two, the 'best of three' as it were, which would decide once and for all who was the better of these two heavyweights. Certainly Patterson needed the fight. He ached to be considered a really *great* heavyweight champion, although, Johansson apart, his choice of opponents left little proved. The return was duly arranged, but this time it was not to be held at either of the two New York venues which had staged the first two fights. On 13 March 1961, the two met again, this time at the Miami Beach Convention Hall.

The weigh-in for the fight produced some mild sensations. Both men were heavier than for their first two fights, Patterson weighing 13st 12¾lb, which was to give Johansson slightly less of an advantage than in their first meeting when he was exactly one stone heavier than the champion. Now he weighed 14st 10^1/$_2$lb. The other shock was that it was announced that the mandatory eight count was going to be used. This was a surprise, for it was supposed to be there to protect novice boxers, and since no greenhorns were supposed to fight for world titles, it had never before been used in the States, as far as anyone could remember. An academic point, one might say, but before the fight was over, that ruling on the 'standing count' was going to have a very significant bearing on the outcome.

In the first meeting between these two, the opening round was nothing more than a powder-puff encounter. Not so here. Johansson almost at once decided to launch the Hammer of Thor. It came across, but not so fast as the time it caught Patterson in the Yankee Stadium. Patterson saw it coming and was able to block it. At once there was the feeling that the Swede had launched his rocket too soon. The early-warning system inside Floyd Patterson's brain had sent its message down the nerves and ensured that the missile exploded harmlessly. Now what was Ingemar Johansson to do? 13,984 people began to wonder as Patterson twice more raised his gloves and allowed the Swede's most deadly weapon to detonate itself in mid-air, far from its intended target. The only effect that this early assault did have was to send Patterson off-balance. It meant that the champion could not counter-attack. Before he could right himself, Johansson shot out his right again, this time hitting home and sending Patterson to the canvas. The champion got up at five, and was then allowed another three seconds respite under the mandatory count ruling. It was a good job that Patterson was allowed that extra breather for in the next second another cracking right floored him again. He jumped up even more quickly than the first time and was again allowed the standing count, though he would probably have stayed down for longer had that not been in operation.

Then Patterson let fly with his own version of the Hammer of Thor. His was not a

right, but a wicked left hook. It bowled the challenger off his feet and now it was the Swede's turn to luxuriate in a compulsory count of eight. This was a tremendous first round with more action packed into 180 seconds than in half the full span of some world title fights. The bell heralded the end of the first frantic three minutes and the boxers went hurriedly to their stools. There had been very little in the scoring, but it is safe to assume that the officials must have given Johansson the edge on the strength of those two knockdown punches.

The second round opened with Patterson flat-footed and unable to land his left, though he threw many a punch of that variety. The challenger did not even have to

Floyd Patterson desperately wanted to become a truly great world champion.

take evasive action, for Patterson was a man who could not slip into the correct rhythm. They clinched and Patterson went to the canvas for a third time, but the referee did not take up the count since the champion had been half-wrestled to the floor as they came out of the clinch. Then punches were swapped and both men got home, with Johansson again marginally in front as the round ended. In the third round Johansson hammered Patterson under the heart and the champion went down, but again it was more the result of a slip than from the direct result of the body punch. Then Patterson had his day. A cut appeared over the Swede's right eye and near the end of the round, Patterson bent his knees with a looping left hook, followed by a right. It was with a volley of rights that Patterson ended his best round so far.

The fourth round saw both men slacken their pace, for truly, this had been a breathtaking first three rounds. Then a right to the head made Johansson dizzy, a left hook drove him on to the ropes, and Ingemar covered up. Then he came back, slammed a right to the champion's head and a left to the jaw, though neither punch seemed to bother the champion who raised a bump over

The roles are reversed and now it is Johansson's turn to taste the resin.

Johansson's left eye with short, stabbing right. Still the Swede came on, scoring to the face with lefts and then a right. Patterson looked confused, but by the end of the fourth he was back into the swing of things and the round ended just about even. The fifth was more ponderous. Johansson seemed hampered by his extra weight and although Patterson got home several good rights, none of them were particularly punishing, though they did score points. Both champion and challenger seemed to be abandoning their usual styles now.

Ingemar Johansson came out for the sixth round looking to land as many punches as he could, whooping up like some Red Indian war party intent on taking the settlers by sheer surprise. Two rights to the champion's head were useful blows, putting Patterson on the retreat. Around the ring they went, Patterson backpedalling fast like a football referee trying to get back into position for a goalkick without wanting to take his eyes off the play; Johansson followed him, jabbing out that irritating left of his and then catching the champion by surprise with two good rights, the second of which was a rare uppercut, for Johansson had not been seen to land one so far this night.

Then it happened. There were over two minutes of the round gone when Patterson landed a smarting left hook, then two successive rights to the side of the head, one landing so quickly after the other that they were almost one and the same punch. They did not appear to carry an excessive dose of venom, but they were enough to send the Swede tumbling forward and down. It was an unusual knockdown, not backwards or sidewards as is usual, but forwards like a nosedive. Johansson landed heavily on his right knee with his left leg stuck out backwards. By the time the count reached five the Swede had managed to bring his left leg down and was now kneeling, almost ready to get back to his feet. But the strength required to do this was not there. Sure, he got to his feet eventually, but he took so long about it that the count of ten had been reached before he scrambled back. There   143 were a few shouts that the count was 'short', Johansson made a token attempt at complaining. The fact remained, however, that he was counted out, though no one can be quite sure why he did not make it back. Men have been struck more vicious blows and risen in time to fight on. So Patterson was still champion, but he had still not proved himself a great one. Johansson? Well he carried on fighting for two more years and won all of his four bouts, one of them to regain the European title which he had relinquished on assuming the world crown. That came in June 1962 when he knocked out Britain's Dick Richardson. A fight against another Briton, Brian London, was his last. Having beaten London on points in April 1963, the Swede laid the Hammer of Thor to rest and devoted his career to less dangerous pursuits. For Patterson there was the grim shadow of Charles 'Sonny' Liston, looming on the horizon.

FLOYD PATTERSON v SONNY LISTON
World Heavyweight Championship
25 September 1962

There can have been no more sinister figure to hold the heavyweight boxing championship of the world than Charles 'Sonny' Liston. There was certainly no challenger more fearsome than the man Floyd Patterson faced in Chicago's Cominskey Park in the Fall of 1962. Consider the statistics alone: at fifteen inches in circumference, Sonny Liston's fists were bigger than any world champion since John L. Sullivan began the modern title eighty years earlier; his reach of eighty-four inches was longer than any champion with the exception of the freak, Primo Carnera; and his weight of 15st 4lb gave nearly a two-stones advantage over Patterson that night.

There was much more to Sonny Liston than the fact that he looked as though he had just emerged from some primeval swamp, more than the simple physical attributes which gave him the look of a man from the dawn of history. Charles Liston was a man with a murky past, too. Born, it is alleged, one of a family of twenty-five children, although some sources reckon it was only twenty-three, he was the son of an Arkansas farmworker, though, again there have been doubts as to the actual place where Sonny first saw the light of day and even his mother was never quite sure, though one can hardly blame the poor woman for not remembering exactly where in the order of things her boy Charles appeared. With a start in life like that, Liston was always likely to get into trouble, and he did. Again the records are sketchy and one must be careful not to repeat stories 'enhanced' for the sake of convenience. Certainly, however, Liston served two terms in jail, one for armed robbery and one for assaulting the police, though by all accounts the police treated him none too kindly at times. An occasion is recalled when he was in the first year of his teens and desperately searching St Louis for his mother, where the police were 'less than kind'. When he was older he was one of a gang of teenagers who beat up the owner of a candy store for a pittance; later still he grabbed a policeman's gun and the officer had his leg broken in the struggle. Clearly, Sonny Liston was no 'regular kind of a guy'.

The only attribute which Sonny Liston possessed was his massive physique. Many

Sonny Liston, the meanest champion of them all.

boys on the wrong trail in life have been rescued by organised boxing, for it seems a good idea to channel youthful aggression which might be used the wrong way, into a clean, healthy, manly pursuit like amateur boxing. So it was while Liston was doing a stretch in the Missouri State Penitentiary that the institution's athletics director, the Catholic priest Father Alous Stevens, saw something in this young man and guided him into the boxing arena. It was a laudable thing to do. Five years later, in 1953, Liston won the Golden Gloves and shortly afterwards turned professional. His first professional fight came in St Louis on 2 September that year when Don Smith became the first paid fighter to feel the immensity of the Liston KO punch. Smith went down in the first round and stayed down, the first of a long line of men who failed to go the distance with Sonny Liston. Liston had thirty-three bouts between that fight and his challenge for the title. Twenty-three opponents were knocked out and only one man, Marty Marshall, beat him. Marshall was given the decision in an eight-rounder in Detroit in September 1954.

Inevitably, Liston became involved with some of the more unsavoury characters in the American underworld, men who cared nothing for the young man, but who saw him as a tool with which to earn considerable sums of money for themselves. These ruthless, greedy men manipulated Liston who despite his physical prowess, was not very well educated and could read and write only with great difficulty. So, as Liston's ring career continued apace, these men began to push their man for a crack at the world title. It was not an unreasonable suggestion. After all, Liston had quite easily disposed of most of the other challengers. Nino Valdes had been KO'd in three rounds, Cleveland Williams stopped in three and then in two, alligator-wrestling Roy Harris did not last the first round, Zora Folley was knocked out in three rounds in Denver in July 1960, and less than two months later Eddie Machen was beaten on points in Seattle. In fact, ever since Liston scored a six-round knockout over Mike De John at Miami Beach in

February 1959, he had been pressing for a title fight. Yet, as his claim grew stronger, there was a body of opinion which held that the last person boxing needed as a world champion was this gorilla of a man with his law-breaking background and seedy, sinister connections.

But could he be ignored? On 23 February 1960, Liston stopped Howard King in seven rounds at the Miami Beach Municipal Auditorium. Just over a year later, Liston met King again at the same venue, just five days before Patterson's third fight with Johansson at the nearby Convention Hall. Posters advertising Billy Graham's forthcoming arrival on a crusade were all over the Florida city. That night Liston 'murdered' King and knocked him out in three rounds. Afterwards he held a press conference and mounted his own crusade for the world title. If Floyd Patterson beat Johansson in this third fight, he told reporters, that would prove conclusively that the black man was the outright champion, best of three and all that. Then, said Liston, he would be prepared to fight Patterson for the title *and not claim one penny for himself*. 'Look', he told the world's boxing press, 'Johansson has said that if he wins he will give me the chance to fight for the title. But it's Patterson who's the champ and I reckon he'll stay champ. What's more, I don't reckon he'll fight me. He'll duck out. So I say this to him: Fight me as the champ and you can keep all the purse — I don't want the money, I want that title.' Fine words indeed, and Liston probably meant them, but after he had demolished King, and Patterson went 2-1 up over Johansson, there was no need for such gestures. Patterson had fought no one else of note apart from the Swede and now Gus D'Amato had to agree to a fight with Liston. The fact that, if he won, Liston would be without doubt the most unpopular world heavyweight champion since Jack Johnson did not enter into it. Justice had to be done, and if anything was just it was Liston's claim to fight Patterson.

Before the fight was arranged, however, Patterson had one more title defence against a 'nothing' fighter. In Toronto on 4 December 1961, 7,813 people watched Tom McNeeley, an average heavyweight with a couple of dozen wins over inferior boxers, beaten by the world champion in four rounds. McNeeley was a game, courageous fighter with lots of strength, but he was woefully short of the class needed to take part in a world title fight and he was down ten times in all before he was counted out. On the same evening, in Philadelphia, Liston met the German heavyweight Albert Westphal, twice national champion of his country. Liston removed him in the first round and a feature of both fights was that they televised live on a huge screen. So fight fans saw both men in action that night. Their next fights would be against each other.

When that day arrived, 25 September 1962, Sonny Liston was 5-1 favourite, the record odds for a challenger in a heavyweight title fight. The days before the bout had been spent in training, of course, but what a contrast there had been between Liston's camp and that of the reigning champion. Liston used a disused race track nearly forty miles from the Windy City,

Liston repeats his first-round defeat of Floyd Patterson in Las Vegas.

Patterson toned up the muscles and the wind in a Roman Catholic centre for poor children. So while the challenger did his stint among the dry, overgrown scrub grass, the champion worked out in pleasant farming country. As the day for the fight drew closer, the financial arrangements were made public. Whereas Patterson was on forty-five per cent of everything, with a two-million dollar guarantee, the challenger stood to make only one-tenth of that: his figure was twelve and a half per cent with a guarantee of $200,000. If he won, Liston would get only one quarter of that, the rest being saved until he met Patterson in a return match. Still, after offering to fight for nothing, perhaps Sonny was well satisfied, though the challenger later said that he had offered to fight Patterson for nothing *in a gym*, not before a world-wide audience.

All this served to stoke up the pre-fight drama, as if any addition was needed. Then came the night of 24 September. At Cominskey Park, in the heart of Chicago's black quarter, the fans were threading their way towards the baseball stadium where, a quarter of a century earlier, Joe Louis had emerged from under the stands which supported the White Sox fans, into the arena to beat Jim Braddock and become one of the world's most popular black champions. Now, as the wind whipped up off Lake Michigan, an entirely different kind of champion was about to be crowned. There can have been few more dissimilar figures than Joe Louis and Sonny Liston. Even to speak of them in the same breath seems almost sacrilegious. Yet the Brown Bomber was there that night. So too were Rocky Marciano, Jim Braddock, Ezzard Charles, Ingemar Johansson, and Archie Moore, that great light-heavyweight who never made it to the top at the ultimate weight class. Five heavyweight champions of the world made it a glittering occasion, but once they had been introduced for old time's sake, all attention turned to the ring where Liston was first in, his head hooded by a white towelling gown. That cloak made Liston appear even more sinister.

Floyd Patterson had enjoyed some fairly easy title defences. But now he was going to pay for them all. The bell's ring was carried away on the night air and suddenly the champion was alone in the ring, alone, that is, except for the presence of the boxer who was Charles 'Sonny' Liston — the person who thought up that nickname must have had a peculiar sense of humour — and right away it was Liston who threw the first punches. The weigh-in had revealed that Liston scaled 15st 4lb to Patterson's 13st 7lb, but the first couple of jabs from the challenger did not carry anything like that weight and Patterson easily ducked them and tried to get nearer to Liston — brave man! Liston looked to be concentrating hard and he let go a swinging right to Patterson's head and followed up immediately with a left uppercut which perhaps just brushed the skin on Patterson's chin. Had it landed it would surely have lifted the champion's head off his shoulders and sent it sailing up into the inky blackness above the floodlights. Patterson was a complex man and perhaps saw himself as the White Knight riding valiantly against the Black Knight in search of justice. It was certainly going to be a Black Night for the champion, though. As he tried to hammer in a left to Liston's body, the challenger scorched his head with two rasping rights and Patterson was forced to bow, almost in acknowledgement.

This was sufficient for Liston to move in again, slamming a tattoo of body punches into the submissive figure of the world champion. Liston was a machine gun now, only he spat not lead, but leather. Patterson bowed his head still further and looked for an escape, but there was none. Liston seemed born for just this moment. All the early years of pain and deprivation, humiliation and anger, had been but a preparation for this time. With each punch there went a little bit of Sonny Liston saying 'I'll never be a bum in a slum'. Patterson had now somehow wriggled towards his own corner, and Liston followed him and slammed in a left hook to the face. Then a right uppercut, and finally another huge left and the champion was down. Ten seconds, that is all it takes for a man to lose his world crown and for another man to pick it up.

That is how long it took Patterson's to fall and Liston's to be placed upon his tight black head. From start to finish the fight had lasted 126 seconds. Patterson could only don dark glasses and a false beard and slink away from the stadium and drive through the night to his wife. Sonny Liston did not want to hurry away though. He was the new heavyweight champion of the world and he wanted to stay a while and enjoy the limelight. It was the third-fastest KO in the history of the title, but Patterson had to go through the motions of trying again. In the Las Vegas Convention Hall on 22 July 1963, Patterson lasted a little longer; Liston KO'd him in two minutes and ten seconds of the first round this time, and now no one could deny that 'Old Stoneface' was the champ. Patterson boxed on for another ten years and never gave up hope of regaining the title again. He fought for it twice more. Those two defeats were included in the eight he suffered during a career of sixty-four fights. His last fight, and his last defeat, came in September 1972 when a man called Muhammad Ali stopped him with a cut eye in seven. Previously, Ali had been known as Cassius Clay, a man who Sonny Liston was soon to know all about.

SONNY LISTON v CASSIUS CLAY
World Heavyweight Championship
25 February 1964

There was hardly anyone in boxing who thought that Sonny Liston would have any problems in disposing of the brash young challenger Cassius Clay when the champion with the prehistoric look came to defend his title for the second time, in the winter of 1964. In Britain, especially, boxing experts in particular and the public in general, felt that the sign painter's son from Louisville, Kentucky, would not last overlong with the most monstrously devastating champion that they had ever seen, on cinema and television screens of course. The reason for the British opinion harked back to a fight in the open air of Wembley Stadium the previous summer when Clay had come within an ace of losing to the British champion, Henry Cooper. In the fourth round a vicious left hook had lifted Clay off his feet and, although he was up at four, the bell prevented Cooper from moving in for what everybody expected to be the kill. By the time Clay's glove had been repaired in the interval, thus allowing the American far more than the usual sixty seconds respite, he was ready again. A badly cut eye ended the fight for Cooper in the very next round. To add injury to insult to the brave Cooper, the glove was never replaced and that eye was damaged by the almost bare knuckles of the Kentucky man.

When Floyd Patterson was winning back his world heavyweight title in the summer of 1960, only a few people in amateur boxing had ever heard of Cassius Marcellus Clay, born 17 January 1942, in Louisville. Clay had started boxing at the age of twelve and six years later he was the Olympic light-heavyweight champion. His amateur career had been highly successful all around. He had won 108 amateur bouts, six Kentucky Golden Gloves titles and, in 1960, the International Golden Gloves title. Returning to Louisville from the Olympic Games in Rome at the end of that year, he became the National American Athletic Union light-heavyweight champion and National Golden Gloves heavyweight champion, turned professional and on 29 October had his first paid fight against Tommy Hunsaker in Louisville. Clay won on points over six rounds at the start of an astonishing professional career.

The former triple amateur champion continued his professional career and his first nineteen fights all resulted in victory, fifteen of them inside the distance. But the only real *name* he had fought in that time was the former world light-heavyweight champion, Archie Moore, and Moore was looking forward to his fiftieth birthday when Clay beat him in four rounds. So, despite his one hundred per cent record, Clay hardly looked a realistic challenger and there were many who felt that another eighteen months in the ring were needed before Cassius Clay would be ready for such an awesome task. After all, he was but a boy and to put him in against a boxer such as Sonny Liston was tantamount to premeditated cruelty. But if one thing speaks louder than anything else in boxing it is money. Dollar bills, pound notes, have it in any currency you like, but the sound of the cash crashing and rustling into the box office till is more likely to get two fighters in the ring than any amount of skill and experience. With a dearth of likely opponents, Clay's unbeaten record, and the Louisville Lip's own inimitable publicity machine, a Liston-Clay fight was a natural if you happened to be a promoter. For the Louisville Lip, Mighty Mouth, or Gaseous Cassius, call him what you will, had been bragging that he would 'whup' the ugly bear that he recognised as Sonny Liston. Clay had already told London audiences, 'If he wants to jive, he'll fall in five', before finishing Henry Cooper in that round. He now mounted a similar campaign against Liston.

Promoter Bill MacDonald arranged the fight for Miami on 25 February 1965. Actually it was a financial flop from his point of view as only 8,297 people turned out to see what they thought would be another speedy Liston win. The events which led up to the two men touching gloves were some of the most remarkable, amazing, and downright bizarre in the history of boxing. The Beatles were there to watch Clay work out in his gym and there was a background rumour that the challenger had joined a religious sect called The Black Muslims, headed by one Elijah Muhammad, though at the time Clay refused to confirm or deny that he had joined the Muslim faith. Then there was Clay chasing Liston through the streets carrying a bear trap, and finally the incredible scenes at the weigh-in. Clay arrived in a blue boiler suit with the legend 'Bear Huntin' embroidered in red on it, carrying what looked like a totem pole. The challenger ranted and raved, was wild-eyed and staring and prompted medical opinion to voice the view that he was emotionally unbalanced.

One of the medical experts who felt that Clay was 'scared to death and living in mortal fear' was none other than the Boxing Commission's top man, Dr Alexander Robbins. If Robbins did think that Clay was, to use his own words, 'burning up energy at a furious rate', then it did not stop him from allowing Clay to go ahead with the fight. With Clay in the dressing room stripping for the weigh-in, Liston refused to come out again until the challenger was on the platform. When they were both back in the tangle of media hardware and software which is present at all such big-fight weigh-ins, Clay tried to attack his opponent and had to be forcibly restrained. Liston per-

mitted himself one baleful stare and then signalled silently that the fight would be over in two rounds. Clay had already told the world of Liston: 'Sure as fate, he'll fall in eight.'

If Clay was 'scared to death' at the weigh-in, where, incidentally, he scaled 15st ½lb against Liston's 15st 8lb, then he did not show it immediately before the fight. Perhaps the fact that he had been fined $15,000 (£900) by the Miami Boxing Commission for his behaviour at the weigh-in might have calmed him down; perhaps it was all a charade anyway. I think it probably was, and there was medical evidence to prove that Clay's pulse rate was exactly the same as Liston's just before the start of the fight. Perhaps he had listened too hard to Eddie Machen's claim that it was possible to rile Liston. Machen was the only man to have gone the distance, twelve rounds, with Liston in the previous two years and he advised Clay to call him names, ask him where that big punch was: 'Once you get him excited, he'll go mad — and no one in his corner will be able to stop him', was Machen's inside information. Well if that was true, as I'm sure Machen felt it was, Liston showed precious little sign of getting mad when Clay baited him unmercifully. Almost all the experts felt that Clay would be crucified, that Liston would pick up another easy paycheck. To the general spectator, Clay was but an affable clown who should not be allowed into the ring with an ex-convict who would tear him to ribbons. Clay was a good-looker and it would be a pity to spoil those pretty features. He might have a lightning pair of hands, but he could not punch the way a heavyweight challenger has to punch if he means to take the title. He might be light on his feet, but could he stay out of the way of the gorilla who faced him? They were all points which were about to be answered.

Joe Louis had scored a hat-trick of one-round victories in the late 1930s — was Liston about to do the same? Clay came into the ring first dressed in a short white robe with 'The Lip' emblazoned across the back.

Almost five minutes elapsed before Liston appeared in that hood which only added to his frightening appearance. The first round answered many questions. For a start, Cassius Clay *could* stay out of the way of Liston's wicked left hooks. Left after left came flashing from the champion in those first three minutes, but almost all of them were well wide. Liston did manage to land a hard right to the body but Clay had already left-hooked him, then hammered rights and lefts to the head, followed by a half-dozen or so left jabs — bang, bang, bang — to the jaw. At the end of the round Clay had not only managed to last longer than Patterson, he had taken the round into the bargain.

In the second round Liston caught Clay with a left hook to the chin, but the challenger danced away to the ropes and when Liston poked out another left to that chin, it wasn't there. Liston now knew that he would have to work hard to hit Clay. He settled down and opened Clay's mouth with a right to the ribs, followed by more to the same place and then a left to the side of the rib cage. The round went to the champion and Clay had hardly landed a punch in anger. Instead he had danced around the ring, mouth open and eyes staring like a rabbit who has been hypnotised by car headlights on a country lane at night.

Round three saw Liston cut. Clay hooked him twice with his left, then launched a two-handed attack which had the champion on the retreat. He tried to duck away from another left hook, but succeeded only in ducking into it, and when he moved away there was the sensational sight of blood pumping from a cut under the champion's left eye. No one could remember the last time they had seen Liston's skin smeared red, unless it was the blood of some hapless opponent being smashed into oblivion. But the champion fought back well enough to get on even terms by the end of the round, helped by three right uppercuts in the dying seconds. Clay had shown a certain amount of inexperience in allowing himself to be caught so near the end of the round and when a more mature fighter would have ensured

no further punishment for himself. Nevertheless, it was now proved that Sonny Liston was human. He bled like anyone else, and after three rounds he had failed to stop the fight.

The fourth round saw the cut under Liston's eye fail to re-open, though the challenger kept pegging away at it. Then the champion managed to set a steam hammer of punches to work on Clay's rib cage. The challenger took it all and more. Liston caught him with a right, then a left, to the head. Clay, meanwhile danced and boxed cleverly; Liston kept hammering away in the same old way, and it was enough to give him the round. Cassius Clay had done a lot of skipping about up to this stage, without laying too many punches. At the end of the round there was consternation in Clay's corner where the challenger was complaining to his manager, Angelo Dundee, that he could not see properly. Apparently some of the solution used to stem the flow of blood

Ali's second fight with Sonny Liston and the Louisville Lip stands snarling over Liston as their title bout comes to a sensational end.

151

from Liston's cut had been transferred via the gloves into Clay's eyes and the challenger was in tears as they smarted. But Clay went out at Dundee's insistence and for the next three minutes the challenger danced backwards around the ring, keeping Liston at bay with a stabbing left. The champion took the round easily and at times it had seemed that Clay would be knocked down.

Again, Cassius Clay complained that he could not see and was almost too late in answering the bell. But in the sixth he seemed to regain much of his composure and a series of uppercuts — lefts and rights — put the champion on his heels. That apart, however, there was little action to report until Liston cracked in a left hook and then Clay responded with a trio of jabs. The fight was slowing down now and when the bell ended the round both men were level pegging in most people's eyes, including those of the referee and two judges. And that was it! In this book we have been learning of great punches ending fights. This one finished in an anti-climax with Liston sitting on his stool. The champion was cut, his left shoulder was hurting like hell, he said, and he was quitting there and then. Clay could have the title. But how could this be? Liston had never been off his feet and he had hurt Clay far more than Clay had hurt him. Liston said that his shoulder was so painful and that he could not feel his hand. Yet one of the last punches he threw was a *left* hook. Was this not the man who had once fought, against Marty Marshall in 1954, with a broken jaw? What had gone on in that big man's mind in the moments after he slumped on to his stool are as much a mystery now as it was then. The reason why Sonny Liston gave up the title in that way has never been satisfactorily explained.

Fifteen months later, in Lewiston, Maine, Cassius Clay, by now known as Muhammad Ali, KO'd Sonny Liston in a return fight for the title. It was another unsavoury episode and Ali finished his opponent in one minute and forty-two seconds of a bout which the World Boxing Association did not recognise. They set up their own world title fight in which Ernie Terrell outpointed Eddie Machen in Chicago in March that year. The WBA objection was that Liston was a major shareholder in the company staging the rematch. Liston had been allowed to keep his purse after the first fight when medical evidence diagnosed bursitis and a probe by the DA had revealed no evidence of a fix. The rematch was originally scheduled for Boston but had to be postponed when Ali suffered a hernia. When it did take place it was hardly worth waiting for, it was such a fiasco. The referee was Jersey Joe Walcott who seemed as confused as everyone else when Liston went down to an innocuous right to the head. I say that Liston was KO'd in 102 seconds, but no one has ever been sure how long it took since at one stage he got up and carried on fighting, Walcott having waved Ali to a neutral corner and then started counting again instead of picking up the timekeeper's call. The only blessing was that this 'fight', staged as it was in a high school hockey rink on the New England coast, was watched by fewer than 2,500 people.

Sonny Liston carried on fighting for another five years, winning fourteen fights mostly by the KO, until in December 1969, he had risen somehow to number three in the world ranking and faced Leotis Martin in Las Vegas. Liston was ahead by the end of the eighth round. In the ninth, a right cross and a left hook delivered the knockout and the fourth defeat of his career. Six months later he stopped Chuck Wepner in ten rounds in Jersey City. It was Liston's last fight. Seven months later his wife found him dead in their Las Vegas home. In the kitchen was a balloon of heroin. Liston died, as he had lived, in the shadiest of circumstances.

MUHAMMAD ALI v JOE FRAZIER
—————————— World Heavyweight Championship ——————————
1 October 1975

The third time that Muhammad Ali, the former Cassius Clay, met Joe Frazier, in the Philippines in October 1975, gave final confirmation, if such was needed, that Ali was a truly *great* champion. He had been telling us for years that he was The Greatest, and that night in Manila he came as near to proving it as ever he did. Joe Frazier, too, fought well that night and it can go down, without doubt, as one of the greatest of all fights for the heavyweight world title. But, oh, what a winding road took Ali and Frazier to that meeting by the South China Sea. Along the way was a world-wide controversy which split the American nation in two, and some great fights.

The way in which Muhammad Ali became world champion, and first defended his crown, were met with open cynicism by the boxing public. Liston had given up the title sitting on his stool, and then abdicated his right as challenger in a less-than-one-round farce. So Ali was still considered something of a joke champion and he had to set about proving himself. He did so in two ways, by beating the best that America had to offer and by taking his title around the world in a way that no other champion, save perhaps Tommy Burns who was high-tailing it from Jack Johnson at the time. Ali started off by tormenting ex-champion Floyd Patterson in Las Vegas in November 1965, six months after stopping Liston in one round. Patterson was hammered around the ring for almost twelve rounds before referee Harry Krause put an end to the former king's misery. Hampered by a back injury, Patterson was glad to hear that bell and one had the feeling that Ali could have won it in half the time, had he chosen. It was in 1966 that Ali took off

around the world to prove himself a truly 'global' champion, though the reasons for his tour had as much to do with politics as with boxing.

In February that year, one month after Ali had divorced his wife, the former model Sonji Roy, because 'she is not a good Muslim', the world champion was informed by a newspaper reporter that the local draft board had passed him A1, and that very soon he could expect his call-up papers for the US Army. At this time the United States was embroiled in the Vietnam War and Ali told the reporter that, as a Muslim, he had a conscientious objection to the war: 'Besides, I ain't got no quarrel with them Vietcong — they never called me a nigger!' The media picked up that remark and a wave of patriotism swept America and sent Ali to seek opponents on foreign shores, for at that time there was not the questioning of the war which later came to dominate United States foreign policy and ultimately resulted in them pulling out and leaving South Vietnam to the Communists from the North.

For almost a year, while he waited for a decision on his appeal against the draft, Ali fought abroad. In March that year he went up to Toronto and outpointed George Chuvalo, the tough but limited Canadian. Then it was to London and a second fight with Henry Cooper, the man who came within a whisker of changing the whole course of world heavyweight title history at Wembley three years earlier. Now Cooper met Ali for the title at another famous soccer ground, Arsenal's Highbury. The stadium was packed with people waiting to see if Cooper could become the first Englishman since Bob Fitzsimmons in 1898 to hold the

Muhammad Ali looking as pretty as ever despite his battles with some of the toughest boxers in the world.

Joe Frazier tells reporters that he is confident he will once again be the world heavyweight champion when he meets Muhammad Ali in Manilla in one week's time.

world heavyweight crown. Cooper lost his meeting with Clay with a cut and he lost this fight in the same way. The referee stopped it in the sixth round with Cooper bleeding badly from the left eye. The crowd paid £210,000 to watch that fight and although disappointed that 'Enery had lost, they were proud of their man. Not so three months later when 11,000 people booed Brian London as he was KO'd in the third round of his title fight with Ali. The following month found Ali in Frankfurt where he met the German southpaw and European champion, Karl Mildenberger. Mildenberger managed to hurt Ali with two hard lefts to the body, but in the twelfth round Teddy Waltham stopped the fight with Ali well ahead on points and the German battered and bloody. Muhammad Ali then returned to the States where he met Cleveland Williams. The Big Cat lasted until the third round of their fight at Houston, Texas, before Harry Kessler stopped it. Ali

had floored Williams three times in the second and once in the third, punching as devastatingly as anyone had ever seen him.

As the WBA had stripped Ali of the title, so far as they were concerned the true world champion was Ernie Terrell who had outpointed Ernie Machen when Ali took up a return with Liston. Terrell had then outpointed George Chuvalo and Doug Jones to retain this WBA crown and with two claimants, the obvious thing was for Ali to meet Terrell. Terrell was born in Mississippi in April 1939 and was one of ten children. Shortly after he was born the family moved to Chicago's South Side and it was in that tough environment that young Ernie learned his trade. After a fine amateur career, Terrell turned professional under the wing of George Hamid, a successful businessman, and the youngster who was to become champion of the world, according to the WBA at least, also played lead guitar in a profitable pop group known, inevitably, as Ernie Terrell and his Heavyweights.

Terrell had no love for Cassius Clay, as he insisted on calling the champion, and Ali had no love for Terrell who he referred to as an 'Uncle Tom', meaning a black man who is still servile to the white man. It was a 'grudge' fight and Ali told reporters that if Terrell admitted that he, Ali, was the real champion, and if he called Ali by his adopted name, then the fight would be over as quickly as possible with the humane knock-out of the WBA man. On the other hand, if Terrell insisted on calling Ali 'Clay', then he would suffer in the same way that Patterson had suffered. The fight was set for 6 February 1967 in Houston and Ali was true to his word. It was a fight which showed us the less acceptable face of Muhammad Ali. For fifteen rounds he toyed with Terrell but refused to finish him. Ali fought 'dirty', his thumb wandering into Terrell's left eye, his elbows and forearms getting into the action as much as the leather-gloved fists which are supposed to do all the work. By the eighth round Terrell's right eye was cut, his left eye red raw from the attentions of Ali's thumb, and the champion was asking him, 'What's mah name? What's mah name?'. Admittedly, Terrell, too, did his ugly bit. But it was the vindictive side of Ali's nature which gripped the crowd. At the end it was revealed that Ali was so far ahead, the referee might have stopped the fight, given all the ugly incidents, such as the time in the third round when Ali deliberately rubbed Terrell's eye along the rope. It all meant that Muhammad Ali was now the true world champion. The defeat of Terrell removed the last doubts, if anyone had any.

That fight was the end of Ernie Terrell as a top-rate fighter. Two defeats after the Ali fight made up his mind for him and he retired, returning to the ring three years later but then calling it a day once more after a succession of ordinary fights against mostly ordinary fighters. For Ali, too, there was a long lay-off just around the corner. After beating Terrell he took on 34-year-old Zora Folley at Madison Square Garden. It was just six weeks after the massacre of Terrell but that did not stop 13,780 fans paying $244,471 to see the champion retain his now undisputed title by stopping Folley in seven rounds.

Then Muhammad Ali took on his biggest opponent to date — the United States of America. His various requests for draft deferment had all been turned down and on 28 April 1967 he was ordered to report to the Houston induction centre. Ali was there on the appointed day, but he refused to be inducted, claiming that this was a 'white man's war' and that he was a black man and proud of it. On 9 May a Federal Grand Jury indicted Ali on a charge of failing to submit to the draft; a few hours later the World Boxing Association and the New York State Athletic Commission stripped Ali of his title, banned him in the United States and declared the world heavyweight title vacant. In June that year Ali was given the maximum sentence of five years' jail and a $10,000 fine by the US District Court for the Southern District of Texas. Ali appealed all the way up to the US Supreme Court, and lost. He was ordered to surrender his passport, which meant that he could not fight abroad, and every boxing commission in the world stripped him of his title, with the British Board being the last to do so. In a three-and-a-half-year period Ali's only 'fight' was a film version of a computerised fight between him and Rocky Marciano. All the relevant details were fed in and the computer predicted how the fight would proceed. Ali and Marciano then acted it out, filming three different endings, for that was a secret. Sadly, Marciano died in a plane crash before he learned that his unbeaten record was still intact. The computer had Marciano a thirteenth-round KO victor. Ali simply shrugged when he saw it and muttered something about the computer being made in Alabama.

It was ironic, then, that when Ali got back his boxing licence — New York was the first to return it — it was granted to box in the Deep South, at Atlanta, Georgia. Ali had never served a day of that sentence, nor, so far as anyone knew, paid so much as a dollar towards the fine. Older white Americans who had fought in wars from France, through Anzio to Korea and Vietnam, might have been pleased with the Government's stance, but youngsters opposed to the war, and blacks who saw Ali as yet another victim of white oppression were not and it would have been suicidal to have jailed the champion, for that is what he still was in most people's eyes, and might have resulted in racial violence. So, on 26 October 1970, Muhammad Ali was back in the ring to face Jerry Quarry in Atlanta, three years and seven months after he had beaten Folley. He stopped Quarry inside three rounds, and two months later KO'd the Argentinian Oscar Bonavena in the fifteenth round in New York.

So Ali was back. On 28 June 1971 incidentally, the Supreme Court finally ruled in his favour to dot the last 'i' and cross the remaining 't' and he now declared himself the People's Champion. Of course, while he had been away, boxing had found itself a new undisputed world heavyweight champion in Joe Frazier, the 1964 Olympic champion, 27-years old and the man who had emerged from a tangle of claims and counterclaims. The WBA and the New York Commission had both put forward claimants when Ali's title was stripped from him in 1967. Frazier had emerged as the New York man, with Jimmy Ellis, a former sparring partner of Ali's, taking the WBA version of the crown. Ellis had outpointed Quarry, the best of the white challengers, at Oakland in April 1968 to gain WBA support. Frazier, the man they called the Black Marciano, had become New York's man a month earlier when he stopped Buster Mathis in the eleventh round in New York. The world had two champions until February 1970 when Frazier stopped Ellis in five rounds in New York. So Joe Frazier, one of thirteen children from South Carolina, was the undisputed world champion, the successor to Muhammad Ali. One man thought different, Ali himself, and after Frazier had defended the title once, stopping Bob Foster in two rounds

in Detroit in November 1970, he found the People's Champion barring his way.

The meeting between Joe Frazier, official champion of the world and unbeaten, and Muhammad Ali, popular champion of the world and unbeaten, was inevitable. It was set for the new Madison Square Garden on 8 March 1971 and was known quite simply as The Fight. Each man was guaranteed two-and-a-half million dollars, around one million pounds each, simply for stepping in the ring. Ali, we know all about. Frazier was known as Smokin' Joe, on account of his non-stop style, the Golden Gloves winner in 1962, 1963 and 1964 and America's only gold medal winner from the Tokyo Olympics boxing tournament. From that moment he had never looked back as a paid fighter and this meeting with Ali was a 'natural' if ever there was one. Never before had two boxers, two champions, with one hundred per cent records, met for this richest prize in sport. There were 20,445 fans in the newly-built Garden that night, plus another one and a quarter million watching on closed-circuit cinema link-up. Ringside were more champions and ex-champions than anyone could ever remember seeing before, the usual glitter of showbiz stars, even an astronaut, to see Ali 'float like a butterfly, sting like a bee' as he said he would. It was the most fascinating question in modern sport: could Muhammad Ali come back from a three-years lay-off and win back the world title which he had never lost in the ring?

The answer was 'No'. Ali had decided to let Smokin' Joe tire himself out, but the champion was allowed so many direct hits at Ali's body, despite a six and a half inch reach disadvantage, and once Ali had lost his speed, once the old dancing shoes became leaden, then the complexion of The Fight altered. Ali spent more time on the ropes than he had ever done before, and the sixth round ended with the fight still unfinished, though Ali had boasted that it would be round six when he picked up his crown again. After that the going just got tougher for Ali. He wanted to rest but Frazier was still there, poking out his left and scoring

Ali grimaces in pain as Joe Frazier drops him in 'The Fight' at Madison Square Garden in March 1971.

point after point. The fourteenth round found Ali rallying slightly. But the fifteenth round said it all. A left hook sent Muhammad Ali to the canvas and although he got up and was ready long before the mandatory count of eight was finished, it was the signal that Muhammad Ali was mortal after all. Joe Frazier was the unanimous points winner and a worthy champion of the world.

All of boxing shed a tear for Muhammad Ali that night, for no one likes to see a legend destroyed. Yet Frazier was such a fine champion and at least the heavyweight world title had emerged conclusively from the muddle of the previous three and a half years. Both men had to go to hospital after The Fight, Smokin' Joe Frazier having a lengthy stay there, which gave Ali the chance to say how much he had really hurt the champion. Frazier defended the title twice against mediocre boxers, Terry Daniels and Ron Stander, before the next sensation of the age. Frazier took on George Foreman, the black Texan whose professional career had started in 1969. Frazier was 3-1 favourite to retain his crown when they met in Kingston, Jamaica, on 22 January 1973. The fight lasted just two rounds, during which Frazier, the man we all thought was indestructable after his beating of Ali, took a terrible hammering. Smokin' Joe was floored three times in the first round and three times in the second before referee Arthur Mercante led him to his corner and the world celebrated a new champion. George Foreman's first two defences saw him score convincing victories to underline his claim to the crown Ali said was his. Joe Roman was KO'd in one round in Tokyo, Ken Norton stopped in two rounds in Caracas.

While all this was going on, Joe Frazier and Muhammad Ali were deciding who should be the next challenger. They met at Madison Square Garden on 28 January 1974 before 20,476 people who paid $1,053,688 at the gate which was only a drop in the ocean of the estimated $25,000,000 which the fight grossed through subsidiary rights. Such was the magic of these men, for, after all, had not Frazier been smashed down six times by Foreman? Had not Ali suffered his second defeat and a broken jaw at the hands of Ken Norton? But it was fight fever all over again and that night Muhammad Ali produced what was up until then the best fight of his life. In twelve rounds of text-book boxing Ali took the fight on points to erase the memory of that earlier defeat by Frazier. Ali had his scares all right, like the time he was trapped in a corner in the second round and was saved only by the referee halting the fight for twenty seconds because he thought he had heard the bell. But it was a fine performance, earned him a unanimous decision and the right to fight for the title again.

That right was exercised in the most unusual of all fight venues: the Central African state of Zaire, once called the Belgian Congo. Television ruled the stage now and just before dawn on 30 October 1974, 62,000 fans and several British and American closed-circuit television teams, packed the Twentieth of May Stadium in Kinshasa where President Mobutu's country had a nine-million dollar interest in the fight. George Foreman went into the fight as the 3 1 favourite and then proceeded to fight a strange battle against the former champion. Unbeaten Foreman knew only one way to fight; an all-out attack on the former champion who he expected to dance away. But Ali stood his ground and instead of 'floating like a butterfly', he evolved a new-for-him style of fighting off the ropes. Ali used his speed, not to dance away, but to counter-attack. Ali lay on the ropes, let Forman come at him, and then fought back. In the hot, humid African night, this led Foreman towards exhaustion.

From the fifth round his punching powers faded while Ali stood flat-footed and continued to fight it out. In the eighth round Ali lay back on the ropes as if he too was exhausted. Then he looped over a tremendous right which sent Foreman to the canvas. There he was counted out, probably as much by exhaustion as by the KO quality of the punch, and Ali became the second man in history to regain the heavyweight championship of the world, although one cannot compare him with the first man who did it, Floyd Patterson.

Ali had come along a winding road to what was to be probably his greatest fight. First he had to defend the title against Chuck Wepner (whom he stopped in fifteen rounds in Cleveland in March 1975), Ron Lyle (stopped in the eleventh round in Las Vegas in May 1975), and Britain's Joe Bugner (so clearly outpointed in Kuala Lumpur in July 1975). With those three out of the way, Muhammad Ali now faced a third meeting with Smokin' Joe Frazier. On their first meeting Frazier had confirmed his right to be called champion; on the second Ali had earned his right to a crack at Foreman and that exciting fight in Africa. But this third meeting was to be the greatest of all, perhaps the greatest fight Muhammad Ali ever fought. On 1 October 1975 they faced each other before 28,000 people in the Philippine Coliseum, Manila, with an estimated 700,000,000 more people watching on television in almost seventy countries. Ali told the world: 'It'll be a thriller, a chiller and a killer when I get the "goriller" in Manila.' At almost eleven o'clock on that October morning he set about proving it.

Ali, guaranteed four and a half million dollars to Frazier's two million, had promised to stand and hit Smokin' Joe from the start, for he considered that Frazier was over the hill as a fighter. Muhammad Ali kept his word and from the first bell he attacked the challenger, bending the hinges on his knees as early as the first minute. It was the same in the second round, and in the third it seemed that Frazier was on his way out. The challenger held on and midway through the fourth, though Ali was still knocking back Frazier's head with left after left, the former champion was still there. Indeed, he actually took the fifth round, burrowing through Ali's fists and sending the champion back to the ropes with a series of lefts.

In the sixth round Frazier came even more into his own and he hammered Ali with two fearsome left hooks to the face which spun the champion back on his heels. For the next four rounds Joe Frazier hammered away relentlessly at the champion. All Muhammad Ali could do was to fight back when he was allowed, which was not very often as Frazier bored into the attack and hit the champion with punch after punch, many of the most ferocious power. With the fight two-thirds of the way through, the two men stood absolutely equal, though it was Ali who looked the worse for wear. Frazier had taken all that early barrage from Ali and had now slowly worn him down to a point where we all began to think that the champion had missed his chance.

That though, is to reckon without the remarkable abilities of Muhammad Ali. In the eleventh round he began to fight back and long-range punches from the champion brought blood to the challenger's face. Swellings appeared over Frazier's eyes and below them too. His cheeks began to puff up and his eyes got smaller, like the proverbial 'water' holes in the snow. Three more rounds of such

punishment followed with Frazier getting more tired, his energy spilling from him like a sack of grain with a hole in it. Ali called upon his last reserves and gained the upper hand. It was the champion who was now in total charge and when Frazier sat on his stool for the rest between the fourteenth and fifteenth rounds, he did so with an almost resigned air, as though he knew what was about to happen. In fact, he had to be helped back to his seat by referee Carlos Padilla and that said it all.

Any boxer who has to be supported by the referee knows what is coming. Despite protests from Frazier his manager, Eddie Futch, would not, quite correctly in my opinion, allow the half-blinded challenger to subject himself to another three minutes of torture. It had been a terrific fight, one of the best ever and certainly a classic. It had taken a great deal out of both men. Ali, in particular, spoke of the intense mental and physical pressure on him in this fight. But he had proved himself, beyond all measure of doubt, to be, if not *the* greatest, then certainly one of the greatest. We will never know if Joe Louis in his prime would have beaten Muhammad Ali; or whether Rocky Marciano really would have knocked him out, just like the computer said. Nor would we want to know. For each in their own time gave boxing some of its most classic moments.

EUSEBIO PEDROZA v BARRY McGUIGAN
_____ WBA Featherweight title _____
8 June 1985

Something had to give when Barry McGuigan took on the legendary Eusebio Pedroza for the WBA featherweight title at the QPR football ground, Loftus Road, in June 1985.

Pedroza was a giant in the division. Pound for pound he was one of the all-time greats. He had defended his title all over the world — twenty times to be precise — making more defences than any man since the great Joe Louis. His was the classic boxing story of a hungry fighter, a man born in poverty in Panama, having to fight to survive. He was cunning and crafty, but time finally caught up with him when he met McGuigan.

'The Clones Cyclone' had revived Irish boxing with a string of stirring all-action displays at the King's Hall in Belfast. He had become a national hero and all Ireland — split by the troubles — was at least united for one night and willing the little man to victory.

Pedroza's handlers tried a few tricks of the trade before the fight to try and unsettle the McGuigan camp. There were trivial disputes over the type of gloves to be used, the amount of tape, etc. There was a row at the weigh-in, but McGuigan's manager, Barney Eastwood, was overruled. Round one to the champion.

McGuigan knew he dared not fail and there were 25,000 present on a magical night to cheer him on. The champion, used to fighting on foreign soil, looked cool, calm and impassive. McGuigan entered the ring to the strains of _Rocky_ and 25,000 people went wild. Then the late Pat McGuigan, Barry's father, took the microphone to sing his own unique version of _Danny Boy_.

It seemed to inspire McGuigan, who chased the champion round the ring for the first three minutes. McGuigan landed the first solid blows in the neutral corner, but Pedroza perhaps shaded the round with his counterpunching. McGuigan tried to close the champion down again in the second round and forced him to open up in the third. A fearful punch under the heart even failed to slow McGuigan down and he continued to pour forward, taking Pedroza's best punches in his stride, slipping under his jab and hooking powerfully to the body.

Pedroza's punches seemed to be having no effect on McGuigan, who was boxing like a man possessed. The champion decided to change his tactics in the fifth, standing toe to toe. But he was clearly no match for the younger man. McGuigan, who had been troubled by an elbow injury, shook Pedroza with a powerful body blow. He was badly hurt at the end of the seventh round but was up by the count of three.

Pedroza tried to take a breather on the ropes, using all his experience to keep McGuigan at bay. He let McGuigan know he was still around with a useful right in the eighth round. This stung McGuigan back into action and he unleashed a flurry of blows which sent the champion staggering across the ring — his corner claiming that he was hit after the bell.

By the end of the thirteenth round Pedroza was surviving on his instincts and was literally holding onto his title. Amazingly, he managed to stay on his feet and take it the distance, but there could only be one winner. Pedroza, a true gentleman, hugged McGuigan at the end, recognising the better man and the end of an era.

*McGuigan in attacking mood in the third
round (Allsport/Steve Powell)*

He had held the title since April 1978 when he stopped Cecilio Lastra in Panama. Now little Barry McGuigan was champion of the world. Near to tears he wanted to thank just about everyone. Afterwards he dedicated the fight to the memory of Young Ali, a boxer who died after fighting McGuigan in 1982. McGuigan's victory over Pedroza — plus impressive wins over the likes of Charm Chiteule and former WBC Champion Juan Laporte — had made him a big favourite with the American fight fans. The large Irish contingent wanted to see more of him. He made two defences — battering the previously unbeaten American Bernard Taylor and stopping Danilo Cabrera, a substitute, in Belfast.

Ironically, McGuigan was to come unstuck against another late substitute, Steve Cruz, in Las Vegas, on 23 June 1986. Looking back McGuigan was ill-advised to tackle Cruz in the unbearable 110 degree heat in Las Vegas. He was floored three times that disastrous afternoon as the heat visibly sapped his strength. McGuigan, who was also said to be suffering from ankle and ear trouble, was taken to hospital on a stretcher.

It was one of the biggest upsets in the history of the division, for Cruz, a Texan plumber, had only had twenty-six professional fights. Ranked as number nine in the world, he had taken the bout at short notice and had not had long to prepare.

For a time it seemed as though McGuigan would never fight again as he tried his hand at driving cars and finally parted company with manager Barney Eastwood, his long-time guide and mentor.

Cruz, incidentally, lost the title at the first time of asking when he was beaten by Antonio Esparragoza (Venezuela) in the twelfth round in Fort Worth, Texas.

SUGAR RAY LEONARD v MARVIN HAGLER
_____ WBC Middleweight title_____
6 April 1987

Sugar Ray Leonard, Marvin Hagler, Thomas Hearns and Roberto Duran were four of the greatest names in modern-day boxing who combined to produce a series of classic, contrasting fights which gripped the imagination of fight fans all over the world. It all culminated in the second 'Fight of the Century', between Hagler and Leonard in April 1987.

Marvelous Marvin had ruled the middleweight division for almost seven years, making twelve successful defences. The long awaited showdown with Leonard took place at Caesar's Palace and what a fight it turned out to be, Leonard taking a twelve-round split decision to take the coveted WBC crown.

It was a fight which shocked the boxing world in more ways than one. Hagler was regarded as one of the fiercest middleweights of all time, so how could Leonard possibly come out of retirement to challenge him? Some thought the bout should never have been allowed on medical grounds. There was trouble for Hagler before the fight when he was stripped of the WBA and IBF titles for failing to meet Britain's Herol 'Bomber' Graham.

It was a fight everyone wanted to see. Some 15,336 paid 7.9 million dollars — average price $500 a seat — and all the seats were sold out six months in advance. The event was said to have been watched by an audience of 300 million world-wide and grossed over 100 million dollars. Hagler was reported to have been paid over 18 million dollars and Leonard 12 million for the 'Super Fight'.

Leonard, not surprisingly after such a long lay off, started as the 3-1 underdog.

Amazingly, he weighed-in only ½lb under Hagler. Hagler took the initiative early on, with Leonard boxing on the retreat. Then Leonard started to show his class, baffling Hagler with his speed and unleashing a dazzling array of shots. He taunted the champion to try and hit him and Hagler replied with an uppercut and some typical hooks which rocked Leonard. Typically, Leonard fought back in the ninth round, despite looking tired and punching only in bursts. But he got his tactics just right and it was enough to give him a split decision after twelve punishing, compelling rounds.

Surprisingly, one judge gave Hagler only two rounds, while another awarded it to Hagler by two points. The other gave it to Leonard by two, to cap one of the most remarkable comebacks in the history of the sport. Leonard, having proved his point, immediately announced he was retiring again. The rest, as they say, is history.

Leonard, born in Wilmington, South Carolina on 17 May, 1956, was undoubtedly the biggest personality in boxing since Muhammad Ali. An outstanding amateur, he won Golden Gloves titles and the Olympic light-welterweight gold in 1976.

He was unbeaten for two years as a professional before he got his title shot, ending the reign of the legendary Wilfred Benitez in the dying seconds at Caesar's Palace on 30 November 1979.

The one blot on his copybook came when he lost the welterweight title to the rugged Roberto Duran in Montreal in June 1980. It was a memorable encounter as Leonard decided, unwisely to, to try and slug it out with Duran. The crowd of 46,317 went wild as Leonard turned on the style. But it was

Duran who held on for a shock unanimous points win (145-144, 146-144, 148-147).

The pair were rematched five months later in the New Orleans Superdrome for a joint purse of 13 million dollars. Amazingly, iron-man Duran stunned the boxing world by turning his back on Leonard, who had been in superb form, and walking back to his corner in the eighth round muttering 'No More'.

Duran, after a majestic 20-year career was on the decline in the 1980s, but his fortunes were linked directly with those of the other three as he moved through the weights. In 1983, Duran had the distinction of taking Hagler the distance but was knocked out in only two rounds by Hearns. Hearns, like Leonard took his place in boxing history by capturing five world titles. When 'The Hit Man' knocked out Juan Roldan (Argentina) in the fourth round in Las Vegas to take the WBC middleweight title, it was his forty-fifth win in forty-seven contests — thirty-eight of them coming inside the distance. On 16 September 1981, Hearns was stopped in the fourteenth round, by Leonard in Las Vegas. Four years later Hagler destroyed him in the third to set up the 'super fight' with Leonard.

Leonard was guaranteed 8 million dollars and Hearns 5 million. Leonard, the light middleweight title holder, put up a marvelous fight against the WBA welterweight holder. His left eye closed, and behind on points, he launched a superb comeback in the thirteenth round. Hearns was floored and Leonard finished him off ruthlessly after 1 minute 45 seconds of the fourteenth round.

It was labelled the 'Fight of the Century' for Hearns had made four successful defences and there were increasing calls for a unification bout with Leonard. Leonard had moved up to a light-middleweight by this

*Sugar Ray Leonard and Marvin Hagler size
each other up in the early rounds*

time, however, taking the WBA title by stopping Ayub Kalule (Uganda) but he relinquished the title to meet Hearns for what was then the biggest purse in the history of the game.

Hearns met Hagler at Caesar's Palace on 16 April 1985 and they combined to produce one of the most savage fights of the decade. Hearns was, by then, the WBC light-heavyweight champion and was expected to give Hagler, then approaching 33 years old, a rough ride. Hagler decided to attack straight from the start to try and combat Hearn's waspish attacks. The outcome was 8 minutes of pure, controlled savagery. Both men were hurt in the first round and it soon became apparent that it would never go the distance. Hagler was cut by some stinging punches but always looked the stronger of the two. The referee twice inspected damage around the champion's eyes and this spurred Hagler into an even more furious attack. Punishing left and rights stunned Hearns and Hagler moved in for the kill.

Hearns never seemed to carry the same potency after that. His punch resistance seemed low and he was flattened by one punch from Iran Barkley in June 1988. Indeed, he was fortunate to hang on, literally, against James 'The Heat' Kinchen, to take the new WBO super middleweight crown. Hearns took a 12-round split decision after being deducted a point for holding after being felled in the fourth round by a hard right.

MIKE TYSON v LEON SPINKS
World Heavyweight Championship
28 June 1988

It might appear ridiculous, at first sight, to include a bout that lasted only 1 minute 31 seconds in a book like this. But Tyson v Spinks fully merits inclusion — for it was the richest event in the history of the sport with Tyson collecting an amazing 22 million dollars for just over 90 seconds of action.

Although the fight was, in the end, a massive anti-climax, it served to illustrate — once again — the vast power and sheer animal aggression that makes Tyson such a phenomenon. Tyson is not built like a true heavyweight. At 5ft 11in tall he was considered by many experts to be too short to be a top-class heavyweight. He is by no means a classic boxer, but he is one of the most devastating and effective punchers in the history of the fight game. In disposing of Spinks so clinically (it was the third fastest win in heavyweight history) Tyson chalked up his thirty-fifth straight win, with thirty one of them inside the distance.

Before the fight Spinks, who also boasted an unbeaten record, was bragging how he would handle the champion. But he was quickly silenced on the big night as Tyson, just 21 years old and 218¼lb of muscle, went to work. Spinks managed to throw just two worthwhile punches before he was caught high on the head and then put down by a blow in the ribs and a left uppercut. Spinks took a count of eight, but then walked straight into a short right — a classic knock out. He bravely tried to get up, but merely sagged back through the ropes. At least Spinks had some consolation in defeat, with a cheque for 13.8 million dollars.

After the fight, Tyson, who was heading for domestic and personal turmoil, said he might not box again. He almost did not. His next scheduled fight, against Britain's Frank Bruno, was subject to numerous delays. Tyson ran into marital problems, added to a much publicized street brawl and an altercation with a tree.

Tyson finishes the challenge of Spinks after only 90 seconds (Allsport/Simon Bruty)

SUGAR RAY LEONARD v DANNY LALONDE
_____WBC Light-heavyweight and WBC Super-middleweight titles_____
7 November 1988

The incomparable Sugar Ray Leonard immortalized himself when he stopped Canadian Danny Lalonde in the ninth round at Caesar's Palace, for he became the first man in history to officially win World titles at five weights.

Leonard, 32 years old, recovered from a rare fourth round knockdown in a ring on the Palace tennis courts, to outclass and overwhelm the light-heavyweight champion and take his rightful place in the 'Sporting Hall of Fame'. It capped a fairy-tale comeback for the remarkable Leonard, whose career looked to be over when he announced his retirement in 1982 because of a detached retina of the eye. There were many critics who said the fight should not be allowed to go ahead. It was a farce and a sham, for a contrived title. But money talks louder than words in the world of boxing and the fight was guaranteed to be a block-buster even before the first glove was laced.

Leonard, despite fighting for only the third time in seven years, began as a 7-2 on

Sugar Ray Leonard dodges a wild swing from
Danny Lalonde (Allsport/Holly Stein)

favourite. 'I'm excited to be fighting again. I love competing and my level of intensity is the same as when I fought Hagler,' he said before the fight.

Lalonde, who had to weight-in half a stone under the limit to accommodate the new super-middleweight title, boasted that he would knock out Leonard in the eighth round. 'I tell myself I'm fighting a small old man who is past his best,' said the 28-year-old Zen studying vegetarian from Manitoba. Lalonde, who had thirty-three fights, thirty-one wins with twenty-six stoppages, unloaded some of his best shots. His moment of glory came when in the fourth round he caught Leonard high on the head and sent him to the canvas for only the second time in his career.

Leonard, who is said to have earned 12 million dollars for the fight compared to Lalonde's 5 million, recovered to display all his old fire and speed. He was cut on the bridge of the nose, but did not seem unduly worried as he traded punches with Lalonde. Bobbing and weaving, he was scoring well with his own left jab, unleashing left and right hooks that had Lalonde in trouble in the fifth round. Leonard opened up again in the seventh round and Lalonde, mouth open, arms dropping, suddenly started to tire.

Lalonde was an easy target for Leonard's lightning punches in the eighth round, with left and right hooks repeatedly jerking his head back. Lalonde who had been troubled by knuckle and shoulder injuries appeared to be banking on one big punch to settle the issue. Both men were eager to come out in the ninth round, but Leonard soon got to work again, piling up points with his jab. Lalonde tried a desperate gamble, standing toe to toe, but then Leonard opened up with a barrage of twenty-one punches with just a minute to go. A left put Lalonde down and, with 40 seconds to go, he was down again. There was no need to count this time.

Amazingly, one judge actually had Lalonde ahead on points at 76-75. The other two were scoring 77-74, 77-75 to Leonard. 'I was surprised at Leonard's ability,' said Lalonde. 'He is a very determined man, he just kept coming back. I never thought I could lose. Ray's a great champion.'

Two questions had to be asked, however. Was it such a glorious victory for the old ring-master in front of 12,000 fans? Or was it just a hollow victory for a paper crown against a second-rate opponent? Leonard, after all, had not fought for 18 months since he beat Hagler. The titles and the money clearly meant little to millionaire Leonard. A week later he gave up the light-heavyweight title, thus becoming the first man in history to win and then relinquish five world crowns. He gave up the welterweight and light-middleweight titles in 1982 and never defended the middleweight title he took from Hagler.

LLOYD HONEYGHAN v MARLON STARLING
WBC Welterweight title
5 February 1989

Lloyd Honeyghan's world fell apart when he took on American Marlon Starling at Caesar's Palace on 5 February 1989. Honeyghan was expected to win, but he got the tactics wrong and was battered to a ninth round defeat. He had gambled his fight future and lost. Around £2 million blew away in the Nevada desert, because manager Mickey Duff had lined up a three-fight package with American TV and there was talk of two Hollywood acting roles.

He ended the fight bruised, battered and bewildered — failing a drugs test into the bargain — and was taken to the Valley Hospital where the other battered Britons, Maurice Hope and Barry McGuigan, had been taken after losing their world crowns.

It was all a far cry from 27 September 1986 when Honeyghan produced one of the most sensational wins in the history of world welterweight boxing by beating America's Don Curry in Atlantic City. For Curry, from Fort Worth in Texas, was unbeaten in twenty-five contests and was considered, pound for pound, one of the best fighters in the world.

Curry 'The Cobra' was quickly installed as the red-hot favourite, even though he was rumoured to be having weight problems. But Honeyghan, who was also unbeaten, did not fear him. He left his house in Kent to train in the quiet of the Catskill mountains and it also served to give him a break from his somewhat tangled love life.

Jamaican-born Honeyghan was the best of British on the night. He attacked straight from the bell and totally outgunned the shell-shocked champion who retired at the end of the sixth round. It was not pretty, but it was effective and Britain soon had a new world champion to salute. Unfortunately, he did not reign long as undisputed champion. He gave up the WBA version rather than defend against the number one contender, Harold Volbrecht of South Africa.

Honeyghan made three successful defences before losing his crown on a technicality in October 1987. He was on top against the rugged Jorge Vaca when the challenger was cut in the eighth round in an accidental clash of heads. Because Vaca was ahead on points at the time he was awarded the fight. But Honeyghan exacted quick revenge and battered Vaca to a third-round defeat in the re-match at Wembley.

Honeyghan, who had excited the Americans by demolishing Johnny Bumphus and Gene Hatcher, was then lined up to meet former champion Starling on a double-header. The winner was to tackle WBA champion Mark Breland, who took only 54 seconds to dispose of South Korean Seung-Soon Lee earlier on the bill at Caesar's Palace. Honeyghan with a 33-1-22 record, was 2-5 on favourite against 30-year-old Starling in what promised to be a real grudge match. There was certainly no love lost on either side and there had been a hate campaign leading up to the big fight.

Honeyghan followed his usual tactic of going off for the quick knock-out, but this time it did not pay off. He wanted to humiliate Starling and this proved to be his undoing as he threw caution to the wind. Honeyghan unleashed an amazing 115 punches in the second round. He threw 695 in all but landed only 107. Honeyghan was like a man possessed, throwing punches from all angles and leaving himself off balance and open to the challenger's crafty counter punches. Starling, by comparison, was boxing superbly, protecting himself in classic fashion as Honeyghan bored in.

Honeyghan continued to pour forward, but how long could he keep up the pace? He started to concentrate on punches to the head, but it did not seem to worry Starling, who was starting to taunt the champion in the fourth round.

Starling, with a 43-5-1-26 record, was ice cool and composed. Honeyghan, under orders from manager Duff, gambled on a desperate change of tactics in the fifth, trying to jab and run and keep away from Starling's damaging punches. Starling, drawing comparisons with the great Sugar Ray Robinson, continued to outbox Honeyghan, a fact acknowledged by the champion who was in pain after apparently damaging a nerve in the side of his face, which began to swell grotesquely.

Honeyghan, also swollen around the right eye, continued to take punishment in the sixth round. He tried to dance and keep out of trouble, but he had run out of ideas and looked a dejected man.

He was hardly throwing a punch in the seventh round, while Starling was confident and strong. There was no hope for Honeyghan, but he bravely insisted on carrying on even though he was behind on all three judge's cards. But, when he sagged to his knees in the ninth round, the end was not far away. Starling opened up and although Honeyghan was not in desperate trouble, it was something of a mercy when referee Mills Lane called a halt after 1 min 19 secs of the round. Marlon 'Magic Man' Starling was again champion of the world.

Honeyghan was full of praise for Starling the boxer — if not the man — after the fight and his sportsmanship won him many admirers. 'My face was swollen and every time he hit me it felt as though he was cutting me with a knife,' he said. 'I made a bad start and just could not get into it. I let my aggression get the better of me. I was just not thinking, I tried everything but it was just too late.'

At least Honeyghan — who was bidding for a record seventh world title win for a Britain — had the consolation of a £400,000 pay day. Down, but not out, he planned one more fight, against Starling or Breland, before retiring.

DENNIS ANDRIES v TONY WILLIS
_____ WBC Light-heavyweight title _____
21 February 1989

Britain's Dennis Andries earned himself a place in the record books when he stopped Tony Willis in Tucson on 21 February 1989 to win the WBC light-heavyweight title. It was possibly one of the most unmemorable fights in the history of the division, but it was a dream come true for Andries who became only the third Briton — behind Ted Kid Lewis and Lloyd Honeyghan — to recapture a world crown. What made it even more remarkable was that Andries — an unfashionable and generally underrated boxer — was possibly closer to 40 years of age rather than the 35 quoted by some sources.

It looked as though he had reached the end of a long hard road when he was 'destroyed' by Thomas Hearns in ten rounds in Detroit on 7 March 1987. But the dedicated Andries was no quitter. He stayed on in Detroit, cut himself off from his wife and children for almost two years and slogged his way back to the top. 'I could not go out like that,' said Andries. 'I was humiliated. I had to do something about it.' And he did. Under the guidance of Team Kronk — whose colours had been worn by six world champions — he won all six come-back fights, including an excellent victory over former IBF champion Bobby Czyz.

That set up a meeting with Willis for the title vacated by Sugar Ray Leonard. The fight was, not surprisingly, totally overshadowed by Mike Tyson's clash with Frank Bruno a few days later. Andries collected a modest £40,000 compared to Bruno's massive £2 million pay out.

But what followed was like a scene from _Rocky_ as Andries became the first British fighter in 72 years to regain a world title on American soil. One suspects that Andries could hardly believe his luck. He had been a run-of-the-mill fighter since turning professional in May 1978, losing six of his first twenty-one bouts.

He was considered an awkward, ungainly slugger with no class or style. But he plodded on and fame came late in life. Guyanan-born Andries — known as 'The Rock' — won the British title in 1984 and took a Lonsdale belt outright in only 259 days.

In April 1986 he became one of the oldest world champions — he admitted to being 33 — when he beat ex-marine, American J.B. Williamson on points over twelve rounds in London for the light-heavyweight title. He made one successful defence, against the fading Tony Sibson, before unwisely taking on the Hit Man.

Fortunately for Andries, Willis was no Hearns, despite an impressive record of winning twelve of his sixteen professional fights within the distance. The 27-year-old North American Boxing Federation champion had the reputation of a hard-hitting street fighter. But he was a massive disappointment against Andries. He hardly threw a punch and seemed content to hold on, employing spoiling tactics.

Andries, who had a 43-33-2-7 record, started confidently and shook Willis early on. Willis was guilty of holding in a messy second round and there were boos at the end of the round. Willis was finally warned for holding as he frustrated Andries and stopped him getting in his best shots, but he was in trouble in the fourth round after getting trapped on the ropes. His legs had gone and he was only saved by the bell.

Willis walked straight into a right at the start of the fifth round and two lefts and a superb left hook put him down and out after 1 minute 6 seconds of the round. A delighted Andries said 'That was a great moment in my life. I have suffered a lot, but it was all worth it when they raised my hands and said I was a world champion again. No-one can take this away from me.'

And that was still not the end of the fairy-tale for the remarkable Andries, who was lined up for a big money fight with the former champion Danny Lalonde. More than that he was giving inspiration to no-hope fighters in gyms all over the world who had dreams of, one day, winning the world title.

Dennis Andries becomes one of only three Britons who have recaptured a World title

MIKE TYSON v FRANK BRUNO
_____ Undisputed World Heavyweight title _____
Las Vegas, 26 February 1989

Frank Bruno walked away from his much publicized world heavyweight title fight with Mike Tyson as the only loser in history to leave Las Vegas with 3.6 million dollars in his pocket. The big man confounded his critics and certainly earned his money, surviving a first-round knock-down to give Iron Mike some anxious moments.

Bruno shook the champion with a good left, but was caught on the ropes in the fifth round and the fight was rightly stopped to save him from punishment. So much for Bruno's glass jaw and the critics who said that he would not get past the first round. The bookies certainly had no doubts, making Tyson the 1-9 on favourite, despite the fact that he had not fought since June. Bruno, who had not been in the ring since he beat Joe Bugner on October 25 1987, was 6-1.

Bruno had certainly had a long wait for his second title chance. The fight should

_Tyson meets Bruno in a lighter moment before
their World title fight (Allsport/Simon Bruty)_

*Bruno puts on a spirited performance against the
awesome Tyson (Allsport/Holly Stein)*

have gone ahead at Wembley on 3 September 1988, but was subject to numerous postponements while Tyson recovered from injury, a car crash, a brawl and resolved marital differences. Tyson was also involved in court actions with his former manager and trainer and his weight was said to have ballooned to 18 stones. He even 'broke out' of his training camp to get a quick divorce just days before the fight. The sum total of all these personal problems gave a glimmer of hope to Bruno.

But Tyson, who was proud that at 20 years and 145 days he was the youngest world heavyweight champion, shed 16lb within two weeks and looked in good shape on the big night. It was scheduled for twelve rounds but no-one expected it to go too far. Tyson, 22, was having his 9th title fight and boasted a 35-35 record, all but four of his wins coming inside the distance.

Bruno, who had prepared well, looked in the best shape of his career. He was calm and collected as he walked into the ring to a tumultuous reception from the large British contingent in the 10,000 capacity crowd. But it all looked to have gone horribly wrong for him as he tried to mix it with Tyson in the opening seconds. He shook Tyson with a good left and it gave him confidence, but a powerful right and a typical left hook had Bruno in trouble — Tyson being guilty of hitting his man as he went down.

Bruno, who was warned for holding Tyson behind the head, was in trouble again at the end of the second round. He was caught by a clubbing left, but managed to hold on for the final eight seconds. Tyson, however, did not look too happy. He was missing with a lot of wild punches and could not get his timing right as he went for a quick win. Bruno had taken some of his best shots and was still there at the end of the third round. Tyson was warned about the use of his head in the fourth round, but there was nothing wrong with the punch that jerked Bruno's head back.

Bruno again connected with a good left hook, but was not throwing enough punches of his own. Tyson although not at his best, was still too quick for Bruno and was even beating him to the jab. Not surprisingly, Bruno was soon in trouble again, bleeding from his mouth and nose. He tried to hold on and regain his senses, when he should have gone down on one knee to take a breather. But he bravely, and unwisely, stayed on his feet as Tyson unleashed a barrage of punches. Bruno's manager Terry Lawless was already on his way round the ring to throw in the towel as the referee rightly called a halt.

It was the twelfth unsuccessful challenge by a British heavyweight this century. But Bruno, at 6ft 3in tall and 16½ stone in weight, had been a great ambassador for Britain and boxing. Branded as a no-hoper, he had conducted himself with dignity throughout. He had not frozen, he had not crumbled and had been gracious in defeat. He had earned world-wide respect, albeit the hard way!

Bruno said he did not fear Tyson and would like a re-match. 'I was more shaken than hurt in the first,' he said. 'I felt I had a chance, but it slipped away from me. I cannot take anything away from him. When you go in with Mike Tyson you can expect a dirty fight, you cannot expect any favours. He's a strong fast guy.'

Index

Ali, Muhammed, 136, 148, 153-9
Ali, Young, 161
Ambers, Lou, 94, 97
Andries, Dennis, 170-1
Anthony, Tony, 136
Armstrong, Henry, 94-7
Attell, Abe, 16-17

Badoud, Albert, 21
Baer, Buddy, 55, 101
Baer, Maxmillian, 56-9, 71-2, 75-6, 101, 134, 137
Baksi, Joe, 114, 121, 130
Baldock, Teddy, 49-51, 106
Barley, Iran, 164
Baroudi, Sam, 130
Basham, Johnny, 21-4, 32, 43
Beattie, Eddie, 21
Beckett, Joe, 35-8
Bell, Archie, 49, 106
Benitez, Wilfred, 162
Benyon, Len, 68
Berg, Jack 'Kid', 60, 94
Beshore, Freddie, 124
Bettina, Melio, 103, 110
Bill, Black, 80
Blackie, Kid, see Dempsey, Jack
Bonavena, Oscar, 156
Boon, Eric, 89-93
Bowdry, Jess, 136
Bowker, Joe, 16, 18
Braddock, James J., 71-5, 85, 99, 134, 147
Breland, Mark, 168-9
Brennan, Bill, 28, 39
Brown, Al, 107
Brown, Jackie, 67-70, 80-1
Brown, Johnny, 49-50, 106
Brown, Newsboy, 49, 80
Brown, Panama Al, 49
Bruno, Frank, 172-4
Brusso, Noah, see Burns, Tommy
Bugner, Joe, 158
Buonvino, Gino, 129
Bumphus, Johnny, 168
Burns, Tommy, 7-10, 37, 153

Cabrera, Danilo, 161
Cameron, Jim, 90
Canzoneri, Tony, 60
Carnera, Primo, 56-9, 71-2, 137, 145
Carpentier, Georges, 28-39, 47, 95
Charles, Ezzard, 124-5, 129-33, 147
Chatanooga, Golden Terror of, 101
Chiteule, Charm, 161
Chocolate, Kid, 107
Christoforidis, Anton, 103, 110, 130
Clark, Elky, 49, 80
Clay, Cassius, see Ali, Muhammed
Cockell, Don, 132, 135
Coffey, Jim, 36
Conn, Billy, 103, 110-11, 120, 123-4
Cook, George, 37
Cooper, Henry, 138-9, 149-50, 153-4
Corbett, Dick, 67
Crossley, Harry, 53
Crowley, Dave, 89, 91-3, 107
Cruz, Steve, 161
Curry, Don, 168
Cusick, Johnny, 68, 108
Cuthbert, Johnny, 50, 60, 106
Czyz, Bobby, 170

Danahar, Albert, 89-93
Daniels, Gipsy, 108
Daniels, Terry, 157
Davies, Tommy, 108
Dempsey, Jack, 12-15. 28-32, 35, 37, 39-43, 46-8, 58, 105, 115-16, 120, 126, 134
Di-Biase, Mike, 136
Dixon, George, 17
Downey, Jack, 12
Doyle, Jack, 52-5, 101
Driscoll, Jim, 16-20, 106
Duran, Roberto, 162-3

Ellis, Jimmy, 156
Erskine, Joe, 139
Esparragaza, Antonio, 161

Farr, Tommy, 74-9,.85, 101, 122, 133
Firpo, Luis 'Angel', 39-42, 47-8, 105, 120
Fitzsimmons, Bob, 7, 43, 89, 94, 114, 125, 153
Flynn, Jim, 7, 11
Folley, Zora, 139, 146, 154, 156
Foord, Ben, 55, 75-6, 86
Forbes, Harry, 17
Foreman, Al, 107
Foreman, George, 157-8
Fox, 'Tiger' Jack, 103, 110
Frattini, Bruno, 43
Frazier, Joe, 153, 156-9

Gainer, Al, 72, 111
Galento, Tony, 98-101
Goddard, Frank, 37
Godoy, Arturo, 98, 122
Graham, Herol 'Bomber', 162
Graziano, Rocky, 115-19
Greb, Harry, 43, 46
Green, Alvin, 132

Hagler, Marvin, 162-4
Harris, Roy, 138-9, 146
Harvey, Len, 50, 52, 55, 63-6, 102-5, 110-11
Hatcher, Gene, 168
Hearns, Thomas, 162-4, 170
Heuser, Adolph, 88
Honeyghan, Lloyd, 168-9
Humery, Gustave, 60-2

Jackson, Tommy 'Hurricane', 136-8
James, Ronnie, 93
Jeffries, James J., 7, 11
Johansson, Ingemar, 137-44, 146-7
Johnson, Harold, 133, 136
Johnson, Jack, 7-12, 36, 74, 120, 125, 146, 153
Johnson, Jim, 11

Jones, Doug, 136
Jurich, Jackie, 84

Kalube, Ayub, 164
Kane, Peter, 80-4, 89
Ketchell, Stanley, 11, 115, 118
Kinchen, James 'The Heat', 164
King, Johnny, 67-70, 107
Kirby, Bert, 67

La Barba, Fidel, 49, 80
La Motta, Jake, 121
La Starza, Roland, 130
Lalonde, Danny, 166-7, 171
Langford, Sam, 7-8, 11
Laporte, Juan, 161
Lastra, Cecilio, 161
Ledoux Charles, 16, 18-20
Lee, Seung Soon, 168
Lee, Tancy, 25
Leonard, Sugar Ray, 162-4, 166-7, 170
Lesnevich, Gus, 103, 110-13, 122, 124, 130
Levinsky, Battling, 26, 28, 46
Levinsky, King, 55, 71
Lewis, John Henry, 63-6, 98, 103, 110
Lewis, Ted 'Kid', 21-4, 32, 43
Liston, Sonny, 136, 144-52
London, Brian, 138-9, 144, 154
London, Jack, 103, 111
Loughran, Tommy, 57, 72
Louis, Joe, 11, 71-9, 83, 85-8, 98-101, 110-11, 116, 120-5, 130, 133-4, 147, 150, 159
Lyle, Ron, 158
Lynch, Benny, 67, 80-4

Machen, Eddie, 139, 146, 150, 152
Marciano, Rocky, 72, 124-39, 147, 155, 159
Marshall, Marty, 146, 152
Mathis, Buster, 156
Matthews, Harry, 129
Mauriello, Tami, 110, 114, 120
Maxim, Joey, 114, 121, 125, 133, 137
McAvoy, Jock, 63, 103, 110
McCormick, Noel 'Boy', 37
McGibbons, Tom, 35
McGuigan, Barry, 160-1

McTigue, Mik, 35
Meen, Reggie, 53
Mildenburger, Karl, 154
Miller, Freddie, 107-8
Milligan, Tommy, 43-5
Mills, Freddie, 102-5, 108, 110-14, 121, 133
Mizler, Harry, 60-2
Moore, Archie, 130-133-7, 147, 149
Moran, Frank, 11, 36-8
Moran, Frank, 11, 36-8
Moran, Owen, 18
Muller, Heine, 53
Murphy, Bob, 133

Neuhaus, Heinz, 139
Neusal, Walter, 75-6, 88
Nicholson, Kid, 49-50
Nilles, Marcel, 32
Norton, Ken, 158

Olson, Carl, 133
Oma, Lee, 110, 125

Palmer, Pat, 81-2
Palmer, Pedlar, 18-25
Paterson, Jackie, 70,84
Pattenden, Alf 'Kid' 49-51, 106
Patterson, Floyd, 136-8, 140-9, 153, 158
Pedroza, Eusebio, 160-1
Perez, Young, 67, 80
Petersen, Jack, 52-5, 63
Peterson, Big Boy, 57
Phillips, Al, 106, 108-9
Phillips, Eddie, 55, 63
Pompey, Yolande, 136

Quarry, Jerry, 156

Rademacher, Peter, 138-9
Reynolds, Bernie, 129
Richardson, Dick, 132, 144
Rinaldi, Giulio, 136
Robinson, Sugar Ray, 43, 133
Roderick, Ernie, 94-7, 107
Roldan, Juan, 163
Roman, Joe, 157
Romero, Johnny, 133
Roper, Jack, 98
Ross, Barney, 94
Rossi, Francis, 18

Savold, Lee, 124, 129
Schmeling, Max, 58, 71-2,

75, 77, 85-8, 98
Schwartz, Izzy, 49, 80
Sharkey, Jack, 25, 47, 57, 72, 79
Sibson, Tony, 170
Siki, Battling, 32-5
Simon, Abe, 120
Smith, Don, 146
Smith, Jewey, 7-8
Smith, Sergeant Dick, 36-7
Spinks, Leon, 165
Spoul, Andre, 11
Squires, Bill, 7-8
Starling, Marlon, 168-9
Sullivan, John L., 145
Sullivan, Tommy, 17
Symonds, Joe, 25

Tarleton, Nel, 68, 95, 106-9
Taylor, Bernard, 161
Terrell, Ernie, 152, 154-5
Thil, Marcel, 43, 115
Thomas, Harry, 85-6
Tunney, Gene, 35, 46-8, 120, 126, 133
Turpin, Randolph, 43
Tyson, Mike, 165, 172-4

Uzcudun, Paolino, 57, 71

Vaca, Jorge, 168
Valentino, Pat, 124
Villa, Pancho, 27, 80
Volbrecht, Harold, 168

Walcott, Jersey Joe, 120-30, 133, 152
Walker, Micky, 43-5, 115
Walsh, Jimmy, 89
Watson, Seaman Tom, 107
Wells, Bombardier Billy, 26, 28, 36-7
Wells, Matt, 21
Wepner, Chuck, 152, 158
Wilde, Jimmy, 25-7, 82, 103
Willard, Jess, 11-15, 28, 36, 39, 47, 58, 74, 120
Williams, Cleveland, 146, 154
Williams, Johnny 'Kid', 25
Williamson, J.B., 170
Willis, Tony, 170-1
Wills, Harry, 39, 46-7
Woodcock, Bruce, 111, 114, 121

Zale, Tony, 115-19, 130
Zivic, Fritzie, 97